GREAT
TRAVEL
VALUES ™

LONDON

FODOR'S TRAVEL PUBLICATIONS

are compiled, researched, and edited by an international team of travel writers, field correspondents, and editors. The series, which now almost covers the globe, was founded by Eugene Fodor in 1936.

OFFICES
New York & London

Fodor's Great Travel Values: London

Editors: Thomas Cussans, Richard Moore, Caz Philcox
Editorial Contributors: Lindsay Bareham, Robert Brown, Sheila Brownlee, Richard Leigh, Mark Lewes, Martha Pichey, Gilbert Wong
Maps: Swanston Graphics

FODOR'S

LONDON

FODOR'S TRAVEL PUBLICATIONS, INC.
New York & London

ISBN 0-679-01484-5
ISBN 0-340-41831-1

MANUFACTURED IN THE UNITED STATES OF AMERICA
10 9 8 7 6 5 4 3 2 1

CONTENTS

FOREWORD

All selections and comments in *Fodor's Great Travel Values: London* are based on personal experiences. We feel that our first responsibility is to inform and protect you, the reader. While every care has been taken to insure the accuracy of the information contained in this guide, the publishers cannot accept responsibility for any errors that may appear.

All prices quoted in this guide are based on those available to us at the time of writing. In a world of rapid change, however, the possibility of inaccurate or out-of-date information can never be totally eliminated. We trust, therefore, that you will take prices quoted as indicators only, and will double-check to be sure of the latest figures.

Similarly, be sure to check all opening times of museums and galleries. We have found that such times are liable to change without notice, and you could easily make a trip only to find a locked door.

When a hotel closes or a restaurant produces a disappointing meal, let us know, and we will investigate the establishment and the complaint. We are always ready to revise our entries for the following year's edition should the facts warrant it.

Send your letters to the editors of Fodor's Travel Publications, 201 E. 50th Street, New York, NY 10022. European readers may prefer to write to Fodor's Travel Guides, 9-10 Market Place, London W1N 7AG, England.

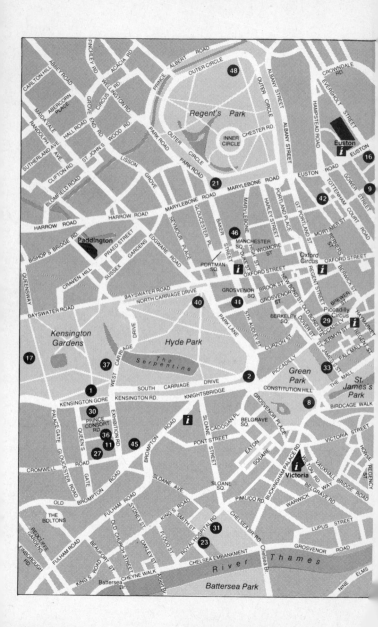

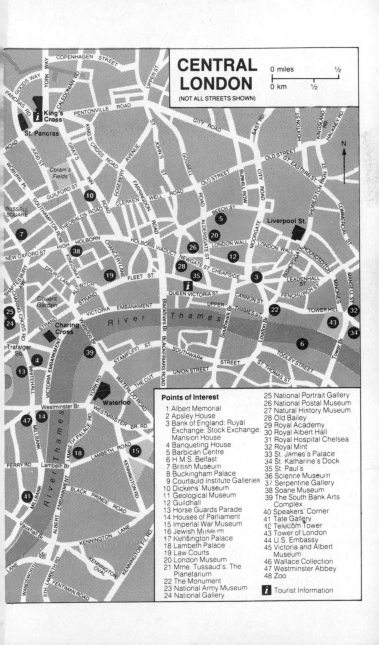

CENTRAL LONDON

0 miles ½
0 km ½

(NOT ALL STREETS SHOWN)

Points of Interest

1 Albert Memorial
2 Apsley House
3 Bank of England; Royal Exchange; Stock Exchange; Mansion House
4 Banqueting House
5 Barbican Centre
6 H.M.S. Belfast
7 British Museum
8 Buckingham Palace
9 Courtauld Institute Galleries
10 Dickens' Museum
11 Geological Museum
12 Guildhall
13 Horse Guards Parade
14 Houses of Parliament
15 Imperial War Museum
16 Jewish Museum
17 Kensington Palace
18 Lambeth Palace
19 Law Courts
20 London Museum
21 Mme. Tussaud's; The Planetarium
22 The Monument
23 National Army Museum
24 National Gallery

25 National Portrait Gallery
26 National Postal Museum
27 Natural History Museum
28 Old Bailey
29 Royal Academy
30 Royal Albert Hall
31 Royal Hospital Chelsea
32 Royal Mint
33 St. James's Palace
34 St. Katharine's Dock
35 St. Paul's
36 Science Museum
37 Serpentine Gallery
38 Soane Museum
39 The South Bank Arts Complex
40 Speakers' Corner
41 Tate Gallery
42 Telecom Tower
43 Tower of London
44 U.S. Embassy
45 Victoria and Albert Museum
46 Wallace Collection
47 Westminster Abbey
48 Zoo

i Tourist Information

INTRODUCTION

◆

Many visitors to London will have heard Dr. Johnson's pronouncement that "when a man is tired of London, he is tired of life." If it were true, then half today's commuters would be busy having their tombstones engraved. The second half of his saying, which is often forgotten, has a lighter ring to it, and is an excellent motto for any guide to budget London—"for there is in London all that life can afford."

London is so rich in history and tradition, in art and architecture, and in the sheer fascination of a great metropolis, that you'll be spending much more time and energy than pounds and pence as you absorb all that it has to offer. Indeed, London has had centuries of practice in keeping seekers happy—the theatergoer, the shophound, the art lover, the royalist, the pub crawler, the historian, and even the gardener. There's more than enough treasure for everyone, whatever particular interest you have, and whatever the size of your pocketbook.

The secret is that London has so many great value offers lined up for Londoners themselves, all you have to do is plug into the network. But plug in with your own situation as a visitor in mind. Never, *never*, phone long distance from your hotel room; the cost can be astronomical. Use a direct-dial phone booth, or go to the special Westminster Communications Center that's set up exactly for this purpose. Take advantage of the many special offers that London Transport has, so that traveling around town isn't the pricey proposition that it could be if, for example, you popped in and out of the tube all day seeing the sights.

One of the greatest draws that London has is its theater scene, with seat prices that will delight you if you compare them with, say, those on Broadway. If you really love the theater, then you could, with the aid of some fairly intensive preplanning, see eight shows in a week of evenings and matinees. (London theaters don't play on Sundays—but there are concerts to take up the slack.)

On the other hand, both restaurants and hotels can be staggeringly costly, largely because so many of them make their profits from expense-account customers. With just a little care you can avoid getting caught. Before going into a restaurant, always read the menu posted outside. Inside, try the house wine, as London wine prices can be inflated, and don't let a waiter con you with the dessert trolley—none of the goodies are priced. We list a selection of economical restaurants, both in the main *Where to Eat* section and as lunch spots after each area that we explore. Hotels in central London are horrendously expensive. To get a room that you feel is within your reach, you may have to stay a little out of the center. But if you choose one that is near to a tube line, then the small cost of a special ticket will be more than offset by your savings.

The amount of London's major offerings that can be seen for absolutely nothing will gradually dawn on you as you read through our lists of attractions. The great majority of the museums have no entry fee; the hundreds of acres of parkland, richly green thanks to a very healthy amount of rain, are open to all comers. But it is London's past that may well be the greatest travel value that the city can provide. The idiosyncratic streets and distinctive squares, ancient buildings and dramatic statues, tell a vivid story that spans over 2,000 years and will unroll before you as you gradually get to know your way about.

Trailing History

It's worth taking the time to get a sense of London's history before you launch into your exploring. One of the very best places to begin unravelling the city's past is at the Museum of London, beside the Barbican Center; happily, it's free of charge. Its intelligently mounted displays follow the story through the centuries from the prehistory of the

London area, through the Bronze Age, and then really getting down to detail when the Romans arrive. All the great events of the following centuries are highlighted, culminating with World War II, and the subsequent rebuilding and development. You will be able to identify, from your progress through the exhibitions, names and sites that you will later see all round you as you circumnavigate the complex streets.

After you have visited the museum, you might want to start your exploration with one of the organized bus tours round the major highlights. They only skim the surface of what there is to see, of course, but they are extremely useful for helping you to understand the general layout of the center of town. Alternatively you could launch yourself on the Thames, the river which was the reason for London existing in the first place. From one of the economical sightseeing boats you will get the best views of the redeveloping docklands east of Tower Bridge, followed by the Tower of London, the Houses of Parliament, and then—if you have time for it—by a cruise up the sinuous course of the river to Hampton Court, half rose-red Tudor brick, half serenely Classical, still buried deep in parkland.

One of the most fascinating things that the Museum of London can tell you is how London grew from its swampy beginnings—swampy, because the Thames originally spread itself out before the Victorians created its straitjacket of embankments in the 19th century—to the metropolis it is today. The growth of the city, slow at first, then speeding up as the centuries passed, can be seen most easily in the way the population changed. In the time of the Romans, say in A.D. 60, the settlement's population was in the region of 50,000. By the time William the Conqueror arrived in 1066, and started to build the first part of today's Tower, the numbers living in the made-over ruins of the Roman town had dropped to just 18,000. The subsequent increase was slow for several centuries. At the end of the 12th there were approximately 25,000, and by 1340, around 50,000; this exploded to 200,000 during the 16th century, when the first Elizabeth was on the throne. By the beginning of the 19th century the figure had reached just under the million mark; we know this because the first census was taken in 1801, and guestimates could give way to solid fact. The Industrial Revolution, which drove people into the city in their thousands, forced the numbers up to 4.5 million by 1901, thus making it the largest population of any city in the world at that time. Today, the figure is around 6.8 million, but, at long last, growth is slowing down.

As to the area that all those millions inhabit—central London is now close to seven miles from east to west, and four miles from north to south, with Greater London spreading out for many miles beyond that. There is a handy rule of thumb for coming to grips with this incredible giant. Its sheer size is much more manageable if you think of it as being broken back down into the succession of villages that it started with. For London grew by the steady absorption over the centuries of dozens of small, distinct communities, fusing them together by the pressure of urban sprawl, though each one has managed to preserve a certain amount of its original identity that can still be recognized, some easily, some needing a more discerning eye.

This amalgamation is the reason for the willfully difficult pattern of London's streets. They trace the long forgotten geographical imperatives of these ancient villages and their surroundings, the edges of fields, the outline of a lord's territory, a path through a wood, the main village street— they all add up to a swirl of spaghetti that is totally confusing to anyone brought up on the rigidity of a grid system. Even Londoners get lost in their own city, and all own at least one dog-eared copy of the indispensable A–Z streetfinder (they come under different names). So, don't feel shy about pulling out your clean, new copy on unfamiliar street corners.

Even though it presents severe problems to anyone trying to find the way round its tangled streets, London is justly famous for its walkability. This has been exploited by the organizers of "theme walks" that cover many aspects of London life and history, such as Jack the Ripper's London, Dickens's London, London Pubs, London Ghosts—the selection is almost endless, and makes a friendly and painless way of coming to grips with an aspect of London that may interest you. You can either join one of these walks for a small fee—the organization is very informal—or plan your own. Even with a pub lunch afterwards, you'll be unlikely to spend more than five pounds for a few healthy and instructing hours.

Listening to the Village Voice

It is as you wander through the streets that you will begin to comprehend the village network that makes up London outside the City itself. The City (note the capital "C," which distinguishes it from the rest of London) was the original settlement, and has kept itself aloof over all the passing centuries as London ate up more and more of the surrounding fields and woods, gorging itself on villages and lone farmhouses, until it reached today's vast size. The City was once ringed with Roman walls, but now its limits are marked by the tall towers of the many financial giants that are its modern raison d'être. At its heart is still the oldest tower of all, the Tower of London, and no one visiting the capital should fail to make a pilgrimage there, it is romantically at the center of so much of Britain's history.

We will concentrate in our exploring sections on several of the villages that were engulfed as London grew. Their names are now enshrined in the names of many of the boroughs, Chelsea, Kensington, Southwark, Chiswick, and Hampstead among them. It would take long acquaintance to grasp the full flavor of each former village, but a distinct sense can be gained on just a brief visit. This will mean, of course, abandoning the main thoroughfares, where the main national chain stores have reduced once-varied shopping streets to a uniform, raucous repetition of identical goods for sale in identical stores. You will have to delve behind these highways and seek out the small side streets, little lanes, hidden mews, and quiet squares that still make up the genuine neighborhood that has stood there for decades, in some cases for centuries.

To take one simple example, Kensington High Street is just such an identikit shopping street as we have described. But if you walk up Kensington Church Street from the lovely Victorian church of St. Mary's for a block, and then turn left onto Holland Street, on your right you'll find Kensington Church Walk, a lane with small, interesting shops, and further on small courtyards with cottage gardens, rambling roses, and all the character of a tiny country town. A period pub, trees everywhere, antique shops . . . all within the area defined by a very few blocks.

By contrast, you will find a totally different side of London's charm down by the Thames, in Chelsea, where famous writers and painters have lived for a couple of centuries, and where people who prefer to escape from the tyranny of four walls are happily ensconced on moored barges.

You will see even more clearly what the villages around London were like if you visit Hampstead or Highgate, high on their hills to the north, with fine distant views over the city below.

Royalty Watching

Every part of London provides its own clues to the city's past, and, while you are gradually piecing the story together, you will be getting a good idea of what daily life is like for the Londoners who love their great, crowded, endless city. You will get a glimpse of the very different life of London's most famous family if you drop by Buckingham Palace. Royalty watching is by no means restricted to fascinated foreigners. You only have to open the tabloid newspapers to see photographs of royal toddlers and read reports of lurid rumors and family spats (in the words of one recent headline, *Dallas at the Palace*) to know that Londoners devour it all with a seemingly insatiable appetite. It amounts to a national obsession.

Whether you are a royalist or a republican, the pageantry of the British Royal Family provides one of the greatest free shows in the world. Don't let the tag of "typical tourist" stop you from watching the Changing of the Guard, or from poking into the Royal Mews for a look at the Coronation Coach. Pomp reaches its zenith in mid-June when the Queen celebrates her official birthday with a parade called Trooping the Color (the "color" is the traditional tall flag of the regiment on parade each year). Queen Elizabeth rides in procession from Buckingham Palace to the Horse Guards Parade on the other side of St. James's Park. Until 1986, she rode sidesaddle, but has since decided it's more comfortable at her age to get there by open carriage.

Plus ça change . . .

Any vibrant metropolis changes, and crowded, noisy, frequently dirty London is no exception. New skyscrapers (if only in Europe's slightly diminutive versions) now puncture the City's skyline, especially the Lloyd's building, gleaming and modern in a way that is difficult to accept in this stronghold of conservatism. The black taxi is being slowly supplanted by a sleeker model, and by versions of the old one in red, white, gold, and other colors. An expected change in pub opening hours will mean that soon you will be able to have a drink in the afternoon without resorting to subterfuge. But all is not under threat; much in London stays thankfully the same. The British bobby is alive and well, still there to help. Cricket is the same slow ceremony very much worth watching, especially with a Pimm's Cup in hand. The tall, red, double-decker buses still lumber from stop to stop, though their aesthetic match at street level, the glossy red telephone booths, are slowly disappearing as British Telecom (no longer the Post Office) replaces too many of them. And, of course, teatime is still a hallowed part of the day, with, if you search hard enough, toasted crumpets in winter still honeycombed with sweet butter.

The London you'll discover will surely include some of our enthusiastic recommendations, but be prepared to be taken by surprise. The best that a great city has to offer often comes to you in unexpected ways. Armed with energy and curiosity, and all the practical information and helpful hints in the following pages, you will find that in London there truly is all that life can afford, and—more often than not—at a very affordable price.

PLANNING YOUR TRIP

Before You Go

NATIONAL TOURIST OFFICES. The major source of information for all aspects of travel to and within Britain is the BTA, the British Tourist Authority. The BTA produces a wealth of tourist literature, the bulk of it free and much of it directed toward low-cost travel, such as all-inclusive bus and train tickets, off-season budget vacations, and economical places to eat. The BTA can be located at the following addresses.

In the U.S.: 40 W. 57th St., New York, NY 10019 (212–581–4700); 875 N. Michigan Ave., Chicago, IL 60611 (312–787–0490); Cedar Maple Plaza, 2305 Cedar Springs Rd., TX 75201 (214–720–4040); World Trade Center, 350 S. Figueroa St., Los Angeles, CA 90017 (213–628–3525).

In Canada: 94 Cumberland St., Suite 600, Toronto, Ont. M5R 3N3 (416–961–8124).

TRAVEL DOCUMENTS. Americans. Major post offices throughout the country are now authorized to process passport applications; check with your local post office for the nearest one. You may also apply in person at U.S. Passport Agency offices in various cities; addresses and phone numbers are available under governmental listings in the white or blue pages of local telephone directories. Applications are also accepted at most county courthouses. Renewals can be handled by mail (form DSP-82) provided that your previous passport is not more than eight years old. New applicants will need:

1. A birth certificate or certified copy thereof or other proof of citizenship;

2. Two identical photographs two inches square, full face, black and white or color, on nonglossy paper, and taken within the past six months;

3. $35 (same for a repeat passport) plus a $7 processing fee if you are applying in person (no processing fee if application is made by mail). For those under 18 the cost is $20 for the passport; same fee arrangements as above.

4. Proof of identity, featuring a photo and signature, such as a driver's license, employment ID card, previous passport, or government ID card. Social Security cards and credit cards are *not* acceptable.

U.S. passports are valid for 10 years. Passports issued for persons under 18 are only valid for five years. You should allow a month to six weeks for your application to be processed, but in an emergency, Passport Agency offices can have a passport readied within 24–48 hours, and even the postal authorities can indicate "Rush" when necessary.

If you expect to travel extensively, request a 48- or 96-page passport rather than the usual 24-page one. There is no extra charge. Record your passport's number, date, and place of issue in a separate, secure place. When you have pictures taken for passports, have extra copies made, especially if you plan to travel extensively. The loss of a valid passport should be reported immediately to the local police and to the Passport Office, Dept. of State, 1425 K St. NW, Washington, DC 20524, or to the nearest U.S. consular office when abroad.

Canadians. Canadian citizens may obtain application forms for passports at any post office; these should then be sent with a remittance of $21, two photographs, and evidence of Canadian citizenship to the Bureau of Passports, Complexe Guy Favreau, 200 Dorchester W., Montreal, PQ H2Z 1X4 (514-283-2152). You may apply in person to the regional passport offices in Edmonton, Halifax, Montreal, Toronto, Vancouver, or Winnipeg. Canadian passports are valid for five years and are nonrenewable.

HEALTH AND INSURANCE. Travel insurance can cover everything from health and accident costs to lost baggage and trip cancellation. Sometimes you can buy a blanket policy, while at other times the travel policy might overlap with existing coverage you have for health and/or home. In some cases it is best to buy policies that are tailored to very specific needs. However, insurance is available from many sources and travelers may unwittingly end up with redundant coverage, so be sure to check your regular policies first.

Generally, it is best to take care of your insurance needs *before* embarking on your trip. You'll pay more for less coverage—and have less chance to read the fine print—if you wait until the last minute and make your purchases from, say, an airport vending machine or insurance company counter. Best of all, if you have a regular insurance agent, he is the person to consult first.

Flight insurance, often included in the price of the ticket

when the fare is paid via American Express, Visa, or certain other major credit cards, is also often included in package policies providing accident coverage as well. These policies are available from most tour operators and insurance companies. While it is a good idea to have health and accident insurance when traveling, be careful not to spend money to duplicate coverage you may already have . . . or to neglect some eventuality which could end up costing a small fortune. For example, basic Blue Cross and Blue Shield policies cover health costs incurred while traveling. They will not, however, cover the cost of emergency transportation, which can often add up to several thousand dollars. Emergency transportation *is* covered, in part at least, by many major medical policies such as those underwritten by **Prudential, Metropolitan,** and **New York Life.** Again, we can't urge too strongly that you check any policy carefully before buying. Remember that most insurance issued specifically for travel does not cover pre-existing conditions, such as a heart problem.

Several organizations offer coverage designed to supplement existing health insurance and to help defray costs not covered by many standard policies, such as emergency transportation. Some of the more prominent are:

Carefree Travel Insurance, c/o Arm Coverage, Inc., Box 310, 120 Mineola, NY 11501 (516–294–0220) offers insurance, legal and financial assistance, as well as medical evacuation arranged through InterClaim. Carefree coverage is available from many travel agents.

IAMAT (International Association for Medical Assistance to Travelers), 417 Center St., Lewiston, NY 14092 in the U.S., or 188 Nicklin Rd., Guelph, Ont. N1H 7L5 in Canada.

International SOS Assistance, Inc., PO Box 11568, Philadelphia, PA 19116, has fees from $15 a person for seven days to $195 for a year (800–523–8930).

Travel Assistance International offers a comprehensive program providing medical and personal emergency services, and offering immediate on-the-spot medical, personal, and financial help. Trip protection ranges from $35 for an individual for up to eight days to $220 for an entire family for a year. Full details are available from travel agents and insurance brokers, or from **Europ Assistance**

Worldwide Services, Inc., 1333 F St. NW, Suite 300, Washington, DC 20004 (800–821–2828).

Loss of baggage is another frequent inconvenience to travelers. It is possible, though often complicated, to insure your luggage against loss through theft or negligence. Insurance companies are reluctant to sell such coverage alone, however, since it is often a losing proposition for them. Instead, this type of coverage is usually included as part of a package that also covers accidents or health. Remuneration is often determined by weight, regardless of the value of the specific contents of the luggage. Should you lose your luggage or some other personal possession, it is essential to report it to the local police immediately. Without documentation of such a report, your insurance company might be very stingy. Also, before buying baggage insurance, check your home-owners policy. Some such policies offer "off-premises theft" coverage, including the loss of luggage while traveling.

The last major area of traveler's insurance is trip cancellation coverage. This is especially important to travelers on APEX or charter flights. Should you get sick abroad, or for some other reason be unable to continue your trip, you may be stuck having to buy a new one-way fare home, plus paying for the charter you're not using. You can guard against this with "trip cancellation insurance," usually available from travel agents. Most of these policies will also cover last-minute cancellations.

BUDGET PACKAGE TOURS. Your money will go further if you buy a package tour. These range from the traditional bus tour to the independent travel package that provides a hotel room, a map, and not much more. The choice of London tours is particularly broad.

American Express, 822 Lexington Ave., New York, NY 10021 (212–758–6510) explores the country outside London as well as the city itself on its "London and Shakespeare Country" tour. 10 days for $555–$635.

Bennett Tours, 270 Madison Ave., New York, NY 10016 (212–532–5060) gives the traveler maximum freedom on its four-day package tour of the city. The cost is $270–$370.

Cosmos/Globus Gateway, 95–25 Queens Blvd., Rego Park, NY 11375 (718–268–1700) offers "A Week in London." Eight days from $259.

You will also find inexpensive tours from:

CIE, 122 E. 42nd St., New York, NY 10168 (212–972–5600).

Fourways Travel, 878 Bridgeport Ave., Shelton, CT 06484 (800–223–7872).

Pan Am, Pan Am Bldg., New York, NY 10017 (212–687–2600).

Trafalgar Tours, 21 E. 26th St., New York, NY 10010 (212–689–8977).

TWA, 28 S. Sixth St., Philadelphia, PA 19106 (215–925–7885).

FLY-DRIVE PACKAGES. Travelers wishing to brave the traffic in London and willing to fly full-fare economy might consider one of the fly-drive deals currently on offer.

British Airways (800–247–9297) and **Europcar** have two rental programs. If you just want a car, it's $17–$60 a day. Combined with hotel accommodations, however, a minimum stay of five days and nights costs $224 per person; extra days are $45 each person. Hotels can be pre-booked, or booked as you go along.

Pan Am (212–287–2600) and **Kemwell** charge $29 a day for a week's car hire.

TWA (800–438–2929) and **Hertz** offer a week's hire for $168, including tax.

All the above quotes are for unlimited mileage. Apart from the TWA/Hertz deal, they do not include tax.

RAIL TRAVEL BARGAINS. For anyone planning to visit other areas of Britain, the BritRail Pass is excellent value, and gives unlimited travel over the entire British Rail network. The pass is available only to overseas visitors. To obtain one, you must get a voucher in your home country at a BritRail Travel Information Office (addresses below), or from a travel agent. This is exchanged for the pass on arrival in Britain. See "Traveling Outside London" in the *Practical Information* section for price details.

For all information on rail travel, in North America contact BritRail Travel, 630 Third Ave., New York, NY 10017 (212–599–5400); Suite 603, 800 S. Hope St.,

Los Angeles, CA 90017 (213–624–8787); Cedar Maple Plaza, 2305 Cedar Springs, Dallas, TX 75201 (214–748–0860); 94 Cumberland St., Toronto, Ont. M5R 3N3 (416–929–3334); 409 Granville St., Vancouver, B.C. V6C 1T2 (604–683–6896).

WHEN TO GO. The regular tourist season in Britain runs from mid-April to mid-October, and the high season brings with it booked-up accommodations and higher room rates. The spring is the time to see the countryside at its greenest and freshest, while July and August are the months when most of the British take their vacations, though this most emphatically is not to say that London itself will seem empty. The winter can be rather dismal for wandering around the countryside at large, but in London it is a time full of interest, with theaters, opera, concerts, and art exhibitions running at full speed.

In the main, the climate is mild, though the weather is changeable and distinctly unpredictable. London is at its best in spring and fall—cool and fresh. Winter is rarely severe, though often gloomy. Summer temperatures hit the 80s at times, though not very often. You should remember that London buildings have little in the way of air conditioning, and dress accordingly. The annual rainfall in London is 23 inches.

Temperatures. Average maximum daily temperatures in Fahrenheit and centigrade:

Jan.	Feb.	Mar.	Apr.	May	Jun.	Jul.	Aug.	Sep.	Oct.	Nov.	Dec.
45	45	50	55	63	68	70	70	66	61	50	45
7	7	10	13	17	20	21	21	19	16	10	7

SPECIAL EVENTS. Here are some of the major happenings in London for 1988. Many of them are very posh social events, which, as a budget-oriented traveler, you are unlikely to be taking in, though even the most upscale of them offer the chance for the hoi polloi to watch. Take Ascot for example, the ritziest event in the social calendar. It is a race meeting as well as a society get-together, and the wide grass spaces round the track are crowded with people enjoying a free day out. Others, like Guy Fawkes night or the Chinese New Year, are times of general wingdingery, when it's come one, come all. Even the Wimbledon Tennis Championships can be a budget experience as they lower the price of entry after five in the afternoon.

January. 6–17, London International Boat Show, Earl's Court Center, SW5. 7–10, Racing Car Show, Alexandra Palace, N22. 20–24, West London Antiques Fair, Kensington Town Hall, W8. 29–1 Feb., International Silver and Jewelry Fair, Dorchester Hotel, W1.

February. 11–14, Crufts Dog Show, Earl's Court Center, SW5. 17, Chinese New Year—Year of the Dragon.

March. 8–7 Apr., Ideal Home Exhibition, Earl's Court Center, SW5. 10–13, Wind, Surf & Water Sports, Alexandra Palace, N22. 15–26, Chelsea Antiques Fair, Chelsea Old Town Hall, SW3. 28–30, London Book Fair, Olympia, W14. 26, Oxford v. Cambridge Boat Race, Putney to Mortlake.

April. 3, Easter Parade, Battersea Park, SW11. 17, London Marathon.

May. 1, London to Brighton Historic Commercial Vehicle Run, from Battersea Park, SW11. 12–15, Royal Windsor Horse Show, Home Park, Windsor. 14, FA Cup Final (soccer), Wembley Stadium, Middlesex. 24–27, Chelsea Flower Show (members only on 24), Royal Hospital, SW3.

June. 1, Derby Day, Epsom. 2–11 (closed 6), Fine Art and Antiques Fair, Olympia, W14. 8–18, Antiques Fair, Grosvenor House Hotel, W1. 10–13, International Ceramics Fair, Dorchester Hotel, W1. 11, Trooping the Color, Horse Guards Parade, SW1. 14–17, Royal Ascot, Berks. 20–3 July, Wimbledon Lawn Tennis Championships, All England Club, Wimbledon. 21–23, Antiquarian Book Fair, Park Lane Hotel, W1. 29–3 July, Henley Royal Regatta, Henley-on-Thames.

July. 3–23, Festival of the City of London, various venues. 3–30, Royal Tournament, Earl's Court Center, SW5. 22–17 Sept., Henry Wood Promenade Concerts, Royal Albert Hall, SW7. 23–7 Aug., Festival of London, Alexandra Palace, N22.

August. 7, London Riding Horse Parade, Rotten Row, Hyde Park, W2. 17–21, West London Antiques Fair, Kensington Town Hall, W8.

September. 13–24, Chelsea Antiques Fair, Chelsea Old Town Hall, SW3.

October. 2, Pearly Harvest Festival, St. Martins-in-the-Fields, WC2.

November. 5, Guy Fawkes night (bonfire and fireworks), Primrose Hill, NW3, and all over London. 6, London to Brighton Veteran Car Run, from Hyde Park, W2. 12, Lord Mayor's Show, City of London. 13, Remembrance Sunday Ceremony, Cenotaph, Whitehall, SW1. 22–26, City of London Antiques Fair, Barbican Center, EC2.

December. 5–8, Royal Smithfield Show, Earl's Court Center, SW5. 7–11, Masters Doubles Tennis Championship, Royal Albert Hall, SW7. 15–19, International Showjumping Championships, Olympia, W14.

National Holidays. Jan. 1 (New Year); Apr. 1, 4 (Easter); May 2 (May Day); May 30 (Spring Holiday); Aug. 29 (Late Summer Holiday); Dec. 25, 26 (Christmas and Boxing Day).

WHAT TO PACK. The first principle is to travel light. The restrictions by size or weight that are imposed on air travelers are an added incentive to keep baggage within the bounds of common sense. Don't forget that porters are scarce these days, and that you may have to carry your cases yourself.

Britain is often cool even in midsummer. In winter you will want sweaters, and you will certainly need rainwear; a foldaway umbrella will be useful. Ordinary, everyday dress runs very much to the casual, and these days it is increasingly unusual to dress formally in the evenings.

If you wear glasses or contact lenses, bring a spare pair. Also make sure you have enough medicines to see you through. Emergency hospital and emergency dental treatment is not free, contrary to popular belief. In most cases you will be required to pay on a private basis; however, this is usually considerably less expensive than in America. But it means that your insurance is all the more important.

Baggage. Regulations concerning baggage on transatlantic flights vary slightly from one airline to another, so check with yours before you go. In general, however, passengers are allowed to check two pieces of luggage and carry on one. Checked luggage is restricted by weight (an average maximum of 22 kilos) or by its total dimensions—the height, width, and depth totaling no more than 62″ on the first case, and 58″ on the other. Carry-on baggage must be small enough to fit either under the seat or in the baggage compartment overhead. These rules apply to economy-class passengers; first- and business-class passengers have a larger allowance. The charge for excess baggage is usually $66. These rules apply to transatlantic flights only. Remember to have your name and address marked clearly on both the outside and the inside of your baggage.

TIME ZONES. London and the U.K. operate on Greenwich mean time, which is five hours ahead of eastern standard time and eight hours ahead of pacific time (i.e., 12 noon in London is 7 in the morning in New York, 4 in Los Angeles). From about the end of March to the end of September, Britain puts its clocks forward one hour for British summer time, which is also five hours ahead of daylight saving time.

TRAVEL FOR THE DISABLED. Thousands of disabled people who are physically able to travel do so enthusiastically when they know they will be able to move about with safety and comfort. A growing number of travel agents specialize in this market, with tours that generally parallel those for the non-disabled traveler. The tours are taken at a more leisurely pace, with everything checked out in advance to eliminate inconvenience, whether the traveler is deaf, blind, or in a wheelchair.

The **Information Center for Individuals with Disabilities,** 20 Park Plaza, Rm. 330, Boston, MA 02116 (617–727–5540) is a helpful organization.

The **Society for the Advancement of Travel for the Handicapped,** 26 Court St., Brooklyn, NY 11242 (718–858–5483) can supply a complete list of travel agents who arrange such travel.

The **Travel Industry and Disabled Exchange,** 5435 Donna Ave., Tarzana, CA 91356 (818–343–6339) is another possibility.

The **Travel Information Center,** Moss Rehabilitation Hospital, 12th St. and Tabor Rd., Philadelphia, PA 19141 (215–329–5715) offers Travel Accessibility information packages detailing travel problems and possibilities to various destinations. The cost is $5; allow a month for delivery.

Several publications are available, including the excellent *Access to the World: A Travel Guide for the Handicapped* by Louise Weiss. It's published by Henry Holt & Co., but has to be ordered through your local bookstore. *The Itinerary,* a bimonthly magazine for travelers with disabilities, is published by Whole Person Tours, PO Box 1084, Bayonne, NJ 07002 (201–858–3400).

A number of car rental companies offer cars with hand controls, including Avis (800–331–1212), Hertz (800–654–3131), and National (800–328–4567). All of the above have London divisions.

Within London, there are several organizations worth knowing about.

Artsline, 5 Crowndale Rd., London NW1 1TU (tel. 01–338 2227) provides a handy service. Call Mon.–Fri. 10–4 or Sat. 10–2 for free information about movies, theaters, exhibits, lectures, concerts, festivals, and other entertainment suitable for the disabled.

Mobility International, 228 Borough High St., London SE1 1JX (tel. 01–403 5688) gives all kinds of information for the handicapped traveler.

The Royal Association for Disability and Rehabilitation (RADAR), 25 Mortimer St., London W1N 8AB (tel. 01–637 5400) is a useful source, particularly for guides (see below).

Of the London-produced literature, *Access in London,* largely researched by disabled people and published by Nicholson, costs £2.25. For the same price you can get *London Made Easy,* a guide that's aimed at both the disabled and the over-60s. It's produced by the London Tourist Board, and is widely available. *Access to the Underground* from London Regional Transport (01–222 5600) gives information on the Tube system. Visually disabled travelers are also catered to: The Talking Underground

Map and now the Talking Underground Station Guide are two tapes available from LRT. The second tape lists the stations alphabetically, telling you what line the station is on, and what type of access there is to the platform. Copies are free from the Unit for Disabled Travelers, London Regional Transport, 55 Broadway, London SW1H 0BD (tel. 01–227 3312). Finally, RADAR (address above) publishes several guides, including the excellent, regularly updated *Holidays for the Disabled* (£2 excluding postage).

STUDENT TRAVEL. Britain is particularly well attuned to students and young travelers, offering discounts to many historical sites and stately homes and gardens, as well as having a wide variety of low-priced, quality accommodations. Hostels, bed-and-breakfasts, and universities (the latter when school is not in session) tend to be the most popular.

An *International Student Identity Card* will get you discounts at all museums (though most of these are free anyway), concerts, and theaters, as well as qualifying you for discounts on inter-European student charter flights and for youth rail and bus passes, available from travel agents all over the U.S. Depending on where you live, apply for an ISI Card from one of the following:

The Council on International Educational Exchange, 205 E. 42nd St., New York, NY 10017, or 312 Sutter St., San Francisco, CA 94108.

The Association of Student Councils, 187 College St., Toronto, Ont. M5T 1P7.

A number of travel agents specialize in student travel:

Arista Student Travel Assoc., 11 E. 44th St., New York, NY 10017.

Bailey Travel Service, 123 E. Market St., York, PA 17401.

Harwood Tours & Travel, 2428 Guadelupe, Austin, TX 78705.

Osborne Travel Service, 3379 Peachtree Rd. NE, Atlanta, GA 30326.

Finally, the following are worth bearing in mind for

student flights, educational opportunities, and other information.

American Youth Hostels, PO Box 37613, Washington, DC 20013, grants its members entry to the worldwide network of youth hostels. The organization publishes an extensive directory listing hostels, many in Britain.

The British Tourist Authority (BTA), 40 W. 57th St., New York, NY 10019, publishes the immensely useful *Young Visitors to Britain,* which contains a thorough listing of courses and activities in Britain.

The Council on International Educational Exchange (address above) provides information on summer study, work/travel programs, and travel services for college and high school students, as well as a free guide to charter flights. The organization's *Whole World Handbook* ($7.95 plus $1 postage) is an excellent listing of both work and study possibilities abroad.

The Institute of International Education, 809 United Nations Plaza, New York, NY 10017, concentrates on study opportunities including scholarships and fellowships for international study and training. The New York office has a visitors' information center; satellite offices are located in Chicago, Denver, Houston, San Francisco, and Washington.

Getting to London

BY PLANE. As the air route between North America and Britain is one of the world's most heavily traveled, the passenger has many airlines (and fares) to choose from. But fares change with stunning rapidity, so consult your travel agent on which bargains are currently available.

The best buy is not an APEX (advance purchase) ticket on one of the major airlines. APEX tickets carry certain restrictions: they must be bought in advance (usually 21 days); they restrict your travel, usually with a minimum stay of seven days and a maximum of 90; and they also penalize you for changes—voluntary or not—in your travel plans. But if you can work around these drawbacks (and most can), they are among the best-value fares available. Mid-1987, the New York–London APEX fare was $680.

Virgin Atlantic has become the standard bearer for low-cost, low-frills flying. Mid-1987, New York–London cost $558 round-trip. These tickets carry fewer restrictions than APEX fares.

Airlines to contact:

Air Canada, 1166 Ave. of the Americas, New York, NY 10036 (212–869–1900).

British Airways, 245 Park Ave., New York, NY 10167 (212–687–1600).

British Caledonian, 10700 N. Freeway, Ste. 700, Houston, TX 77037 (800–231–0270).

Pan Am, Pan Am Bldg., New York, NY 10017 (212–687–2600).

TWA, 605 Third Ave., New York, NY 10016 (212–290–2141).

Virgin Atlantic, 43 Perry St., New York, NY 10014 (212–242–1330).

A third possibility is a charter flight. Seats on charter flights are inexpensive, but can only be found with the help of a travel agent. Easier to obtain are the last-minute seats sold at cut-rate by tour operators left with empty places on a particular flight. These are sometimes advertised in the travel section of the Sunday papers. A number of brokers specialize in such tickets, and usually charge an annual membership fee of $35–$45. Names to look for are:

Discount Travel International, 114 Forrest Ave., Narberth, PA 19072 (215–668–2182).

Moments Notice, 40 E. 49th St., New York, NY 10017 (212–486–0503).

Stand-Buys Ltd., 311 W. Superior, Ste. 414, Chicago, IL 60610 (312–943–5737).

Worldwide Discount Travel Club, 1674 Meridian Ave., Miami Beach, FL 33139 (305–534–2082).

Leaving London

CUSTOMS ON RETURNING HOME. Americans. U.S. residents may bring in $400 worth of foreign merchandise as gifts or for personal use without having to pay duty, provided they have been out of the country more than 48 hours and provided they have not claimed a similar exemption within the previous 30 days. Every member of a family is entitled to the same exemption, regardless of age, and the exemption can be pooled. For the next $1,000 worth of goods, inspectors will assess a flat 10% duty based on the price actually paid, so it is a good idea to keep your receipts; above $1,400 duties vary with type of merchandise.

Included in the $400 allowance for travelers over the age of 21 are one liter of alcohol, 100 cigars (non-Cuban), and 200 cigarettes. Any amount in excess of those limits will be taxed at the port of entry, and may additionally be taxed in the traveler's home state. Only one bottle of perfume trademarked in the U.S. may be brought in. However, there is no duty on antiques or art over 100 years old—though you may be called upon to provide verification of the item's age. Write to U.S. Customs Service, Washington, DC 20229 for information regarding importation of automobiles and/or motorcycles. You may not bring home meats, fruits, plants, soil, or other agricultural items.

Gifts valued at under $50 may be mailed to friends or relatives at home, but not more than one per day (of receipt) to any one addressee. These gifts must not include perfumes costing more than $5, tobacco, or liquor.

If you are traveling with such foreign-made articles as cameras, watches, or binoculars that were purchased at home, it is best either to carry the receipt for them with you or to register them with U.S. Customs prior to departing. This will save much time (and potential aggravation) upon your return.

Canadians. In addition to personal effects, the following articles may be brought into Canada duty-free: a maximum of 50 cigars, 200 cigarettes, or two pounds of tobacco and 40 ounces of liquor, provided these are declared to customs on arrival. The exemption is $300, and gifts mailed to friends should be marked "Unsolicited Gift—value under $50."

VAT REFUNDS. See *Shopping,* page XX.

PRACTICAL INFORMATION FOR LONDON

CUSTOMS ON ARRIVAL. There are two levels of duty-free

allowances for people entering the U.K.: **one,** for goods bought outside the EEC or for goods bought in a duty-free shop within the EEC; **two,** for goods bought in an EEC country but *not* in a duty-free shop.

In the first category you may import duty free: 200 cigarettes or 100 cigarillos or 50 cigars or 250 grams of tobacco *(Note* if you live outside Europe, these allowances are doubled); plus one liter of alcoholic drinks over 22% vol. (38.8° proof) or two liters of alcoholic drinks not over 22% vol. or fortified or sparkling or still wine; plus two liters of still table wine; plus 50 grams of perfume; plus nine fluid ounces of toilet water; plus other goods to the value of £32.

In the second category you may import duty free: 300 cigarettes or 150 cigarillos or 75 cigars or 400 grams of tobacco; plus 1½ liters of alcoholic drinks over 22% vol. (38.8° proof) or three liters of alcoholic drinks not over 22% vol. or fortified or sparkling or still wine; plus five liters of still table wine; plus 75 grams of perfume; plus 13 fluid ounces of toilet water; plus other goods to the value of £250. *(Note* though it is not classified as an alcoholic drink by EEC countries for Customs purposes and is thus considered part of the "other goods" allowance, you may not import more than 50 liters of beer.)

In addition, no animals or pets of any kind may be brought into the U.K. The penalties for doing so are severe and are strictly enforced; there are *no* exceptions. Similarly, fresh meats, plants, and vegetables, controlled drugs, and firearms and ammunition may not be brought into the U.K. There are no restrictions on the import or export of British and foreign currencies.

Anyone planning to stay in the U.K. for more than six months should contact H.M. Customs and Excise, Dorset House, Stanford St., London SE1 9PS (tel. 928 0533) for further information.

CURRENCY. The monetary unit in Britain, the pound sterling, is divided into 100 pence, usually abbreviated to "p." There are banknotes of £50, £20, £10, and £5; the coins are £1, 50p, 20p, 10p, 5p, 2p, and 1p. Don't confuse the seven-sided 50p piece with the similarly sized 10p piece. The old two-shilling and one-shilling coins are still in

use and are equivalent in size and identical in value to 10p
and 5p, respectively.

CHANGING MONEY. Banks at all main airports and rail
stations are open from early in the morning to late at night
for changing money when you first arrive. Otherwise,
within London itself, your best bet is to head for any
branch of the major banks. They will always change money
for you at reasonable rates. Banks close at 3:30 P.M.,
however, and most do not open on weekends, so it's
important to change money in advance to avoid being
caught out. There is a series of small change offices
throughout the West End, most of them open daily and
closing late. But they should be used only in emergencies as
their charges are little short of robbery.

TIPPING AND TAXES. Some hotels will add a service charge
of about 10–12.5% to your bill; be sure to find out if this
applies to you when you check in. Generally speaking, you
will find that few of the hotels suggested in this book make
a service charge.

As you are on a budget vacation, the only tips you will
need to give are to the hotel porter (25p per case), 20p to
the bellboy if he hails you a taxi, and about 25p for drinks
or sandwiches brought to your room. If you have spent
several days in the same hotel, £1 for the chambermaid
would not go amiss, but use your discretion.

In restaurants a service charge of 10–15% is usually
included in the bill; if not, leave 10%. There's no need to
tip if you are just having a coffee. At teatime leave 10 or
20p if the waitress is pleasant, nothing if you fetch it
yourself from a counter.

Hairdressers in London get 12–15%, elsewhere 10% is
plenty; station and airport porters—if you can find them—
get about 30p a bag, but it's smarter to find a luggage
trolley. Do not tip in pubs, though you can buy the barman
a drink if you are on friendly terms; do not tip cinema or
theater ushers, elevator operators, or, unlike most European countries, washroom attendants. The latter do sometimes display a saucer, and if you feel like leaving 5p or 10p
that's fine, but you don't have to. Taxi drivers get about
10%.

GETTING IN FROM THE AIRPORTS. From **Heathrow,** there

are three forms of transport into Central London: by coach (bus), by underground (tube), or by taxi. From **Gatwick** you can take the overground train or a choice of buses. Though the trip *can* be done by taxi, the distance involved makes it extremely costly, and the very opposite of a great travel value!

London Regional Transport runs a special "careline service" carrying disabled passengers between Central London and Heathrow Airport.

By Bus. From Heathrow, LRT runs double-decker Airbuses from all four terminals. The hotel areas of west London are well served: the A1 goes to Victoria Station, with intermediate stops along the Cromwell Road and Sloane Street, Chelsea; the A2 finishes up at Euston Station, calling at Marble Arch and Russell Square. Trip time is 40–60 minutes, depending on the traffic. The A1 leaves Heathrow every 20 minutes between 6:20 and 12:50, then every half hour until 10:20 P.M.; the A2 every 20 minutes in the morning and then half-hourly until 9:05. Fare is £3 one way; you can also pay in U.S. or Canadian dollars.

An alternative to the Airbus, and serving Gatwick and Luton as well as Heathrow, is the Flightline Coach, which finishes up at Victoria Station. Coach 767 departs Heathrow every 20 minutes from 6:40 to 12:40, then half-hourly until 9:05, taking approximately 45 minutes. The 777 leaves Gatwick every 30 minutes between 6 A.M. and 10 P.M. (again, hourly in evening); it takes about 70 minutes.

By Tube. There are two Underground stations at Heathrow; one for terminals 1, 2, and 3; and the other for the new terminal 4. During the day trains run roughly every five minutes, and the ride to the center takes about 40 minutes. The fare to any central zone station is around £1.60. Problems for the visitor can be the long lines for tickets and minimal space for luggage; the Underground does not directly serve the main tourist hotel areas, and there are no carts for bags at the other end. All this can be a bit daunting after a transatlantic flight. However, tubes run 20 hours a day (slightly less on Sundays) and are easily reached by moving walkways at Heathrow.

By Train. The British Rail overground train is unquestionably the best way of getting into town from Gatwick;

the ride to Victoria takes but 30 minutes and costs £4.60 (£6.90 first class). The station is inside the airport, just a short walk from the Arrivals Hall. Between 5:30 A.M. and 11:30 P.M. there are four trains an hour to Victoria.

By Taxi. As already mentioned, this is not really feasible from Gatwick given the mileage involved. However, from Heathrow the cost of a cab into Central London should work out at about £16–£18 depending on the time of day and traffic conditions.

TOURIST OFFICES. The **London Tourist Board,** 26 Grosvenor Gdns., SW1W 0DU (tel. 730 3488) gives details for London and Britain. The LTB also has a useful center at Victoria Rail Station for tickets, theater, and tour bookings, plus a bookshop, and an accommodation service including the Book-a-Bed-Ahead scheme. Open daily 9–8:30, including Sun. July and Aug. 8–10. There are Information Centers at Selfridges and Harrods (only open during store hours), at Heathrow Airport terminals 1, 2, and 3, and at the Tower of London, Apr. through Oct.

The **British Travel Center** is at 12 Regent St., SW1Y 4PQ (tel. 730 3400).

CITY FACTS. London sits in the southeast of England, 40 miles from the coast. The city and suburbs that make up Greater London radiate either side of the river Thames for 625 square miles. Today, however, suburban growth has slowed right down, taking second place to the urban renewal of inner London—a renewal encouraged by Londoners less and less willing to endure the rigors of daily commuting from the suburbs.

Just as suburban expansion has dwindled, so has London's population growth. About 6.8 million people now live in the capital, roughly a third of whom were born in some place other than London itself.

Greater London is divided into 32 boroughs—33, when you consider the City of London, which has all the powers of a London borough. More useful for finding your way around, however, are the subdivisions of London into various postal districts. Throughout the guide we've listed the full postal code for places you're likely to be contacting by mail, although you'll find the first half the most important. The first one or two letters give the location:

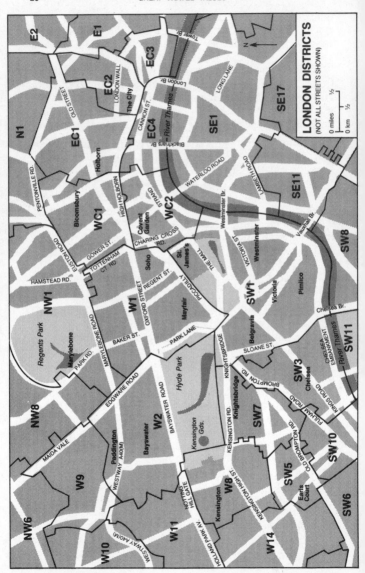

LONDON DISTRICTS
(NOT ALL STREETS SHOWN)

N=north, NW=northwest, etc. Don't expect the numbering to be so logical, however. You won't, for example, find W2 next to W3.

USEFUL ADDRESSES. Airlines. Air Canada, 140 Regent St., W1R 6AT (tel. 759 2636); British Airways, 75 Regent St., W1R 7HG (tel. 439 9584); Pan Am, 193 Piccadilly, W1V 0AD (tel. 409 0688); TWA, 200 Piccadilly, W1Z 0DH (tel. 636 4090); United (tel. 734 9282); Virgin Atlantic, The Virgin Megastore, 14–16 Oxford St., W1N 9FL (tel. 631 3757).

Changing Money. American Express, 6 Haymarket, SW1Y 4BS (tel. 930 4411), and 89 Mount St., W1Y 6AY (tel. 499 9584); Hogg Robinson/Diners Club, 176 Tottenham Court Rd., W1P 0DE (tel. 580 0437); Thomas Cook, 45 Berkeley St., Piccadilly, W1A 1EB (tel. 499 4000), or 378 The Strand, WC2R 0LW (tel. 836 0811). There are other branches of all of the above.

Credit Cards. If you lose or have your credit cards stolen, here are some numbers to call. Access/Mastercard (tel. 0702–352255); American Express (tel. 0273–696933 for credit cards, 0273–693555 for travelers checks); Barclaycard/Visa (tel. 0604–21288); Diners Club (tel. 0252–516261).

Embassies. American Embassy, 24 Grosvenor Sq., W1A 1AE (tel. 499 9000); Canadian High Commission, Canada House, Trafalgar Sq., SW1Y 5BJ (tel. 629 9492).

Lost Property. For items lost on tubes and buses, try the LRT lost property office, 200 Baker St., NW1 5RZ (tel. 486 2496), open Mon. to Fri. 9:30–2. All the main British Rail stations have lost property offices, although after a week items go to the office at Waterloo Station (tel. 922 6135), open Mon. to Fri. 8:10–7. If you leave something in a taxi, contact the Public Carriage Office, 15 Penton St., N1 9PU, open Mon. to Fri. 9–4.

Medical Emergencies. The following hospitals all have 24 hour casualty departments: Guys (tel. 407 7600), The Royal Free (tel. 794 0500), St. Bartholomew's (601 8888), St. Thomas's (tel. 928 9292), University College (tel. 387 9300), and Westminster (828 9811). Drugstores (chemists) that open late include Bliss Chemist, 55–56 Willesden Lane NW6 7FX (tel. 624 8000), open daily 9 A.M.–2 P.M.

Closer at hand to the center of London is the branch at 5 Marble Arch W1H 7AP (tel. 723 6116), open daily 9 A.M.–midnight. Inoculations can be had at short notice at British Airways, 75 Regent St. W1R 7HG (tel. 439 9584). Allow two to three days for an appointment, or else walk in and take your turn. Open Mon. to Fri. 8:30–4:30. Alternatively, try Thomas Cook at 45 Berkeley St. W1A 1EB (tel. 499 4000).

MAIL. Post offices are open Mon. to Fri. 9–5:30, Sat. 9–12:30. Postage stamps can be bought from main post offices or sub-post offices (always part of a shop), and from stamp machines outside main post offices. You cannot buy stamps anywhere else. Mailboxes are known as post- or letterboxes and are painted red; you will find the familiar tubular ones set on the edge of sidewalks. Smaller boxes are set into post office walls.

At press time, summer 1987, postage rates were as follows. Airmail letters up to 10 grams to the U.S. and Canada, 31p; postcards and aerograms, 26p. Letters and postcards up to 20 grams to EEC countries, 18p; to the rest of Europe, 22p. Letters within the U.K. cost 18p first class and 13p second class and for postcards.

TELEPHONES. Britain's telephone booths come in three types. The traditional **Pay-on-Answer** phone takes only 10p coins. Lift the receiver and listen for the dial tone (a purring noise). Dial the complete number, including the code. If you get an interrupted single tone (beep beep beep), then the line is engaged. A repeated ringing (brr-brr, brr-brr) means that you've got the line. When someone answers you will hear rapid pips—put the coin in the slot immediately, then speak. If you hear the pips before you've finished the call, put in another 10p. Should you have any difficulty with your call, dial the operator at 100.

The blue **Press Button** phone takes 2p, 5p, 10p, 50p, and £1 coins, and can also be used for international calls. Use a lot of smaller coins rather than one coin of a larger amount, as you only get change if a coin has not been used at all. Put your money in first, dial, and your coins will be used up as you speak—no pips with this system. A sign flashes when you need to put in more coins.

The third type is the **Cardphone.** Post offices or newsagents stock phonecards, which come in values of £2, £5, £10, and £20. An indicator panel shows how many units you're using; at the end of the call the card will be returned to you.

The three charge rates are: peak rate Mon. to Fri. 9 A.M.–1 P.M., standard rate Mon. to Fri. 8 A.M.–9 A.M. and 1 P.M.–6 P.M., and cheap rate Mon. to Fri. 6 P.M.–8 A.M. and all day Sat. and Sun. International calls are cheaper during some parts of the day; exactly when depends on your telephone destination, so check with the international operator (tel. 155) before dialing.

London numbers are often given with the code 01– at the beginning. Ignore this unless you are phoning into London from elsewhere in the country.

Note. Bear in mind the huge surcharges that hotels levy on calls made from guest rooms; pay phones are found in most hotel foyers. The **Westminster Communications Center** at 1 The Broadway, SW1H 0AY (opposite New Scotland Yard and St. James's Park Underground) has an overseas calls service. Open daily 9–7.

IMPORTANT TELEPHONE NUMBERS.

999	Fire, police, or ambulance
283 3400	Samaritans
837 1600	Rape Crisis Center
142	London directory inquiries (Information)
192	Directory inquiries (Information) outside London
123	The correct time
730 3488	London Tourist Board
730 0791	Teletourist Service
222 1234	London Regional Transport travel inquiries
387 7070	Euston/St. Pancras train information
278 2477	King's Cross train information
283 7171	Liverpool Street train information
262 6767	Paddington train information
928 5100	Victoria/Waterloo train information
353 4242	Daily Telegraph general information service
246 8026	Financial Times Index and Business News Summary
246 9091	Local weather report
246 8021	Road conditions within 50 miles of London

Getting Around

TICKET BARGAINS. London is split into five concentric fare zones, and though individual ticket charges continue to rise, LRT has tried to limit any increase in the rates of various "bargain" travel cards and passes. Get a zonal map from LRT or British Rail before deciding which of the various offers best suits your travel plans. Individual trips in the central zone cost 50p; if you cross into the next zone it's 70p. These two zones cover most visitors' needs.

One Day Off-Peak Travelcard. This allows unrestricted travel on both bus and tube from 9:30 A.M. onward, Mon. to Fri., and at all times during the weekend and on public holidays. It costs £1.70 or £2, depending on the number of zones covered.

One Week Travelcard. This is a less expensive version of the Visitor's Travelcard. A week's travel in two zones is £6; for all five zones you pay £14.30. This card allows travel in the rush hour. You need a photograph.

Visitor's Travelcard. If bought before you arrive in Britain, this card is available for three, four, or seven days, for $11, $15, or $24, respectively. Only the seven-day card is available in Britain. The card can be used on bus and tube in all zones, and includes the Airbus service between Heathrow and Central London.

Capitalcard. This is for the traveler planning the odd trip out of Central London via British Rail's overground train service; it also includes bus and tube travel. One day's travel in all zones costs £2.50. Seven days' travel costs £7 for two zones, £10.20 for three, £13.20 for four, and £16.30 for all five. (See *Traveling Outside London.*)

Network Southeast Card. See *Traveling Outside London.*

Cheap Day Return. This is available for bus or tube as well as for British Rail. It is less expensive than two singles, and is useful for the odd day out.

TRAVEL INFORMATION. London Regional Transport Travel Information Centers can be found at the following tube stations: Oxford Circus, Mon. to Sat. 8:15–6, closed Sun.; Piccadilly Circus, Mon. to Sun. 8:15–9:30; Victoria (upstairs), Mon. to Sun. 8:15–9:30; King's Cross, Sun. to Thurs. 8:15–6, Fri. to Sat. 7:15–6; Euston, Mon. to Sat. 7:15–6, Sun. 8:15–6. Opening times at Heathrow Airport are: Heathrow Central, Mon. to Sat. 7:15–6:30, Sun. 8:15–6:30; Terminal 1, Mon. to Fri. 7:15–10:15, Sat. 7:15–9, Sun. 8:15–10; Terminal 2, Mon. to Sat. 7:15–9, Sun. 8:15–10; Terminal 3, Mon. to Sat. 6:30–1:15 (lunchtime), Sun. 8:15–3; Terminal 4, Mon. to Sat. 6:30–6:30, Sun. 8:15–6:30.

BY UNDERGROUND. Known colloquially as "The Tube," London's Underground train system is extensive, covering the entire central area and many of the suburbs. All stations, both those on the surface and those underground, are clearly marked with the London Underground symbol and the word "Underground." Trains are all one class, and smoking is not allowed either on the trains or in stations.

There are nine basic lines—all named—plus the East London line that runs from Shoreditch and Whitechapel across the Thames as far south as New Cross. The Central, District, Metropolitan, Piccadilly, and Northern lines have branches, so check which branch your particular destination is on. Signboards tell you the final destination and route of the next train; some central stations also have signs indicating how long you have to wait for the train to arrive.

LRT issues a useful pocket map of the whole system. Every platform should have at least one enlarged map on the wall, although these can be defaced beyond recognition. There should also be a map in every carriage.

Tickets can be bought from ticket offices or from automatic ticket machines that also give change. When you pass through the automatic barriers, collect your ticket; it *must* be handed in at the end of your journey. Alternatively, buy one of the travel cards described above.

During the week, trains start just after 5 A.M.; last services from Central London are between midnight and 12:30. On Sun. they start two hours later and finish an hour earlier. Frequency of trains depends on the route and time of day, but you should not have to wait longer than 10 minutes in central districts.

BY BUS. LRT runs London's bus system with its red double-decker buses and a growing number of single-decker buses. The destination is displayed on the front and back of the bus, with the number on the front, back, and

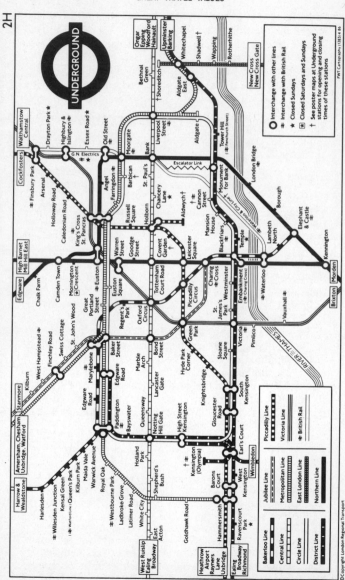

London Regional Transport Underground Map Registered User No. 88/668

PWT Cartography (1383) ii 46

side. Buses don't always run the full length of their route, so check the termination point before boarding. Many buses are now "one-man operated"; you pay the driver as you enter. This can cause considerable delay.

Buses stop only at clearly indicated stops. Main stops have a white background bearing a red LRT symbol; buses should stop automatically. There are also request stops with a red background and white symbol, with the word "Request" added. At these you need to hail the bus to make it stop. Just stick your arm out.

Smoking is not allowed on the lower deck of double-decker buses and is discouraged on the top deck, save at the back.

Traveling by bus you see much of the town, but London traffic often slows buses to a crawl. In addition, at peak times you could find yourself waiting 20 minutes for a bus and then find it so crowded you might not be able to get on once it arrives.

If you do go by bus, get hold of the London-Wide Bus Map, free from LRT.

BY TAXI. These unmistakable vehicles, with square bodies and a separate compartment for the driver, are liberally scattered throughout Central and west London. No longer exclusively black, some now come in a variety of colors and carry advertising on their sides. If the taxi flag is up or a "for hire" sign is lighted on the top, then hail the taxi. Cab drivers often cruise at night with their "for hire" signs unlit. This is to enable them to choose their passengers and avoid those they think might cause trouble. If you see an unlit, passengerless cab, hail it. You may well be lucky.

Fares start at 80p when the flag falls; after 990 yards or 3½ minutes the meter clicks up at a rate of 20p per 495 yards or 60 seconds. After six miles the rate changes to 20p per 330 yards (or one minute). Weekday nights 8–12 and Sat. up to 8 P.M. there's a 40p surcharge. This rises to 60p on Sat. nights, Sun., and public holidays. Over Christmas and New Year's Eve the surcharge is £2. If, after reading that, you can bear to, tip the driver around 10 per cent.

BY CAR. Driving in London is not recommended for tourists. Distances are large, parking difficult to come by, and whereas there is some logic in the street planning in North American cities, in London there is none. A minute grid system bequeathed by the Romans and extended in all directions in a haphazard manner over 2,000 years has not been clarified by the plethora of one-way streets. Drivers who get lost and hope to retrieve the situation by returning to base through a series of left-hand turns invariably find themselves somewhere else.

For those who must drive in London, the speed limit is 30 mph unless you see the large 40 mph signs found in the suburbs. Pedestrians have priority on "zebra" crossings. These have black and white stripes between two striped beacons topped with orange bowls (that flash at night). It is an offense to park within the area of zigzag markings on either side of the crossing, or to overtake another vehicle on the approach side. The British mostly take their pedestrian crossings seriously. On other crossings pedestrians must give way to the traffic, but they take precedence over that turning left at controlled crossings.

The red, yellow, and green traffic lights sometimes have arrow-style filter lights directing left- or right-hand turns. It is therefore important not to get into the turn lane if you mean to go straight on (if you can catch a glimpse of the road markings in time). The use of horns is prohibited in all built-up areas between 11:30 P.M. and 7 A.M. You can park at night in 30 mph limit zones provided that you are within 25 yards of a lit street lamp, but not within 15 yards of a road junction. To park on a bus route, side (parking) lights must be shown—but you'll probably be fined for obstruction. In the daytime it is safest to believe that you can park nowhere but at a meter or in a garage. The cost of transgression is now £12. An official toy, much in the news and not exclusive to Britain, is the notorious Denver Boot, which clamps a wheel immovably and costs £37 (including the ticket) to get released. Note that it is now illegal to park on the sidewalk in London.

If you still want to hire a car, see "Traveling Outside London."

BY CYCLE. A good way to see London is by renting a bicycle by the day, by the week, or longer. Try **Dial-a-Bike,** 18 Gillingham St., SW1V 1HU (tel. 828 4040). Current rates start at £5 per day, plus £40 deposit. You'll need identification, so bring your passport. Be warned, though, that unless you are a fairly experienced cyclist, London traffic can be a little daunting. Also, the incidence of bicycle theft is very high.

BY BOAT. See "Escorted Tours."

Traveling Outside London

BY RAIL. All major rail services in Britain are run by British Rail, and most are fast and reliable. The principal services are on the InterCity network that radiates from London, connecting the country's major towns and cities. Unlike many European railways, British Rail makes no extra charge for travel on its express services. Its InterCity 125s are comfortable, air conditioned trains that are widely used and travel up to 125 mph. The remaining InterCity trains, though not as fast as the 125s, are reasonably comfortable and reliable.

Local services present a slightly different picture, with the vast commuter network around London sporting some services that are not always good. However, trains to all major destinations are perfectly satisfactory, although services can be slow, especially at weekends.

One thing must be stressed about rail travel to and from London: The city has no fewer than 15 rail stations, so be absolutely certain which one your train departs from or arrives at. All have Underground stations either on the premises or within a couple of minutes' walk. They are also served by many bus routes.

Check British Rail's *Out and About Britain* booklet for places that can be visited in a day.

Fares. These are high when compared with trains in many European countries. However, there is a wide, and often bewildering, range of ticket reductions. Ticket clerks cannot always be relied upon to know which is best for you, so check at the information office first. Alternatively, get both travel information *and* your tickets in advance from the British Rail Travel Centers in Regent Street, The Strand, King William Street, Victoria Street, and at Heathrow Airport. In addition, many travel agents are authorized by British Rail to sell tickets; they display the British Rail "double arrow" logo in the window.

Britrail Pass. This is only available to overseas visitors (check the *Planning Your Trip* section for North American addresses). The pass can be bought for periods of eight, 15, or 22 days, or for a month; prices are $149, $225, $285, and $355, respectively, for economy class. Visitors over the age of 60 can travel *first* class for $180, $270, $340, or $400, while the less expensive **Youth Pass** for those between 16 and 25 costs $130, $190, $240, or $285, economy class. These passes are useful for those intending to travel widely outside London.

Capitalcard. A week's Capitalcard for all five zones in the Greater London area costs £16.30 and gives you rail access to, say, Greenwich, Blackheath, and Dulwich, as well as tube and bus access to Hampstead, Kew Gardens, and Richmond. Windsor and Hampton Court are outside the Capitalcard area. See the *Getting Around* section for more details.

Cheap Day Returns. These are excellent value if you intend to return the same day, although the tickets cannot be used before 9:30 A.M.

Network Southeast Card. This card is for those wishing to travel within Southeast England. The £10 card allows a third off ticket prices for up to three adults; children travel for £1. You cannot use the card before 10 A.M., Mon. to Fri.

BY BUS. American visitors planning to travel by bus should take note of the difference between buses and coaches. Buses in Britain generally form part of local public transport systems and are used in towns and cities and their immediate vicinity. They stop frequently. Coaches, on the other hand, are more like Greyhounds; they are more comfortable than buses and are used on longer trips. Coaches are quite separate from local public transport and often use different departure points.

The coach and bus network was deregulated in 1986. **National Express,** Victoria Coach Station, Buckingham Palace Rd., SW1W 9TP (tel. 730 0202) leads the way with both its regular coaches and the high-speed *Rapide* service. The London-to-Brighton journey costs £6 for a day return; by British Rail the cost is £7.40. Students with a £3.50

Student Coach Card get a third off the normal fare; senior citizens of any nationality automatically get the same discount, upon presenting a passport. National Express also has an office at 13 Regent St., SW1Y 4RL (tel. 839 1975).

Aside from National Express, **Greenline** coaches operate within a 30–40 mile radius of London. A Golden Rover ticket gives unlimited travel for £3.95. Contact Greenline at Lesbourne Rd., Reigate Surrey (tel. 668 7261).

BY CAR. Although visitors are advised not to rent cars for use in London, some might want a car for the drive to places outside the capital. To rent a car, all you need is your current domestic driving license or an International Driving Permit. In Britain you drive on the left-hand side of the road. To generalize, speed limits are 30 mph in built-up areas, 40 mph in some suburban areas, 70 mph on dual carriageways (divided roads) and motorways, and 60 mph on all other roads, unless otherwise indicated.

The price of gasoline (ask for petrol) when we went to press in summer 1987 was somewhat unsteady, but an imperial gallon came in at about £1.75. Petrol comes in three grades, but the price difference is negligible. Lubricating oil averages £2.30 a liter (less if you buy a five-liter can). The British imperial gallon is larger than the American one—four of the former equal five of the latter.

Car Rental. Numerous car rental firms operate throughout the country; their names and addresses can be found in the yellow pages and at Tourist Offices. Many of the large national firms will meet you with a car at your point of arrival, and there are car rental offices at major airports and seaports.

To give you an idea of charges, a Ford Fiesta from Avis will cost you £168 for a week, including service and tax. Watch out for rates that are exclusive, as the extras can add £50 to your bill in no time. You will also have to pay a deposit. Some firms charge less than this, and nearly all operate an inexpensive weekend scheme, whereby you pick up a car Friday evening and return it Monday morning. A few car rental firms are listed below; most have other branches.

Avis Rent-a-Car, 68 North Row, off Park Lane, W1R 1DE (tel. 629 7811).

Budget Rent-a-Car, 74–78 Culpitt House, Hatfield Town Center, Hatfield, Herts (toll-free tel. 0800–181 181).

Central Rent-a-Car, 48–56 Ebury Bridge Rd., SW1W 8QF (tel. 730 9130).

Godfrey Davis, Davis House, Wilton Rd., SW1V 1LA (tel. 834 8484).

Hertz Rent-a-Car, 200 Buckingham Palace Rd., SW1W 9TJ (tel. 730 8323).

Kenning Car Hire, Central Reservations, Manor Offices, Old Rd., Chesterfield, Derbys (tel. 0246–7724).

The British Tourist Authority produces a free booklet, *Vehicle Hire,* as well as a leaflet entitled *On the Road in Great Britain.*

Where to Stay

Despite the range of places to stay in London, the following list centers on the small hotel, guest house, and bed-and-breakfast market, and on hostel and camping facilities. There are also suggestions for those wanting to stay for a week or more.

If you arrive in London without a hotel reservation, certain booking agencies can help. Gatwick Airport's desk is between the Arrivals Hall and the British Rail Center, Heathrow's is in the underground station. At Victoria Station, the London Tourist Board's accommodations service is in the Tourist Information Center at the front of the station by the Grosvenor Hotel. A deposit must be paid when making a reservation and this will be deducted from your final bill. A nominal, nonreturnable booking fee is also charged.

In London, bed and breakfast does not mean the same as it does in the U.S. Most B&Bs are small, converted, row houses, with standards of decor not unlike a budget motel—in other words, not at all like home. We have tried to include only those that are at least clean and have pleasant management. Being converted houses, few have elevators.

All hotels with four or more bedrooms should display a

price list at reception. These prices should include breakfast, so check. Most hotels in this listing offer full English breakfast (cereal, juice, egg, bacon, coffee); we've noted those that only give the Continental version.

Prices. Rates given below are the *average* cost for two people in a double room; they include breakfast, VAT, and service charges. In the Moderate (M) category, expect to pay £35–£50 a night, and in Inexpensive (I), up to £35 a night. The price of your room is largely determined by whether or not it has a private bathroom—our listings are based on rooms without private bathrooms whenever possible. All rooms have a basin. ● = Highly Recommended.

Hotels and B&Bs

Bayswater
Moderate

Averard, 10 Lancaster Gate, W2 3HL (tel. 723 8877). Lancaster Gate tube. 61 rooms, all with bath. The stately Averard is at the top end of the (M) category, with plush dining rooms, lobby, bar, and reception area, as well as coffered ceilings, chandeliers, marble statues, and elegant furnishings. A wrought iron staircase leads to clean and airy bedrooms, though with somewhat bland decor. Close to Hyde Park.

●**Camelot,** 45–47 Norfolk Sq., W2 1RX (tel. 723 9118). Paddington tube. 34 rooms, 28 with bath or shower. No elevator. Top marks to this affordable hotel, with its beautifully decorated rooms; even the public bathrooms are attractive. The breakfast room has an exposed brick wall, a large open fireplace, wooden trestle tables, and a highly polished wood floor.

Edward Lear, 28–30 Seymour St., W1H 5WD (tel. 402 5401). Marble Arch tube. 30 rooms, half with bath or shower. No elevator. Onetime home of artist/writer Edward Lear (famous for his nonsense verse), this hotel has an imposing entranceway leading to a black-and-white tiled floor. Rooms on busy Seymour Street can be noisy, so ask for a room at the back. The breakfast room has huge

French windows, and the management proudly uses the same butcher as the Queen. Two short blocks north of Oxford Street at the Marble Arch end.

Gards, 36–37 Lancaster Gate, W2 3NA (tel. 402 1101). Lancaster Gate tube. 67 rooms, all with shower. Gards is on a quiet corner, just a block from the Bayswater Road and Hyde Park. The somewhat vibrant carpets in the reception area and hall are toned down in the modern guest rooms, which all have wooden walls. Front-facing, second-floor rooms have French windows and balconies.

Lancaster Hall, Craven Terr., W2 3EL (tel. 723 9276). Lancaster Gate tube. 100 rooms, 80 with bath. The modern, purpose-built Lancaster Hall has spotlessly clean, if rather featureless, rooms. Those in the front can be noisy, but they get the most light. Like the rest of the hotel, the dining area is functional, though perfectly acceptable; open for dinner as well as breakfast.

Parkwood, 4 Stanhope Pl., W2 2HB (tel. 402 2241). Marble Arch tube. 18 rooms, 12 with bath or shower. No elevator. The Parkwood is pleasantly set on a serene residential block of Victorian and Edwardian town houses. It has bright, clean rooms, an accommodating management, and a patio that overlooks the leafy Tyburn Convent courtyard. Glowing comments in the visitors' book. Very close to Hyde Park.

Prince William, 42–44 Gloucester Terr., W2 3DA (tel. 724 7414). Lancaster Gate tube. 42 rooms, all with bath or shower. The Prince William is a handsome, mid-19th-century building on the corner of Gloucester Terrace and Craven Road. It's at the upper end of the (M) category, although prices drop in the low season. Most rooms have their original high ceilings, while those on the second floor have balconies on which to soak up the elusive London sun. There's a cozy dining room.

Inexpensive

◉**Ashley,** 15 Norfolk Sq., W2 1RU (tel. 723 3375). Paddington tube. 52 rooms, 18 with shower. No elevator. Three handsome Italianate terraced houses are now run as a single unit overlooking slightly shabby Norfolk Square. Though many of the rooms are small and somewhat sparsely furnished, the unusually friendly and conscientious management (two brothers) make this a decidedly good choice.

Caring, 24 Craven Hill Gdns., W2 3EA (tel. 262 8708). Between Queensway and Paddington tubes. 26 rooms, 18 with bath or shower. No elevator. The Caring is on a pleasantly leafy side street promising peace and quiet. Rooms are large and modern, the decor verges on the gaudy, but this is a friendly and efficient place to stay.

● **Kingsway,** 27 Norfolk Sq., W2 1RX (tel. 723 7784). 32 rooms, 15 with bath or shower. No elevator. The Kingsway has a surprisingly well-decorated lobby for an (I) hotel. Rooms overlooking the square are the best bet, although all are clean and neat. Many have high ceilings and French windows.

Norfolk Court, 20 Norfolk Sq., W2 1RS (tel. 723 4963). 28 rooms, none with bath. No elevator. This modest, pleasant, and small Regency hotel is less than a minute from Paddington tube. Some second-floor rooms have French windows and balconies overlooking the square, and admirers of Art Deco will enjoy the touches in the landing windows and in the breakfast room. The Norfolk Court has been family-run for 50 years.

Ruddiman's, 160 Sussex Gdns., W2 1UD (tel. 723 1026). Paddington tube. 32 rooms, half with shower. No elevator. Don't be put off by the small, dark reception area; the rooms are a definite improvement, except for the loud carpets. Many rooms have high ceilings, French windows, and wood paneling; try for one looking over leafy Sussex Gardens. There's a heavy, Bavarian-style, breakfast room.

Bloomsbury

Moderate

Crichton, 36 Bedford Pl., WC1B 5JR (tel. 637 3955). Russel Sq. tube. 62 rooms, 39 with shower. No elevator. Parts of the Crichton date back over 225 years, though the modern interior belies the fact. The overall effect is quiet, clean, sedate, and a little spartan. The public bar is open until 5 A.M.—a boon for nightowls. The management is very accommodating.

Ruskin, 23–24 Montague St., WC1B 5BN (tel. 636

7388). Russell Sq. tube. 35 rooms, 7 with shower. Immediately opposite the British Museum, the family-owned Ruskin is both pleasant and quiet—all front windows are double glazed. Bedrooms are clean, though nondescript; back ones overlook a pretty garden. Note the bucolic mural (c. 1808) in the public sitting room. Well run, and very popular.

St. Margaret's, 26 Bedford Pl., WC1B 5JL (tel. 636 4277). Russell Sq. tube. 64 rooms, 5 with bath. No elevator. This hotel is on a tree-lined Georgian street, and has the air of elegance just slightly gone to seed. You'll find spacious rooms and towering ceilings, with the added benefit of a wonderful location just half a block from Russell Square.

Thanet, 8 Bedford Pl., WC1B 5JA (tel. 636 2869). Russell Sq. tube. 12 rooms, 3 with bath. No elevator. The Thanet, with its bay trees in front, gives good value for money, reasonably sized rooms, and simple, understated decor. All rooms have radios and color TV. The management is pleasant.

Wansbeck, 6 Bedford Pl., WC1B 5JD (tel. 636 6232). Russell Sq. tube. 35 rooms, none with bath. No elevator. The Wansbeck is made up of three stately, terraced, Georgian houses. The rooms are clean and neat, some with original fireplaces, and the recently redecorated breakfast room is a striking black, white, and red. Staff verge on the brusque. Close to major Bloomsbury sites.

● **White Hall,** 2–5 Montague St., WC1B 5BU (tel. 580 5871). Russell Sq. tube. 80 rooms, 20 with bath or shower. An imposing entrance promises good things, which the interior more than lives up to. There's an elegant lobby with arched windows and a marble floor, and a garden bar leading onto a patio and a not-too-manicured garden. It's a definite winner, though the beer posters strike an odd chord. A fine dining room offers both Continental and English breakfast (neither included in the rates).

Inexpensive

Georgian, 67 Gower St., WC1E 6HJ (tel. 580 7060). Goodge St. tube. 19 rooms, none with bath. No elevator. The rooms here are oddly proportioned: They're small, yet with very high ceilings. There's not even one picture on the

Wedgewood blue walls, but the hotel is clean and obviously well cared for. It's acceptable, considering the low rates.

Gower House, 57 Gower St., WC1E 6HJ (tel. 636 4685). Goodge St. tube. 14 rooms, none with bath. No elevator. Somebody here likes the color blue—it's on the walls and in the rugs and furnishings. The hotel is in good shape; rooms, though small, are clean. Close to the British Museum, and a short walk from the Oxford Street shops.

Maree, 25–27 Gower St., WC1E 6HG (tel. 636 4868). Goodge St. tube. 31 rooms, 3 with shower. No elevator. This is a family-run establishment, with low prices and adequate accommodations. Back rooms overlook a neat garden with a lawn and roses, which guests are allowed to use.

☙**Morgan,** 24 Bloomsbury St., WC1B 3QU (tel. 636 3735). Tottenham Court Rd. tube. 17 rooms, 9 with bath or shower. No elevator. This Georgian terrace hotel near the corner of busy and attractive Bloomsbury Street is family-run with charm and panache. Rooms are small and functionally furnished, yet friendly and cheerful overall. The tiny paneled breakfast room comes straight from a doll's house. Back rooms overlook the British Museum.

Ridgemount, 65 Gower St., WC1E 6HJ (tel. 636 1141). Goodge St. tube. 15 rooms, none with bath. No elevator. The Ridgemount's kindly owners, Mr. and Mrs. Rees, keep their hotel neat and clean. The public areas, especially the family-style breakfast room, have a friendly, cluttered, Victorian feel. Some rooms overlook a leafy garden.

Chelsea

Moderate

Flaxman House, 104–105 Oakley St., SW3 5NT (tel. 352 0187). 21 rooms, none with bath. No elevator. Flaxman House is just off King's Road—it's not convenient for the tube, but good for bus routes. The hotel is slightly down-at-heel, and the rooms are on the small side, but the smart pink-and-gray modern decor makes a change from the gaudy florals of many similar places.

Willett, 32 Sloane Gdns., SW1 8DJ (tel. 824 8415). Sloane Sq. tube. 18 rooms, 15 with bath or shower. No elevator. This hotel is in an attractive block of redbrick mid-19th-century houses. Though blandly decorated inside Willett maintains high standards of cleanliness and service. The rooms are small and a bit pokey, though many include original features. Some look out onto a pretty public garden.

Inexpensive

●**Annandale,** 39 Sloane Gdns., SW1 8DJ (tel. 730 5051). Sloane Sq. tube. 12 rooms, 10 with bath or shower. No elevator. The Annandale is efficiently run by the affable Mr. and Mrs. Morris. It's excellent value for money, and the many repeat visitors attest to the hotel's popularity. Breakfast is a tasty choice of kippers, Welsh rarebit, crumpets, cereals, and authentic Scottish porridge.

Oakley House, 71–72 Oakley St., SW3 5HF (tel. 352 9362). 24 rooms, one with bath and shower. No elevator. This is impeccably Victorian outside, and a bit dark inside—though not at all dreary. The manager is bright and personable, and the rooms, while small, have attractive moldings and colorful Indian print bedspreads. The public showers are clean and absolutely gigantic. Self-service breakfasts. Close to the Chelsea Embankment; no good for tubes.

Earl's Court

Moderate

Amsterdam, 7 Trebovir Rd., SW5 9LS (tel. 370 2814). Earl's Court tube. 20 rooms, all with bath or shower. The Amsterdam provides modern, clean, and relatively quiet accommodations. Rooms are reasonably furnished, with painted bamboo headboards and bedside tables. The bathrooms are unusually spacious.

Henley House, 30 Barkston Gdns., SW5 0EN (tel. 370 4111). Earl's Court tube. 20 rooms, 8 with bath or shower. No elevator. Henley House is not exceptional for the price (low M), but its convenient location goes a long way to make up for the rather dull rooms and drab hallways. Continental breakfast. It's in a particularly pretty redbrick square just two minutes from the tube.

Rushmore, 11 Trebovir Rd., SW5 9LS (tel. 370 3839). Earl's Court tube. 20 rooms, 16 with bath or shower. No elevator. The Rushmore is a bit shabbier than its sister establishment, the Amsterdam, but perfectly adequate for the price. Most rooms have TV, and those in the back overlook a rather overgrown brick-walled garden. The bathrooms are nicely tiled.

Kensington
Moderate

Clearlake, 19 Prince of Wales Terr., W8 5PQ (tel. 937 3274). High St. Kensington tube. 20 rooms, all with shower. The Clearlake nestles in a quiet Victorian street, a block from Hyde Park. It is an attractive self-catering hotel; the rooms are cozy, with refrigerators, ample storage space, and huge windows. Several of the studios and family apartments have full kitchen facilities.

●**Prince,** 6 Sumner Pl., SW7 3AB (tel. 589 6488). South Kensington tube. 20 rooms, 14 with bath or shower. No elevator. The Prince is unashamedly upmarket, yet offers amazingly reasonable rates for what you get. Furnishings are all to a very high standard, and the bathrooms were installed so as to preserve the lovely cornices. The halls are papered in a mint green Regency stripe, and the garden/conservatory is straight out of *World of Interiors.* Close to the antique shops and florists of the Old Brompton Road.

Inexpensive

●**Abbey House,** 11 Vicarage Gate, W8 4AG (tel. 727 2594). High St. Kensington or Notting Hill Gate tubes. 15 rooms, none with bath. No elevator. The Abbey House is in a fine residential block. Standards are high, with unusually spacious and high-ceilinged rooms. While not as attractively decorated as the nearby Vicarage, it still offers excellent accommodations for a reasonable price. Close to Kensington Palace and Gardens.

●**Vicarage,** 10 Vicarage Gate, W8 4AG (tel. 229 4030). High St. Kensington tube. 19 rooms, none with private bath. No elevator. Family-owned and -run for nearly 30 years, this is the undisputed highlight of our London hotel listing. The charming young owners make their guest house feel like a real home. The Vicarage is beautifully decorated, in a quiet location overlooking a magnificent garden square. Close to the Kensington shops.

Swiss House, 171 Old Brompton Rd., SW5 0AN (tel.

373 2769). Gloucester Rd. tube. 17 rooms, 8 with bath or shower. No elevator. The picturesque facade is misleading, for the interior of the Swiss House, though adequate and clean, is by no means plush. But, for the price, it is acceptable, and the location is a plus. Breakfast is not included.

Knightsbridge

Moderate

Claverley, 13–14 Beaufort Gdns., SW3 1PS (tel. 589 8541). Knightsbridge tube. 32 rooms, 20 with bath and shower. This is a gracious hotel that's decidedly upper class, and a dash ritzy. There's charming stenciled decor throughout the ground floor, and the hallways are lined with brass lamps. Rooms are well decorated; ones with a bath can be a bit pricey, though. Pleasant and intelligent staff. A short stroll away from Harrods.

Knightsbridge, 10 Beaufort Gdns., SW3 1PT (tel. 589 9271). Knightsbridge tube. 20 rooms, 13 with bath or shower. No elevator. This hotel is pleasantly decorated in plain rather than paisley tones. Front-facing rooms on the second floor have balconies overlooking the leafy square. Continental breakfasts are served in the small, cozy breakfast room.

Victoria

Moderate

Elizabeth, 37 Eccleston Sq., SW1V 1PB (tel. 828 6812). Victoria rail and tube station. 24 rooms, 7 with bath or shower. No elevator. The Elizabeth, overlooking lushly grown Eccleston Square, stands out thanks to its fresh coat of yellow paint. Public areas are attractively decorated, though bedrooms are a bit drab. Front-facing rooms have double glazing to reduce the considerable traffic noise. Guests can use the tennis courts in the square.

Morgan, 120 Ebury St., SW1W 9QQ (tel. 730 8442). Victoria rail and tube station. 11 rooms, none with bath. No elevator. The Morgan offers a warm and personable welcome to its many repeat guests. It is pleasantly sited on bustling Ebury Street (Mozart composed his first symphony in 1764 at #180), and front-facing windows are, by necessity, double glazed. The charming breakfast room should get the day off to a good start.

Sir Gâr House, 131 Ebury St., SW1W 9QQ (tel. 730 9378). Victoria rail and tube station. 11 rooms, 3 with bath or shower. Rooms here are small, and those in the front could be noisy. But overall the Sir Gâr is perfectly adequate. Guests can sit in a very pretty brick-walled garden, ablaze with geraniums, roses, and creepers. The tiny breakfast room is full of Victorian bric-a-brac.

Woodville House, 107 Ebury St., SW1W 9QU (tel. 730 1048). Victoria rail and tube station. 13 rooms, none with bath. No elevator. The personable new owners have done much to Woodville House, with pleasing results—though it's slightly overpriced for what you get. Most of the rooms are small but well decorated. There's a tiny garden complete with a huge, gnarled tree. Homemade muesli and fruit compote is there for those who can't face another English breakfast (fresh ground coffee, with cream, yet).

Inexpensive

Chesham House, 64–66 Ebury St., SW1W 9QD (tel. 730 8513). Victoria rail and tube station. 23 rooms, none with bath. No elevator. This, another Ebury Street contribution, is modest, clean, and with reasonably sized if somewhat spartan rooms. Friendly staff; full English breakfast.

Youth Accommodations

This is guaranteed to be inexpensive, and is in great demand in London. Reservations, particularly for groups, should be made at least six weeks in advance. Prices range from £9 to £18 per person, per night, but most are about £12 for bed and breakfast. Lower rates are sometimes available to International Student Card holders. Most universities and college residences accept both groups and individuals during vacations. The following are just a few to try.

Astor College (Middlesex Hospital Medical School), 99 Charlotte St., W1P 1LD (tel. 580 7262). 236 beds, mostly single. Open all year. Facilities here include a lounge, TV, washing and ironing rooms, games rooms, squash courts, and a garden. Good central location.

Carr Saunders Hall (University of London), 18–24 Fitzroy St., W1P 5AE (tel. 580 6338). 300 beds, mostly singles. Open Mar. through Apr., and July through Sept. The hall is modern and central. Parking lot.

Central University of Iowa Hostel, 7 Bedford Pl., WC1B 5JA (tel. 580 1121). 31 beds, no singles. Open mid-May through Aug. Here you'll find a lounge, TV, and washing and ironing facilities.

King's College Campus Vacation Bureau (King's College), 552 King's Rd., SW10 0UA (tel. 351 2488). 1,400 beds. Open mid-Dec. to mid-Jan. (excluding Christmas), with one month at Easter, and then July through Sept. This is highly recommended, with facilities including squash and tennis courts, croquet, gym, TV, bar, and lounge.

Westfield College (University of London), Kidderpore Ave., NW3 7ST (tel. 435 7141). 600 beds. Open mid-Mar. to mid-Apr., and July through Sept. Although it's not central, the campus is attractive. There's a bar, lounge, washing and ironing facilities, sports field, games room, and garden.

Young Men's Christian Association, Barbican, EC2 8BR (tel. 628 1697); London Central, 112 Great Russell St., WC1B 3NO (tel. 637 1333). Other hostels can be found at Ealing, Hornsey, Stockwell, Waltham Forest, and Wimbledon.

Young Women's Christian Association, Central Club, 11 Great Russell St., WC1B 3LR (tel. 636 7152). There are also hostels in Acton, Chelsea, Euston, Hampstead, Kensington, Regent's Park, and Victoria.

Youth Hostels

You don't have to be a student to stay at one of London's youth hostels, though you must belong to the Youth Hostel Association. Annual membership for internationals costs £6; citizens of England and Wales pay £1 (under 16), £3.50 (16–20), or £6 (21 and over). Join at the *Youth Hostel Association,* 14 Southampton St., WC2E 7HY (tel. 836 8542), or at individual hostels.

Five London hostels open year-round, and all are within easy reach of the center. Charges range from £3.75 to £5.50 per night according to age. When food is available, breakfast costs about £1.60, dinner £2–£2.80, and a packed lunch £1.20. Bookings received at a hostel that's already full will be transferred automatically to another hostel.

Carter Lane, 36 Carter Lane, EC4V 9AD (tel. 236 4965). 300 beds. Open daily 7–10 A.M. and 11:30 A.M.–midnight. Right in the City, close to St. Paul's Cathedral; in fact, this was formerly the choirboys' home. No cooking facilities, and no set meals.

Earl's Court, 38 Bolton Gdns., SW5 0AQ (tel. 373 7083). 111 beds. Open daily 8–10 A.M. and 5–midnight, though the reception is open at other times. This is a town house in London's inexpensive hotel district. No evening meals, except for advance group bookings.

Hampstead Heath/Golders Green, 4 Wellgarth Rd., NW11 7HR (tel. 458 9054/7196). 220 beds. Open daily 7 A.M.–midnight. The location is not central, but the Heath is close by. Breakfast, packed lunches, and evening meals.

Highgate, 84 Highgate West Hill, N6 6LU (tel. 340 1831). 62 beds. Open daily 7–10 A.M. and 5–11:30 P.M. Again close to Hampstead Heath. The village atmosphere of Highgate makes this Georgian House an attractive option. Breakfast only.

Holland House, King George VI Memorial Youth Hostel, Holland House, Holland Walk, Kensington W8 7QY (tel. 937 0748). 190 beds. Daily 7 A.M.–1 A.M. Modern hostel incorporating part of ancient mansion, and set in lovely park. Breakfast, packed lunches, and evening meals.

Camping

Camping in England can be damp. If you're still game, there are several sites within easy reach of the city by public transport. The city center has no sites, and sleeping out in the parks is illegal. Most sites open summer only.

Contact the **Camping and Caravan Club,** 11 Grosvenor Pl., SW1W 0EY (tel. 828 1012). £14 buys membership of the Club, Mar. through Oct., plus a Member's Handbook recommending over 1,000 sites.

Caravan Harbor, Crystal Palace Parade, SE19 1UF (tel. 778 7155). Open all year.

Hackney Camping, Millfields Rd., Hackney Marshes, E5 0AA (tel. 985 7656).

Lee Valley Park, Eastway Cycle, Circuit, Temple Mills Lane, Newham, E15 2EN (tel. 534 6085).

Picketts Lock Campsite, Picketts Lock Leisure Center, Picketts Lock Lane, Edmonton, N9 0AS (tel. 803 4756). Open all year.

Tent City, Old Oak Common Lane, East Acton, W3 7DP (tel. 743 5708). This is the nearest site to the center of town, with handy bus and subway lines.

Outside London, in the Home Counties, there are "country" sites in Hertfordshire, Bedfordshire, Buckinghamshire, Oxfordshire, and Berkshire to the north and west, in Essex and Kent to the east, and in Surrey, Sussex, and Hampshire to the south.

For a Longer Stay

If you are staying in London for more than a couple of weeks, particularly in the summer months, you could consider sharing a flat—the English for apartment. Hard-up flat sharers sometimes let out rooms for a month or so in the summer; try the ads in the *Standard* or *Time Out*. Alternatively, **Aston's Budget Studios,** 39 Rosary Gdns. SW7 7NQ (tel. 352 2221), has about 60 studio apartments with mini kitchenettes. They are in a Victorian block four minutes from Gloucester Road tube. Rates for two from £185 per week (£26 daily).

Where to Eat

WHAT'S ON THE MENU? One of the best places to find English food at budget prices is in a good pub at lunchtime. With more pubs serving food as well as drink, prices are competitive. Pub lunches cost from around £2, making them good value.

A number of larger pubs have been converted into French-style cafés or brasseries. Making rather more of their food than most pubs, they offer breakfasts, teas, snacks, and light bar meals. Brasseries are open all day and, due to the recent change in English licensing laws, now allow you to have a drink with an afternoon meal.

A few traditional dishes should be mentioned. You may

want to try roast beef and Yorkshire pudding with horse-radish sauce or roast lamb and mint sauce, though beef prices have risen so much that roast beef is no longer the Sunday staple it once was. You can still find it in some restaurants, but avoid those which serve it at too low a price as the quality is likely to be poor. Good roasts can be found in carveries; prices are not rock-bottom, but you can usually have a second helping free.

For a good British breakfast try porridge—a Scottish cereal of oats served hot with milk and sugar—followed by kippers, or smoked herring, which is another traditional breakfast food. Marmalade made from Seville oranges is found on most British breakfast tables.

Cockles, winkles, and smoked eels are a Cockney specialty that can be bought in pubs or from stalls in the East End of London and in a few places in Central London. Petticoat Lane market on a Sunday morning is a good place to find them.

Stilton and Cheddar are undoubtedly the best known of Britain's cheeses, but there are many other interesting varieties, including Double Gloucester, Cheshire, Lancashire, Wensleydale (from Yorkshire), and Caerphilly (from Wales). These are not uncommon and are all very tasty, but they may not be easy to find in budget restaurants.

As for drinks, remember that ice is not the common commodity it is in the United States. Beer is generally dark in color, warm, and much stronger than American beer, and comes in a wide variety of forms: mild, bitter, brown ale, light ale, stout, and Guinness. If you want a lighter, more American-type beer, try lager, it might even be cold! And if you find the taste too bitter, try a shandy (beer and lemonade) or lager-and-lime. Cider (with about the same alcoholic strength as beer) is drunk all over the country but it is at its best in the West Country and Hereford, where the cider apples are grown.

RESTAURANT DATA. London has a wide variety of budget eating places, many of which do better than their expensive relations. You are more likely to get tasty dishes at reasonable prices in foreign restaurants—American, French, Greek, Italian, Indian, or Chinese—than at places serving traditional English fare. Remember that meat is expensive, so you'll get better value with concocted dishes than with steak.

Whole-food and vegetarian restaurants generally offer excellent value for money. Pubs and wine bars are also a rich source of interesting food that is not too costly. In most pubs, especially at lunchtime, shepherd's pie or a ploughman's lunch (bread, cheese, and relish) can be had for as little as £2. If you are in Central London or the City, sandwich bars that cater to office workers are a good bet—although these are closed at weekends. There is also a sprinkling of coffee shops and tearooms where you can get appetizing light meals and pastries at modest prices.

Fast Food Chains. Perhaps the most fruitful source of budget meals—mostly at the Inexpensive rate—are the big chain restaurants. The hamburger chains such as **MacDonald's**, **Wendy's,** and **Burger King** are all over the place in Central London, frequently in prime locations. **Garfunkel's** offers greater variety and interest, and again there is no way you can miss them. Then there are the pizza palaces such as **Pizza Hut** and **Pizza Express,** which are probably the best bet for really budget meals. Finally there are the slightly more upmarket restaurants such as the **Spaghetti House** eateries, found in many handy locations, such as the one immediately by the Coliseum Theater, just north of Trafalgar Square.

All the above are fairly reliable for "fuel food"; you know what you are going to get, and you know that the quality is going to be to a set standard. By and large, we have omitted these chains from our listings for the simple reason that there are dozens of them and we don't have enough space. All you have to do is walk along any street in the center of town and the chances are you will come across one.

Lunch Spots. In the *Practical Information* listings at the end of each chapter of our *Exploring London* section you will find some suggested lunch spots. These are places where you can find some lunch while you do your sightseeing rounds. As with all our suggestions, these restaurants or pubs have a variety of dishes at a range of prices, so you can take your choice. Pubs tend to be among the cheapest spots for lunch and, if the pub is a good one, the food can be among the best you'll find for the price anywhere.

Prices. All restaurants are legally required to display their price list—menu—outside. Be sure to look at the bottom of the menu for hidden extras such as an automatic service charge, VAT, minimum charge, and cover charge (especially in Italian restaurants). Drinks, too, push up the price of a meal considerably: bear this in mind when the bill is £5–£10 more than expected. Most house wines are perfectly drinkable and are easier on the pocket than listed ones—and if you are counting the pennies you can usually get just a glass. Beer, too, is a way of having a cheaper drink with your meal.

In general, restaurants are closed on Sundays and Bank Holidays. Licensing hours (that is, when alcohol can be sold) vary, but most pubs are open from 11 A.M. to 3 P.M. and from 5:30 P.M. to 11 P.M. as we go to press. A new Act of Parliament is expected soon, which will allow pubs to be open all afternoon, as well as the current two sessions.

The following listing includes eating places of all styles and atmospheres, where you can get food at reasonable prices. Our two grades cover the approximate price of a meal for two, inclusive of VAT, but without alcohol:

(I) Inexpensive—under £15; (M) Moderate—£15–£20.

The restaurants in the following lists are arranged by area. ● = Highly Recommended.

Bayswater

Moderate

● **Ark,** 122 Palace Gdns. Terr., W8 4RT (tel. 229 4024). The Ark is a pleasant, cozy, bistro-style restaurant offering popular French dishes in informal surroundings. It's near Notting Hill Gate tube station.

Bunga Raya, 107 Westbourne Gro., W2 4UW (tel. 229 6180). Run by a young Malaysian couple who will advise on the spicy, tasty food, this restaurant has special budget meals for children and low-cost meals for those unfamiliar with Malaysian cooking.

Hetty's, 43 Hereford Rd., W2 5AH (tel. 221 9192). Hetty's is open from breakfast till late. *Plat du jour* and fixed-price, three-course meals are served in friendly and informal surroundings. It's north of Bayswater Road.

Hung Toa, 54 Queensway, W2 3RL (tel. 727 6017). This is an extremely popular Cantonese restaurant whose specialties of roast duck, barbequed pork, and fried oysters are so much in demand that you should phone ahead to reserve your dish.

Khan's, 13–15 Westbourne Gro., W2 4UA (tel. 727 5420). This crowded, noisy Indian restaurant offers extremely good-value food. It's always frantically busy so book ahead.

☛**Romantica,** 12 Moscow Rd., W2 4BT (tel. 727 7112). The Romantica is an excellent Greek restaurant which serves a selection of fish as well as good-value Greek dishes in atmospheric surroundings with sheepskins and carpets on the walls.

Inexpensive

Baba Bhel Poori House, 29 Porchester Rd., W2 5DP (tel. 221 7502). Here's a good Indian vegetarian restaurant that serves some appealing dishes; try *masala dosa,* a spicy potato-filled pancake, or *thali,* the vegetarian set meal.

Halepi, 18 Leinster Terr., W2 3ET (tel. 723 4097). This is part of a Greek chain specializing in a wide range of Greek and Middle Eastern dishes, all well presented and tasty. The good-value 15-dish *mezze* is sufficient for at least three people. The Halepi is open till 12:30 A.M.

Standard, 23 Westbourne Gro., W2 4UA (tel. 229 0600). This popular Indian eating house has a menu offering over 80 specialties including tandoori, fish, and vegetarian dishes.

The Wine Gallery, 294 Westbourne Gro., W11 2PS (tel. 229 1877). As the second member of John Brinkley's chain—the others are in Hollywood Road, Chelsea, and Brompton Road—this wine bar/restaurant offers an imaginative, snacky menu and a good choice of wines.

Bloomsbury
Moderate

Brasserie du Coin, 54 Lamb's Conduit St., WC1N 3LZ

(tel. 405 1717). Classic French food—*steak au poivre, moules marinière,* onion soup, and a good-value *plat du jour*—are all served here in a relaxed and pleasant atmosphere.

The Carvery, Hotel Russell, Russell Sq., WC1B 5BE (tel. 837 6470). There are plenty of roast meats to choose from at this hotel restaurant—but watch the budget.

Inexpensive

Hermitage, 19 Leigh St., WC1H 9EW (tel. 387 8034). There's a busy coffee bar upstairs, while a variety of fresh fish dishes are on offer in the restaurant downstairs—though you can ask for almost anything you like at any time of day. It's in a maze of streets not far from St. Pancras train station. Open from 10 A.M.–10:30 P.M.

My Old Dutch, 131 High Holborn, WC1V 6PS (tel. 242 5200). Huge, 18″-diameter Dutch pancakes are served with a choice of sweet or savory fillings—there are 67 varieties to choose from. The surroundings are traditionally Dutch.

North Sea Fish Restaurant, 8 Leigh St., WC1H 9EW (tel. 387 5892). You can take out or eat in at this pleasant restaurant which serves freshly caught and well-cooked fish and chips—french fries. It's a popular cabbie haunt, and is just down the road from the Hermitage.

Chelsea

Moderate

Blushes, 52 King's Rd., SW3 4UD (tel. 589 6640). At the Sloane Square end of this famous shopping street, this large, noisy, and popular wine bar serves reliable international "fuel" food.

Lou Pescadou, 241 Old Brompton Rd., SW5 9HP (tel. 370 1057). This is mainly a fish restaurant, but you can also dine on pizzas, pastas, omelets, and fresh salads. The owner hails from Cannes and has recreated a fairly authentic southern French setting. It's open till midnight and is near Earl's Court.

Inexpensive

Chelsea Pasta Bar, 313 Fulham Rd., SW10 9QH (tel. 352 6912). The Pasta Bar gives generous portions of pasta and there's a variety of Italian sauces to choose from. It's handy for the movies opposite and is crowded on Saturdays. Take the 14 bus from South Kensington tube station, and get off at the Canon cinema complex.

Nineteen, 19 Mossop St., SW3 2LY (tel. 589 4971). This popular, informal bistro serves consistently high-standard international food in attractive English country-cottage surroundings. It's between South Kensington and Sloane Square.

⊜**Parsons,** 311 Fulham Rd., SW10 9QH (tel. 352 0651). Parsons has a wide-ranging and good-value menu of soups, burgers, salads, vegetarian and game pies, and pasta—and there are free second helpings if you order a spaghetti dish. The directions for getting there are the same as the Chelsea Pasta Bar above; they're next door to each other.

The City
Moderate

Coates Café, 45 London Wall, EC2M 5TE (tel. 256 5148). This noisy, busy, and informal bar is much favored by the young City set and offers good set meals. There's nonstop pop music and the share-price index is displayed, but there's no food in the evenings.

Rouxl Britannia, Triton Court, Finsbury Sq., EC2A 1RR (tel. 256 6997). Sophisticated, vacuum-packed food is served with élan in this large, ultra-swanky café in a posh office block. It's run by the Roux brothers; try it for snacks and light meals. It's open until 9 P.M.

⊜**Rudland and Stubbs,** 35–37 Greenhill Rents, Cowcross St., EC1M 6BN (tel. 253 0148). This restaurant is in an old sausage factory in the heart of London's Smithfield meat market. It mostly serves fish, though there are also two meat dishes a day. You can lunch at the bar on fishy snacks, from jellied eels to oysters.

Inexpensive

East/West Restaurant, 188 Old St., EC1V 9BP (tel. 251 4076). Macrobiotic/whole-food dishes are served here by knowledgeable staff. There are good soups, pastries, stuffed pancakes, and a daily fish dish, as well as salads and quiche, all served in a pleasant, bustling café atmosphere.

Covent Garden
Moderate

Ajimura, 51 Shelton St., WC2E 9HE (tel. 240 0178). This popular Japanese spot is relaxed and informal. The menu is easy to follow and offers good advice on how to order. Excellent *tempura* and *sushi* are served at the bar or at tables.

●**Bertorelli's,** 44A Floral St., WC2E 9DA (tel. 836 3969). Open from noon to midnight, this is a popular and stylish restaurant, newly decorated, and serving the usual Italian fare from fresh pasta to *osso buco.* Otherwise just drop in for a coffee.

Cafe des Amis du Vin, 11–14 Hanover Pl., WC2E 9JP (tel. 379 3444). A very popular spot near the Opera House, this café has a genuinely French feel to it. There is a good menu offering an interesting choice of regional dishes, salads, snacks, and wines. The upstairs restaurant is pricier, and you'll need to book ahead.

Café Bordeaux, 245–249 Shaftesbury Ave., WC2H 8HE (tel. 836 6328). You'll find this restaurant at the top end of Shaftesbury Avenue, off New Oxford Street. It specializes in food and wine from Bordeaux but has dishes from other regions, too.

Le Café du Jardin, 28 Wellington St., WC2E 7BD (tel. 836 8769). Just off the Aldwych, this pleasant and attractive restaurant serves good French country-style food. It's handy for the theaters and the pre-theater dinner is fast and good value.

Café Pelican, 45 St. Martin's Lane, WC2N 4EJ (tel. 379 0309). This is the closest you'll come to an authentic French brasserie in London. It's a good spot for breakfast, snacks, and full meals throughout the day; the set tea and *café complet* are both excellent value. It's open from 11 A.M. to 12:30 A.M.

●**Joe Allen,** 13 Exeter St., WC2E 7DS (tel. 836 0651). This famous American basement café, behind the Strand Palace Hotel, is a great place to spot stage and screen personalities. It's open for lunch and is good for pre- and post-theater dining with excellent burgers and fries. The desserts shouldn't be missed either. You must book a couple of days ahead though as it's always very busy.

L.S. Grunt's, 12 Maiden Lane, WC2E 7NA (tel. 379 7722). This noisy, jokey, popular haunt is best late at night, but it's good value at any time for giant pizzas with a variety of toppings, salads, and all the familiar favorites.

Mon Plaisir, 21 Monmouth St., WC2H 9DD (tel. 836 7243). You'll find a very Gallic atmosphere in this traditional French café that serves reasonably priced classic dishes such as *coq au vin,* snails, frogs' legs, and onion soup. They are closed at weekends and very busy at other times, so book ahead.

Inexpensive

Bar Sol, 11–12 Russell St., WC2B 5HZ (tel. 240 5330). You can make the most of the excellent Spanish habit of *tapas* here—a wide range of excellent appetizers that can be ordered as a snack to accompany a drink or as a full meal. It's in the basement of Tuttons.

India Club, 143 The Strand, WC2R 1JA (tel. 836 0650). Very popular with students, this restaurant serves generous and inexpensive portions of regional dishes from all parts of India. Everything is good value, but try the daily specials.

Maxwell's, 25 Coventry St., W1V 7FG (tel. 839 1374). This is the downtown—just off Piccadilly Circus—version of the Hampstead eatery. Burgers, fries, and salads are the standard fare, in brash and busy surroundings.

Palm's Pasta on the Piazza, 39 King St., WC2E 8JS (tel. 240 2939). Low-priced Italian food is served here in spacious and lively surroundings. This is an ideal spot for a quick meal before or after the theater, and it's open until midnight.

Porters, 17 Henrietta St., WC2E 8QH (tel. 836 6466). And here is a budget spot for traditional English fare: pies with imaginative and generous fillings, followed by marvelously sticky puddings. It's open on Sundays, too.

Kensington

Moderate

Costa's Grill, 14 Hillgate St., W8 7SR (tel. 229 3794). In summer if the weather's good you can eat outside—the Greek food's good and the prices are reasonable. At #18 there's **Costa's Fish Restaurant** (tel. 727 4310) for excellent-quality fish-and-chips in generous portions, either to take out or to eat in. Near Notting Hill Gate tube.

● **Michel's Bistro,** 6 Holland St., W8 4TL (tel. 937 3367). Large portions of well-cooked, everyday French food will be served to you here in a very pleasant atmosphere by efficient and friendly staff. They have a simple and sensible system of set menus.

Phoenicia, 11–13 Abingdon Rd., W8 6AH (tel. 937 0120). Tasty and spicy Lebanese food is served in a relaxed and westernized setting. There's a good lunchtime buffet with as much as you can eat for about £6 per head. It's down a street opposite the Commonwealth Institute.

Siam, 12 St. Albans Gro., W8 5PN (tel. 937 8765). Excellent Thai food will be served to you on bended knee while you recline Roman-style and watch traditional dancing. Prices are at the top end of the moderate range, but it is possible to dine more simply in the restaurant upstairs.

Star of India, 154 Old Brompton St., SW5 0BE (tel. 373 2901). This is one of London's oldest Indian restaurants serving authentically prepared dishes such as *tandoori chicken.* The decor is very attractive and the service efficient.

Texas Lone Star, 154 Gloucester Rd., SW7 4TD (tel. 370 5625). Tex Mex food such as steak sandwiches, ribs, and hickory-smoked burgers, nonstop music, and western videos are all part of this lively spot. Cocktails are served in half-pint mugs.

Inexpensive

Bistro Vino, 1 Old Brompton Rd., SW7 3HZ (tel. 589 6590), or 303 Brompton Rd. This long-established and very popular bistro serves extremely good-value international food and daily specialties in a relaxed and informal atmosphere. You'll probably even be able to afford some wine to go with your meal.

Daquise, 20 Thurloe St., SW7 2LT (tel. 589 6117). The haunt of mid-European emigrés, this inexpensive restaurant serves marvelous goulash, stuffed cabbage leaves, and other specialties to make them feel at home. It's a handy place for coffee and cake before tackling the museums at South Kensington.

● **Geale's Fish Restaurant,** 2 Farmer St., W8 7SN

(tel. 727 7969). All sorts of different fish are prepared in the classic English style here and are served with excellent french fries. It's in comfortable surroundings just behind the Gate movie house in Notting Hill Gate.

Khyber Pass, 21 Bute St., SW7 3EY (tel. 589 7311). This is a good-value Indian restaurant where the food is attractively presented and the atmosphere relaxed. It's near South Kensington tube.

Knightsbridge
Moderate

Borscht'n'Tears, 45 Beauchamp Pl., SW3 1NX (tel. 589 5003). This long-running eatery with jokey menu and ads serves familiar Russian dishes such as *beef Stroganoff* and *chicken Kiev,* as well as food with an international theme— steak, roast duck, and scampi. There's occasionally live balalaika music, too.

La Brasserie, 272 Brompton Rd., SW3 2AW (tel. 584 1668). Authentically Gallic onion soup, pâté, omelets, croissant, and other French café specialties are served here from 8 A.M.–1 A.M. on Sat. and from 10 A.M.–1 A.M. on Sun. You can eat outside in summer, and inside the Art Deco surroundings add to a genuine French feel.

Grill St. Quentin, 136 Brompton Rd., SW3 1HY (tel. 581 8377). You'll find this restaurant in a huge, stylish basement where you can snack on a French sandwich or try one of the barbeque grills with *pommes allumettes.* It's near the Brompton Oratory and is open from noon to midnight.

Luba's Bistro, 6 Yeoman's Row, SW3 2AL (tel. 589 2950). This Russian bistrovich has a long-established reputation for generous portions and good value. There is no liquor license so take your own. It's always busy so book ahead, and be on time or you might lose your table.

O Fado, 50 Beauchamp Pl., SW3 1NY (tel. 589 3002). Live music from Portuguese guitars adds to a pleasant atmosphere in this family-run restaurant offering excellent-value traditional Portuguese food and some international dishes. There's a good wine list to choose from, too.

Windy City Bar and Grill, 163 Knightsbridge, SW7 1DW (tel. 584 1255). With a menu of U.S. sandwiches, salads, eggs Benedict, and steaks, this 200-seater restaurant also serves lunch specials such as corned beef hash and wonderful desserts.

Inexpensive

Pizza Pomodoro, 51 Beauchamp Pl., SW3 1NY (tel. 589 1278). Delicious homemade pasta with classic Italian sauces is served here in a relaxed atmosphere. It's just a couple of blocks down from Harrods and is open until 1 A.M.

Stockpot, 6 Basil St., SW3 1AA (tel. 589 8627). Whitewashed walls, pine tables, and benches provide an informal atmosphere here in which to enjoy filling homemade soups, casseroles, and puddings. The prices are modest and the portions very generous.

North London

Moderate

⊖ **Le Bistroquet,** 273 Camden High St., NW1 7BX (tel. 485 9607). A high standard of French brasserie-type food is on offer in this wine bar and café/restaurant, with a nouvelle cuisine accent to most dishes. Teas and a special weekend brunch menu are also available. It's close to Camden Lock market and antique shops.

⊖ **Harry Morgan's,** 31 St. John's Wood High St., NW8 7NH (tel. 722 1869). This is one of London's best Jewish restaurants with good-value specialties such as hot salt beef, gefilte fish, meatballs, and potato latkes, all served in generous portions. Before the open-air theater perhaps? It's just across the road from Regent's Park.

Inexpensive

Diwana Bhel Poori House, 121 Drummond St., NW1 2HL (tel. 387 5556). You'll find tasty, aromatic, vegetarian cooking in this bright and lively Indian eating house. Particularly popular are the *thalis,* the excellent *samosas,* and the *bhel poori* choices.

Earth Exchange, 213 Archway Rd., N6 5DN (tel. 340 6407). This large basement café/restaurant, decorated in country-kitchen style, serves outstanding vegetarian food. There's also a bookshop, and live music, cabaret, or poetry reading most evenings.

Manna, 4 Erskine Rd., NW3 3AJ (tel. 722–8028). Here's another vegetarian restaurant with specialties such as Hizki-seaweed, vegetable casseroles, and spinach pancakes, all excellently cooked and served in generous portions. It's near Primrose Hill.

Minogue Bar and Dining Rooms, 60 Liverpool Rd., N1 0QX (tel. 359 4554). Handy for Camden Passage antiques market, this new Irish pub stocks an outstanding choice of whiskeys, beers, and, of course, draught Guinness. The dining rooms have excellent Irish dishes such as steak and kidney pie, fresh mussels and fish, and Irish cheeses. The weekend brunch is particularly memorable.

Moussaka on the Green, 23 Islington Green, N1 8DU (tel. 354 1952). Again close to Camden Passage, this is a cosy, bistro-style Greek cafe with superb *mezze* and low-cost traditional Greek dishes. The set meal is good value.

Pasta Underground, 214 Camden High St., NW1 8QR (tel. 482 0010). This busy and attractive spot serves a variety of freshly made budget-priced pastas and sauces.

⬤**Seashell Fish Bar,** 35 Lisson Gro., NW1 6UH (tel. 723 8703). This superior "chippy" has a reputation as one of the best fish-and-chip shops in London. Large portions of freshly caught fish and perfectly cooked chips make an excellent-value meal, with cheerful service at both the restaurant and take-out counter.

Trattoria Aqualino, 31 Camden Passage, N1 8EA (tel. 226 5454). You'll find this welcoming Turko-Italian place tucked between two antiques shops down a quaint passage. It serves spareribs, pasta, kebabs, and good vegetarian dishes. It's always very busy so book ahead.

Soho

Moderate

Compton Green, 14 Old Compton St., W1V 5PE (tel. 434 3544). Imaginative international vegetarian food is attractively presented in this lively new spot. Portions are generous and the atmosphere relaxed. Some of the paintings on the walls are for sale.

Garuda, 150 Shaftesbury Ave., WC2H 8HL (tel. 836 2644). This chic Indonesian restaurant serves *satay* and main rice or noodle dishes, which are all excellent and filling. There is plenty of choice for vegetarians, too. Indonesian beers are also available.

Joy King Lau, 3 Leicester St., WC2H 7BL (tel. 437 1132). You may have to line up at this popular and superior Cantonese restaurant for *dim sum* at lunchtime or for a full and wide-ranging menu in the evening.

Manzi's, 2 Leicester St., WC2H 7BL (tel. 734 0024). Bright and breezy, Manzi's is a very popular Italian fish restaurant, just off Leicester Square. There's a wide variety of good-value dishes including oysters, scallops, and smoked eels, all served with a flourish.

●**Mayflower,** 68 Shaftesbury Ave., W1V 7DF (tel. 734 9207). Here's another Cantonese restaurant, comfortable and informal, and always busy. The food is worth the wait—the set meals are reliable and particularly good value (it's popular with the Chinese, which is always a good sign). The menu is one of the longest in Soho, and it's useful for late meals as it doesn't close until 3:30 A.M.

Mykonos Greek Taverna, 17 Frith St., W1V 5TS (tel. 437 3603). You'll find excellent moussaka, kebabs, and other familiar Greek dishes, accompanied by ouzo and Greek wines, at this popular family-run taverna.

Soho Brasserie, 23 Old Compton St., W1V 5PJ (tel. 439 9301). You can have a drink and snack in the bar, or enjoy a full meal of top-quality nouvelle cuisine in the restaurant, though watch the budget as it can be quite pricey. The Brasserie is open for breakfast, snacks, and meals all day, making this a very popular spot.

●**Le Tire Bouchon,** 6 Upper James St., W1V 3HF (tel. 437 2320). This is another busy brasserie but with a short and simple regional French menu. The set meal is good value as are the various *plats du jour.* You'll find it by Golden Square, behind Regent Street, and it's best to book as it's always busy.

Inexpensive

Amalfi, 31 Old Compton St., W1V 5PL (tel. 437 7284). Marvelous fresh pasta is the specialty of the house at this Italian café/restaurant, and the pastries are exquisite—you can have them with a cappuccino, on their own, as a sweet, or to take home.

Canton, 11 Newport St., WC2H 7JG (tel. 437 6220).

Authentic Cantonese dishes—*dim sum,* roast duck, barbequed pork—are served at this 24-hour restaurant near
Leicester Square tube. The food is well cooked and very
good value.

Chicago Meatpackers, 96 Charing Cross Rd., WC2H
0JG (tel. 379 3277). This vast basement is decorated with
railway memorabilia (tiny trains run round on suspended
tracks), and serves authentic American food masterminded
by one who knows—Chicagoan Bob Payton.

●**Chuen Cheng Ku,** 17 Wardour St., W1V 3HD (tel.
437 1398). This restaurant is part of a large complex and is
always full at lunchtime and on Sun. It's a good place for
dim sum, or for large portions of delicious fish.

Cranks, 8 Marshall St., W1V 1LQ (tel. 437 9431). The
doyen of vegetarian restaurants, Cranks offers a self-service
buffet counter during the day and candlelit dining in the
evenings, in pleasant natural pine surroundings. Just a
couple of blocks behind Liberty, Cranks is also open for
morning coffee.

Fatso's Pasta Joint, 12 Old Compton St., W1V 5PG (tel.
437 1503). If you're really hungry, head for Old Compton
Street for as much pasta and sauce as you can eat for
£2.60—from Sun. to Thur. It's open late (to 1 A.M.
on Fri. and Sat., when there's also live cabaret), and is near
Cambridge Circus.

Harry's, 19 Kingly St., W1R 5LB (tel. 734 8708). Here's
a good spot for inexpensive wholesome food: traditional
English breakfasts of fried eggs, bacon, sausages, and
tomatoes for the city's all-nighters, and daily specials for
the daytime clientele at #16. Kingly Street is directly
behind Liberty.

Jimmy's, 23 Frith St., W1R 5PG (tel. 437 9521). This is
a favorite haunt for those who like large helpings of
Cypriot/international food at budget prices. It's opposite
Ronnie Scott's jazz club, off Soho Square.

●**New World,** 1 Gerrard Pl., W1V 7LL (tel. 734 0677).
This is another large and cheerfully decorated Cantonese
restaurant, serving *dim sum* on trolleys at lunchtime, and
marvelous specialties such as whole steamed fish or scallops. There are also good-value specials featured at the start
of the menu.

Nuthouse, 26 Kingly St., W1R 5LB (tel. 437 9471). All the food served here is organically grown and freshly cooked; macrobiotic dishes are also available. The decor is very pleasant and it's handy for shopping in Regent Street.

Wong Kei, 41 Wardour St., W1V 3HA (tel. 437 8408). Genuine Pekinese food is the specialty at this very popular eating house whose specialties include braised duckweb. The noodle set dishes are a good choice for the less adventurous.

Victoria and Pimlico
Moderate

Dolphin Brasserie, Dolphin Sq., SW1V 3LX (tel. 828 3207). Breakfast, snacks, lunch, tea, and dinner are all served in this French-style spot in a vast apartment block. Musical evenings are an added attraction to the splendid Art Deco surroundings. It's across the road from the Thames and not far from the Tate.

Hunan, 51 Pimlico Rd., SW1W 8NE (tel. 370 5712). As you may perhaps guess from the name, this restaurant specializes in the hot and spicy food of central/southwestern China. There are set meals for those not familiar with the fare, as well as better-known Chinese dishes.

Pomegranates, 94 Grosvenor Rd., SW1V 3LE (tel. 828 6560). An interesting and ever-changing menu of truly international dishes from deepest Africa to rural Wales is the great attraction of this restaurant. It's in a comfortable basement and is just down the road from the Tate Gallery.

Tent, 15 Eccleston St., SW1W 9LX (tel. 730 6922). Although there isn't actually a tent here, good value is to be had at this French restaurant with its wide-ranging bill of fare. There are only fixed-price menus, which can work out at the top end of the moderate range.

Inexpensive

Bumbles, 16 Buckingham Palace Rd., SW1W 0QP (tel. 828 2903). There's original British home cooking and some international dishes at this small and friendly eating spot. The prices are reasonable and the restaurant also has an interesting selection of English wines. It's handy for sight-seeing around Buckingham Palace.

West End

Moderate

Café Fish, 39 Panton St., SW1Y 4EA (tel. 930 3999). The cover charge here includes fish terrine, salad, and as much French bread as you can eat. The rest of the menu consists of sandwiches and hot and cold dishes of fish cooked in every way imaginable. It's off the Haymarket.

Café Italien, 19 Charlotte St., W1P 1HB (tel. 636 4174). This is one of London's greatest Italian restaurants (the original Bertorelli's) transformed into a stylish café/wine bar. The pasta, pizzas, and traditional Italian fare are all perfectly cooked—it's a good place for a drink and a snack, too. Just one room of the old restaurant is preserved intact.

Criterion Brasserie, Piccadilly Circus, W1V 9LB (tel. 839 7133). This brasserie has been magnificently restored to its former Edwardian glory, with a mosaic ceiling and semiprecious stones set into the walls. Classic bistro dishes are the order of the day—but it's the surroundings that count, not the food.

●**Fountain Restaurant,** Fortnum and Mason, 181 Piccadilly, W1V 9LB (tel. 734 4938). Delicious light meals, toasted snacks, sandwiches, and ice-cream sodas are all available in this elegant restaurant at the back of the famous store, on the Duke Street corner. It's particularly good for breakfast, high teas, and pre- or post-theater stoking up as it's open until 11:30 P.M., but it is closed on Sun.

Hard Rock Café, 150 Old Park Lane, W1Y 3LN (tel. 629 0382). This is a loud-rocking, long-established favorite, with burgers, fries, and a juke box. It's just as popular with kids as its New York counterpart, so you'll have to stand on line. You may prefer to use the take-out service and eat in either neighboring Green Park or Hyde Park—it faces onto Piccadilly, close to Hyde Park Corner.

Rodos, 59 St. Giles High St., WC2H 8LH (tel. 836 3177). You'll get excellent food and friendly service at this family-run Greek restaurant just off the top end of Charing Cross Road. Great set-price *mezze* can be ordered for two, but will easily feed three. It's very popular so do book ahead.

White Tower, 1 Percy St., W1P 9FA (tel. 636 8141). This

old-fashioned but elegant restaurant serves Greek and Balkan food, though it can work out at the top end of the moderate range. It's halfway between Tottenham Court Road and Goodge Street tubes.

Inexpensive

Agra, 135 Whitfield St., W1P 5RY (tel. 387 4828). You can sample some interesting tandoori fish dishes and an excellent draught Pilsner at this popular and good-value Indian restaurant. It's near Goodge Street tube.

◖**Chicago Pizza Pie Factory,** 17 Hanover Sq., W1R 9AJ (tel. 629 2669). There's a cocktail bar, rock music, and videos in this bright basement spot serving huge pizzas with salad and garlic bread at good budget prices, though the choice of fillings may be a bit limited. You'll find it just off New Bond Street.

Raw Deal, 65 York St., W1H 1PQ (tel. 262 4841). This busy vegetarian eatery serves a wide selection of salads; all the vegetables are organically grown when possible and the pies, cakes, and trifles are all made on the premises.

Virgin Megastore, 14–16 Oxford St., W1N 9FL (tel. 631 1234). Upstairs at this vast record, tape, and video shop, international fast food is served in a modish setting. It's part of the Richard Branson empire, so you can buy airline tickets here, too.

Widow Applebaum's Deli & Bagel Academy, 46 S. Molton St., W1Y 1HE (tel. 629 4649). Here's an import: an American-Jewish delicatessen with an extensive menu where the specialties include hot pastrami, matzo balls, and homemade apple strudel. South Molton is a smart, pedestrian-only shopping street.

Coffeeshops, Crêperies and Snacksville

For those who do not wish to have a complete meal, there are many attractive places, some of them very upmarket indeed, to take tea or coffee accompanied by something light. Most of London's hotels, for example, have a lounge where nonresidents can have morning coffee, afternoon tea, and sometimes lunches, at almost-reasonable prices. But there are plenty of smaller places where you needn't worry so much about what you're wearing and how much it's going to cost.

Bar Crêperie, 21 South Hall, Covent Garden, WC2 8RD. You can watch the cooks tossing the pancakes in this crêperie, and preparing an exciting variety of fillings. You can dine on one of the terraces on the ground floor, or take late morning coffee and croissants outside, if you prefer.

Bar Escoba, 102 Old Brompton Rd., SW7 3RD. *Tapas,* or Spanish appetizers, make a perfect snack meal. This converted pub has taken on the lively and busy atmosphere of its Iberian counterparts.

Bar Italia, 22 Frith St., W1V 5TS. Superb Italian coffee, salami- and Parma ham-filled rolls, brioches, and tartines mean that this tiny café is always crammed.

Bunjies, 27 Litchfield St., WC2H 9NJ. You'll find Italian coffee and a variety of meals and snacks in this cosy basement coffee bar. There's a "folk cellar" in the adjoining room.

Chandos Snack Bar, 60 Chandos Pl., WC2N 4HG. It looks rather basic and functional but this café behind Covent Garden specializes in homemade pastries, cheesecakes, and scrumptious fruit pies.

Crêperie, 56A S. Molton St., W1Y 1HF. Here's another French-style pancake house where you can watch the chef creating at least 80 varieties of crêpe. It also serves soups, salads, and hot savories. There's another branch at 26 James St., W1M 5HS, in the Covent Garden area.

Garbanzo Coffee House, 411 City Rd., EC1V 1NP. The Garbanzo serves several varieties of coffee and handmade chocolates, as well as fresh croissants at noon. It is run by an American couple who saw the need for a civilized atmosphere in which to linger over a good cup of coffee or two.

Habitat Café, 206 King's Rd., SW3 5XP. Some of the tables here overlook the King's Road so you can do some people-watching while you eat. It's self-service with salads, pâtés, quiches, and some hot dishes.

Harrods: Dress, Upper, Way In, and **Leisure Circles,** Knightsbridge, SW1X 7XL. There are quiches, salads, sandwiches, and pastries at these four well-appointed coffee shops. The Way In is the only one that's not licensed for alcohol.

Louis Pâtisserie, 32 Heath St., NW3 6TE, and 12 New College, Parade, Finchley Rd., NW3 5EP. These two spots are well known to pastry connoisseurs; the tea and coffee are good, too.

Maison Bertaux, 28 Greek St., W1V 5LL. This Soho pâtisserie, run by the Vignaud family for several generations, has an irresistible array of French and Continental specialties.

Maison Bouquillon, 45 Moscow Rd., W2 4AH. You'll find savory pies and sweet pastries, imaginative salads, and lunchtime entree at this Continental-style café.

Maison Pechon Pâtisserie Française, 127 Queensway, W2 4SJ. Meringues, brandy snaps, and truffle logs are among the goodies available at this French bakery.

Maison Sagne, 105 Marylebone High St., W1M 3DB. The eye-catching window display of dainty cakes and pastries will be enough to tempt you in here. Light snacks such as omelets and sausage rolls are served at lunchtime.

Muffin Man, 12 Wright's Lane, W8 6TA. In a craft shop, this comfortable retreat is arranged on two levels and offers sandwiches, homemade cakes, soups, pâtés, and hot savory fare.

Pâtisserie Valerie, 44 Old Compton St., W1V 5PB. Enticing Danish pastries and savory snacks make this a very popular place.

Peter Jones Coffee Shop, Sloane Sq., SW1W 8EL. Overlooking Chelsea, this bright café has some unusual open sandwiches, hot snacks, and a variety of salads, as well as cakes and puddings.

Sharaton Pâtisserie, 10 Conduit St., W1R 9TG; 84 Edgware Rd., W2 2EA; 270 Kensington High St., W8 6ND; 157 London Wall, EC2M 5QD. This family-owned chain of pâtisseries has an impressive selection of both sweet pastries and savory fare.

Silver Moon, 68 Charing Cross Rd., WC2H 0BB. For women only, this self-service basement café and meeting place offers a range of exotic and herbal teas, and a variety of whole-food cakes and pies.

Swiss Center, 10 Wardour St., W1V 3HG. The coffee shop here is one of the few places where you can have just a coffee at any time. The food ranges from sausages, cakes, and pastries to Swiss-style salads and hot savories. It has a children's menu, too. The other restaurants in the same complex could be pricey on a budget.

The Veritable Crêperie, 329 King's Rd., SW3 5ES. Taped classical music creates a calming ambiance in this Breton crêperie, which serves sweet and savory pancakes in a huge variety of combinations.

Wine Bars

Wine bars bridge the gap between a restaurant and the traditional pub by providing a relaxed, perhaps candlelit setting for somewhere to eat, drink wine, and listen to music. The food served in most wine bars tends to be simple but good quality—often quiches, pâtés, cheeses, and salad. While many are good value for money, we should warn you that some can be very pricey. The following were selected with the budget-conscious in mind.

Wine bars are usually open normal pub hours: Mon. to Sat., 11–3 and 5:30–11; Sun. 12–3 and 7–10:30.

Boltons, 198 Fulham Rd., SW3 6JL. There's good home-made food and a well-chosen wine list at this small and tastefully designed wine bar.

Bouzy Rouge, 221 King's Rd., SW3 5EJ. You can listen to live jazz here in the evenings, and there's a choice of over 60 wines. It's below the wine shop of the same name.

Bow Wine Vaults, 10 Bow Churchyard, EC4M 9DQ. Sandwiches and excellent set lunches are served at this extremely busy spot. It's behind Bow Church and there's a wine shop attached.

Brahms and Liszt, 19 Russell St., WC2B 5HP. There is very good-value food here, though the wine bar is rather loud and brash. The odd name is Cockney rhyming slang for . . . well, drunk.

Cork and Bottle, 44 Cranbourne St., WC2H 7AN. This popular wine bar serves tasty food and a good selection of wines—look out for the special offers. It's near Leicester Square tube station.

Crusting Pipe, 27 The Market, Covent Garden, WC2E 8RD. Port is the specialty in this maze of converted wine vaults in the Piazza, but there's an excellent selection of other wines by the glass or bottle. There are tables outside, and the food ranges over pâtés, cheeses, game pie, roast beef, and salads, to something from the grillroom.

Draycotts, 114 Draycott Ave., SW3 3AE. It's quietest upstairs at this very popular bar. They have a crùover machine, which means premier crù wines can be sold by the glass, and there's a good selection of food.

The Garden, 29 Maiden Lane, WC2E 7JS. Here you'll find homey British food such as homemade soup, and pork and apple pie, as well as a reasonable wine list.

Julie's, 135 Portland Rd., W11 4LW. This very fashionable wine bar is decorated with Victoriana throughout. It has good food and an interesting wine list, and there's a pretty garden for summer drinking. Tea is served in the afternoon.

The Loose Box, 136 Brompton Rd., SW3 1HY. This busy wine bar is handy if you're shopping around Knightsbridge. There's a modest selection of wines and a good choice of food.

Odette's, 130 Regent's Park Rd., NW1 8XL. There's interesting international food and a good wine list here. It's in a pretty basement below the restaurant of the same name.

Reams, 34 Store St., WC1E 7BS. Reams is more of a cocktail bar, but it serves excellent food. There are half-price offers during the happy hours from 11:30 A.M.–12:30 P.M. and 5:30–7 P.M. Mon. to Fri.

Sloane's Wine Bar, King's Head, Sloane Sq., SW1W 8AX. The reasonably priced food is good, and the wide selection of wines makes this a popular spot. It can be very busy in the evenings, but it's quieter at lunchtime.

Pubs

The pub is a uniquely British institution which, like many traditions, is rather eccentric. Perhaps the strangest thing about it is the opening hours. In London, pubs are open from 11 to 3, and in the evening from 5:30 or 6 to 11. On Sundays the hours are 12 to 2 and from 7 to 10:30. These times may vary in the country and between summer and winter. Efforts are being made to bring England into line with other countries, including Scotland, that allow pubs to remain open all day. The licensing laws should be changed within a year.

Entering a pub you may be confronted by two doors, one marked Saloon Bar, the other Public Bar. This is a hangover from the days when the middle classes used the former and the working classes frequented the latter.

Today, the two doors often lead into the same part of the pub.

Beer may be ordered in two quantities—pints or half pints. If this is your first taste of British beer, then order a half. Some London pubs sell "real ale," which is beer brewed in the traditional way. It is usually stronger and, many would argue, has a better flavor than the mass-produced beer of the large brewing companies. When ordering shorts, Americans may find the measures rather small and may want to order a double.

An important point to bear in mind is that children under the age of 14 are not allowed in pubs and if found they will certainly be asked to leave. Many pubs now have a beer garden or a family room where children are welcome. If the pub is next to a park or the river, drink may be consumed off the premises, so adults can drink while the children play. No one under the age of 18 may order or consume alcohol in a pub.

There are hundreds of pubs in London; sometimes you will find the most surprisingly attractive ones in the least attractive surroundings. These are survivors of an earlier age: there has been a tendency amongst the brewers to modernize, and many pubs have been stripped of their old interiors, leaving them characterless and featureless. Most of the pubs in the following list have managed to survive intact with their own particular aura.

Admiral Codrington, 17 Mossop St., SW3 2LY. There's an interesting display of old Toby jugs in this friendly Chelsea pub. The cooking in the restaurant has an Anglo-French slant and there's a pleasant enclosed patio for summer drinking.

The Anchor, 1 Bankside, SE1 4DN. Shakespeare used to drink in the original Anchor. The restaurant is excellent, though very expensive, and there are lovely views across the river to St. Paul's.

Antelope, 22 Eaton Terr., SW1W 8EZ. This popular watering hole is in *Upstairs, Downstairs* territory and has good food and beer.

Argyle Arms, 18 Argyle St., WC1 8EQ. There are five bars down and one up at this large Victorian establishment with mirrors and mahogany furnishings. It's just south of King's Cross Station.

Baker and Oven, 10 Paddington St., W1M 3LA. The basement of this small pub has been turned into an attractive restaurant specializing in homemade pies cooked in a Victorian baker's oven.

Black Friar, 174 Queen Victoria St., EC4V 4DB. Next door to Blackfriars tube, this pub is a wonderful example of Art Nouveau decor, with a gold-leaf, marble, and mosaic grotto at the back.

Bunch of Grapes, 16 Shepherd Market, W1Y 7HU. There's a colorful crowd at this popular Victorian pub in the heart of Shepherd Market, just off Piccadilly. In good weather drinkers spill out onto the small piazza.

Cartoonist, 76 Shoe Lane, EC4A 3BQ. As the headquarters of the Cartoonist Club of Great Britain, the walls here are covered with an interesting collection of satirical drawings.

Cheshire Cheese, 5 Little Essex St., WC2R 3LD. Original oak beams and a friendly atmosphere make this a good place for tasty bar snacks—it's close to the Middle Temple.

De Hems, 11 Macclesfield St., W1V 7LF. This popular Victorian pub off Shaftesbury Avenue has a fine collection of foreign bank notes suspended from the ceiling.

Dickens Inn by the Tower, St. Katharine's Way, E1 9LB. St. Katharine's was at the heart of London's working dockland, just beyond the Tower, but it is now a yacht marina. The pub looks over the main pool.

Duke of Clarence, 203 Holland Park Ave., W11 4UL. This friendly spot has a lovely garden which is used for barbeques in summer.

George Inn, 77 Borough High St., SE1 1NH. Originally a Victorian coaching inn, the atmosphere here has been preserved with beamed ceilings, leaded windows, and hunting prints. A wine bar serves food, and upstairs there's an excellent restaurant.

George and Vulture, Castle Court, EC3V 9DL. Off Cornhill, this tavern dates from 1175 and consequently is reputed to be the oldest pub in the world. Chaucer and Daniel Defoe were regular visitors, and Charles Dickens wrote part of Pickwick Papers while staying here.

Holly Bush, 22 Holly Mount, off Heath St., NW3 6SG. You'll find real ale in this quaint Hampstead pub. It was built in 1796.

Lamb, 94 Lamb's Conduit St., WC1N 3LZ. This small and atmospheric hostelry is very popular, and gets rather crowded at lunchtime in summer.

Lamb and Flag, 33 Rose St., WC2E 9EB. There's good beer and food in this tiny, beamed haunt down an alleyway near Covent Garden. Dickens used to drink here.

Mayflower, Rotherhithe, SE16 4NF. The Pilgrims allegedly stepped onto the boat for Holland from here. Although the original tavern was blitzed during the war and this is a replacement, it still has the passenger manifest on the wall.

Nag's Head, 10 James St., WC2E 8BT. The Nag's Head is right next door to the Royal Opera House, and is a favorite with the theater crowd.

Pindar of Wakefield, 328 Gray's Inn Rd., WC1X 8BZ. The menu here is limited but good and entertainment comes in the form of authentic old-time music hall and jazz.

Princess of Wales, 145 Dovehouse St., SW3 6LB. This upmarket pub has an attractive forecourt, and is just off the King's Road.

Prospect of Whitby, 75 Wapping Wall, E1 9SP. The original Prospect was an old sailing ship and this pub is right on the riverside. It can be difficult to get to, unless you're a walker, but it's full of character and is a good place for lunch.

Queen's Elm, 241 Fulham Rd., SW3 6HY. Queen Elizabeth I took shelter under a nearby tree in 1597—hence the name. There's also a fascinating collection of pipes and cartoons, and art exhibits upstairs. Books are sold over the bar.

Red Lion, 48 Parliament St., SW1A 2NH. This is one of the few places to eat on Whitehall. You'll get typical pub fare here.

Rose and Crown, 2 Old Park Lane, W1Y 3LL. This 200-year-old country pub is now surrounded by salubrious Mayfair houses.

Salisbury, 90 St. Martin's Lane, WC2N 4AP. In the middle of theaterland, this Edwardian pub is resplendent with sandblasted glass screens, molded ceilings, and red velvet seating. You won't be surprised to hear that it's often been used as a film location. The food's good, too.

Spaniards, Spaniards Rd., Hampstead Heath, NW3 7JJ. This is just the spot for laying the dust after a walk on the Heath with its splendid views across the city.

Star Tavern, Belgrave Mews W., SW1 8HT. The beer's good and there's plenty of atmosphere in this small mews pub.

Sun in Splendor, 7 Portobello Rd., W11 3DA. In the midst of the antique market, this small, attractive pub has a tiny garden at the back, good beer, and excellent food.

Surprise, 6 Christchurch Terr., SW3 4AJ. You'll find strong beer at this small, characterful pub, just around the corner from where Oscar Wilde lived.

Westminster Arms, 9 Storey's Gate, SW1P 3AT. This is a good spot for inexpensive food. There is a wider choice on the menu upstairs.

Windsor Castle, Campden Hill Rd., W8 8LY. A large, paved garden makes this smart but friendly spot perfect for a relaxed summertime drink. It can get very crowded.

Ye Olde Cheshire Cheese, 145 Fleet St., EC4A 2BU. Dr. Johnson maintained that this was his favorite tavern. The specialty of the house is steak and kidney pudding.

Escorted Tours

BUS TOURS. A good way to see the principal sights of London is from the top deck of a bus. LRT runs a sightseeing tour that lasts 90 minutes and covers about 20 miles, taking in most of the capital's landmarks, among them St. Paul's, Westminster Abbey, the Tower of London, Tower Bridge, and the Houses of Parliament. No advance booking is necessary. Pick-up points include Piccadilly Circus (Haymarket), Marble Arch (top of Park Lane, near Speakers' Corner), Victoria Station, and Baker Street underground station. Coach tours of London are also offered by **Evans Evans,** 27 Cockspur St., SW1Y 5BN (tel. 930 2377), and **Frames Rickards,** 11 Herbrand St., WC1N 1EX (tel. 837 3111).

WALKING TOURS. The City Corporation has laid out a walk around the City of London marked by a series of stars set into the sidewalks. Known as the Heritage Walk, it takes in Bank, Leadenhall Market, and the Monument; you will find a map of the walk on the back of *A Visitor's Guide to* *the City of London,* available from the City Information Center opposite St. Paul's Cathedral.

If you want to know more about Jack the Ripper, Samuel Pepys' London, or ghosts in the City, join a walking tour organized by Alex and Peggy Cobban, who offer around 80 guided walks. Tickets are £2.25 for adults, £2 for senior citizens and students, while under-16s go free if accompanied by an adult. Contact **Discovering London,** 11 Pennyfields, Warley, Brentwood, Essex (tel. 0277 213704). A similar organization is **London Walks,** 139 Conway Rd., N14 7BH (tel. 882 2763). Prices are £2.25 for adults, £2 for senior citizens and students; again, under-16s go free if with an adult.

RIVER TRIPS. From Easter through October, boats ply up and down the River Thames, most starting from the piers at Westminster Bridge, Hungerford rail bridge (opposite the entrance to the Embankment underground station), and the Tower of London. Upriver destinations include Kew, Richmond, and Hampton Court, while heading downriver, boats go to the Tower, Greenwich, and the Thames Barrier at Woolwich. A catamaran service run by **Thames Line** (tel. 987 0311) is due to start in summer 1988 and will sail between Greenwich and Chelsea, with eight boarding stages planned en route.

Capital Cruises (tel. 350 1910) has a disco cruise that leaves Temple Pier at 8 P.M., lasts four hours, and includes a two-course buffet. Price is £8.95 Fri. and Sat., £7.45 the rest of the week. Book in advance. Capital also has a sailing barge moored at Temple, just to the east of Charing Cross, that is now a wine bar/restaurant. It's open for lunch and dinner, with barbeques a specialty. Check first, though, as it's mainly used for private parties.

CANAL TRIPS. Summer is the time for waterbus/barge excursions along London's Regent Canal; most vessels run between Little Venice in the west (nearest underground is Warwick Avenue on the Bakerloo line) and Camden Lock (just north of Camden Town tube station). **Canal Boat Cruises,** 250 Camden High St., NW1 8QS (tel. 485 4433/ 6210) plies this section of the canal; the fleet includes the floating restaurant My Fair Lady that operates year-round. Dinner Tues. to Sat. costs £16.95; Sun. lunch is £12.95.

Alternatively, a cruise only on the *Jenny Wren* costs £2 for adults and £1 for children.

Sightseeing Tips

ART FOR FREE. We have listed the most interesting London museums and galleries in the Exploring sections. Admission is free unless otherwise indicated, though there is a growing trend to request a voluntary contribution, particularly at the South Kensington museums. In a few cases compulsory charges now operate. Museums are usually open daily, including Bank Holidays, but not Good Friday, Christmas Eve, Christmas Day, Boxing Day (first day after Christmas), and New Year's Day, or where otherwise stated.

Apart from the institutional galleries and museums, there are dozens of commercial galleries scattered around the West End. These are usually free. Don't bother with the catalogs, which are expensive. Although the galleries are spread around the town, most are in the Bond St., Cork St., and St. James's areas.

Shopping

THE BUDGET APPROACH. If shopping in London conjures up for you an image of dollar signs and endless credit card slips, read on; we may be able to change your mind. It's true, of course, that for Frank Sinatra, say, a shopping spree in London means ordering 50 pairs of handmade shoes at £250 a throw. When Joan Collins heads out to the stores in London, it's to visit Bruce Oldfield to pick up half a dozen of his latest creations. Yours for £1,500 a time.

But London has so much more to offer, and you really don't have to be Imelda Marcos to get the most out of it. However carefully you're counting the pennies, a visit to Harrods' Food Hall, for example, is something nobody should miss. Apart from anything else, it's among the best free shows in the city. And though Harrods may boast that it can supply anything to anyone, anywhere in the world—and is equally proud that this is where the Queen does her Christmas shopping—you needn't feel you have to buy out an entire department. Why not pick up one of the numerous excellent gift items in the store? How about one of the distinctive green-and-gold Harrods' bags to give a touch of class to your shopping back home at the supermarket?

The other vital point to remember as you wander round is that practically all the best shops in London are in areas that are crying out to be explored. You can't beat window shopping. Take a turn down Savile Row or Jermyn Street. These are where every self-respecting English gent has his clothes made, and the fusty, masculine atmosphere is still much as it was 20 or 30 years ago (unlike the prices). Those in search of high fashion—and in London this means high price tags as well as haute couture—should head for the pretty little shops along Beauchamp Place and Walton Street in Knightsbridge or make for still oh-so-classy Bond Street. Again, you may well find that distinctive small gift. And then again, if you feel the need to splurge, well, there aren't many better places to do it.

But don't get the idea that affordable shopping in London means either just window shopping or hunting for tiny gifts in huge department stores. There's much more for the discriminating shopper in search of genuine bargains. Covent Garden, for example, is packed with attractive little stores. You can easily spend a whole day combing them, and you'd be bound to turn up much that is genuinely British *and* genuinely affordable. Likewise, London's street markets, the Portobello Road and Camden Lock preeminently, are tailor-made for hours of happy hunting. You'll find everything from a stuffed parrot to a four-poster bed (though whether you'd want to buy them is another matter). Other great buys can be found in the shops in London's major museums. You can buy copies of ancient Egyptian jewelry at the British Museum; jewelry, scarves, printing blocks, or specially designed porcelain at the Royal Academy; candlesticks, posters, books, soap, and a host of other carefully crafted goods at the Victoria & Albert.

Sales and Refunds: There are two main sales periods: one just after Christmas and into the New Year; the other at the end of June into early July. Some stores may have other, shorter sales at odd times, but these are the two periods when the dedicated bargain hunter can really play the field. With prices reduced by anything between 20 and

50 percent, expensive woolen goods or china suddenly come within reach. Harrods' sales have now become regular institutions, with hundreds of extra staff taken on, immense lines outside, and a ritual sprint to the china and glass departments as the doors open. In fact, the crowds are thick on the ground at all the major stores during the sales. You'll also find that standards of service become ever more perfunctory, and that late arrivals will have little left to pick over. But you can be sure of some terrific bargains.

VAT refunds are the other great boon for the hungry shopper on a budget. All the major stores, and a great many smaller ones besides, have facilities to ensure you needn't pay VAT, Britain's version of sales tax, and a hefty 15 percent, provided you take the goods out of the country. The scheme works like this. 1) Most shops will not refund VAT for purchases of less than £75. 2) Once you've bought your goods, hand over your passport as ID, and the shop will fill out and give you a form (VAT Form 407). 3) Show the form to Customs as you leave Britain (you may have to wait on line for some time, so arrive early). 4) Your refund will be forwarded to you, minus a service charge of around $3. Specify if you want the refund credited to your charge card or if you'd like a sterling check. The latter is slower; plus, U.S. banks will charge a fee to convert it. Note: If you have the goods shipped directly to your home by the store, you have to get the VAT form signed by the Customs, Police, or a notary public once you get home. You'll then have to send it back to the store, which will refund you the money.

Shopping Hours: Most shops are open, Mon. through Sat., 9 or 9:30–5:30 or 6. All the larger stores stay open late at least one night a week, closing at 7:30 or 8. In the West End (Oxford Street, Mayfair, St. James's) they stay open late Thurs. In Knightsbridge, shops stay open late Wed.

St. James's, Piccadilly, and Mayfair

This is the largest and most varied shopping area in London, right in the heart of the capital. At one end of the scale, classic tailored clothes can be found in the plush shops of St. James's and Mayfair; at the other, a short walk to Oxford Street and Regent Street takes you to the center of popular, up-to-the-minute high-street fashions. All these areas tend to be crowded, but none more so than Oxford Street. You'll be hard put to find a square inch of sidewalk here.

As well as the major shopping streets, the area has some intriguing nooks and crannies. Try South Molton Street, for example, or St. Christopher's Place, running south and north of Oxford Street, near Bond Street tube station. Neither offers much in the way of low-cost shopping—these are streets for serious fashion hunters—but both are pretty in a quaintly British way, with elegant brick-built town houses and striking window displays.

Some of the smaller streets running east and west of Bond Street offer much the same kind of experience. Make for Cork Street, unofficial headquarters of London's commercial art galleries. One great travel value point to remember is that you can go free of charge into almost all the commercial art galleries that throng this area, and spend as long as you like looking at the pictures on view. Or head for Burlington Arcade, a fine, covered Regency arcade by the Royal Academy (it can be reached from Old Burlington Street or Piccadilly). The draw here are the many little shops selling woolen goods by the score, silk ties, pipes, stripey pajamas, pens, slippers, and other upscale gift items—the sort of thing you would find in every Rockefeller's Christmas stocking. You may find something more affordable here, but the atmosphere really remains the attraction: formal, old-fashioned, and chic.

Jermyn Street, over the road in St. James's, has much the same kind of cachet as does, on a larger scale, its grander neighbour, St. James's Street. These are the sorts of places where, behind a weathered facade, you'll find a discreet store that's been making hats for the Royal Family since the 18th century. Again, the emphasis here is on atmosphere rather than bargain. But the famous shirt shops along Jermyn Street, for example, sell their multicolored wares at half price during the sales. A £50 shirt becomes significantly more tempting when you can buy it for £25.

But probably the major shopping highlights in this central area are the two well-known stores: Liberty, up on

Regent Street by Oxford Circus, and Fortnum and Mason, grocers and provision merchants to HM the Queen and suppliers of leather and fancy goods to HM the Queen Mother, as they are pleased to describe themselves. Both offer unlimited style and class. A case for your glasses may not sound especially enticing, but it takes on an entirely new dimension when made up in one of Liberty's distinctive floral prints. Likewise, you may not think much of coming home with some tea in your luggage, but that, too, becomes a deal more appealing when it comes in one of Fortnum's delightfully old-fashioned tins, complete with royal coat of arms.

Clothing and Accessories

BHS, 252 Oxford St., W1N 9AG (tel. 629 2011), and branches all over Central London. Head here for classic woolens, bright leisurewear, and good-value crockery and china.

C&A, 200 Oxford St., W1N 9DG (tel. 629 7272); 376 Oxford St., W1N 9DH (tel. 408 0047); 505 Oxford St., W1A 2AX (tel. 629 7272); and other branches. C&A is a large and generally reliable store, which sells clothes for all the family at reasonable prices, with some surprisingly bright fashions for teenagers. You won't find anything startling, but it's always good value.

Fenwick of Bond Street, 63 New Bond St., W1A 3BS (tel. 629 9161). You'll find the best of both worlds at this store, with designer names as well as everyday fashions. There is also an excellent accessories department on the first floor. Considering the Bond Street address, prices are generally quite low.

Hennes, 238 Oxford St., W1R 1AB (tel. 493 8557). There's excellent-value inexpensive fashion here for men, women, and children.

Laura Ashley, 256–258 Regent St., W1A 5DN (tel. 437 9760); 7–9 Harriet St., SW1X 9JS (tel. 235 9797); 157 Fulham Rd., SW3 6SN (tel. 584 6939); 35–36 Bow St., WC2E 7AU (tel. 240 1997); Macmillan House, Kensington High St., W8 5NP (tel. 938 3751); 36 Hampstead High St., NW3 1QE (tel. 431 3215); and other branches all over Central London. Laura Ashley's popularity remains as great as ever. This is the place to come for country-style English dresses, blouses, shirts, and knitwear; the prices are half those of a Laura Ashley in the U.S. Most branches also sell cottage-garden fragrances, while some have home-furnishing departments, too.

Marks & Spencer, 173 Oxford St., W1R 1TA (tel. 437 7722); 458 Oxford St., W1N 0AP (tel. 935 7954); and branches all over London. Marks & Spencer's is still Britain's best-loved high-street store, selling clothes to suit most ages and tastes. You'll find colorful and casual wear as well as sensible work clothes, all at reasonable prices. M&S has also branched out into home furnishings and cosmetics. The food departments have excellent quality produce, but prices are on the high side.

Department Stores

Debenhams, 334–338 Oxford St., W1A 1EF (tel. 580 3000). Debenham's has thrown off its dowdy high-street style to transform itself into a distinctly flashy store with white and gold decorations, a pianist tinkling away, and even that most un-British of additions, a glossy atrium to house the escalators.

Fortnum and Mason, 181 Piccadilly, W1A 1ER (tel. 734 8040). This traditional English store is most famous for its marvelous food halls where English teas, bottled condiments, and biscuits in attractive tins make inexpensive and distinctive presents. Upstairs there are good quality men's and women's fashions, toys, and gifts—you might well find a gift to take home well within your budget.

John Lewis, 278 Oxford St., W1A 1EX (tel. 629 7711). John Lewis prides itself on a hard-won reputation for high quality household goods, fabrics at low prices, and clothing. It's always crowded and often difficult to find your way around, but hard to beat for value—in fact, their slogan is "we are never knowingly undersold."

Liberty, 222 Regent St., W1R 6AH (tel. 734 1234). This is the most splendid store on Regent Street and probably the most desirable and upscale department store in London. Famed principally for its fabrics, Liberty also offers a huge range of Oriental goods, jewelry, textiles, rugs, porcelain, small items of furniture, and much more. There are

affordable gifts to be found here—Liberty print handker-
chiefs, scarves, ties, cushions, or lavender bags. You'll
also find a wonderful selection of soaps, perfumes, and
potpourri.

Selfridges, 400 Oxford St., W1A 1AB (tel. 629 1234).
Selfridges is London's equivalent of Macy's and, in London, is second in size only to Harrods. It is extremely well
stocked and offers a wide choice of goods of every kind.
The food halls have excellent ranges of luxury and basic
provisions.

Specialty Shops

The Cocktail Shop, 5 Avery Row, W1X 9HF (tel. 493
9744). You'll find everything here you could ever need to
shake, stir, or sip a cocktail, as well as some pretty
remarkable recipes. It's just off New Bond Street.

Floris, 89 Jermyn St., SW1Y 4UD (tel. 930 2885). You'll
be hard put to find a more traditional English store than
this. It specializes in delightfully old-fashioned soaps, toilet
waters, and aftershaves. There are also accessories such as
shaving brushes, bowls, and powder puffs.

Hamleys, 188 Regent St., W1R 6BT (tel. 734 3161).
London's premier toy shop, Hamleys sells everything from
marbles to the latest in video games. Kids love it.

Tower Records, 1 Piccadilly, W1V 9PB (tel. 439 2500).
This huge music store has every facility for listening and
seeing before you buy—everything from records, tapes,
cassettes, and compact discs to videos. The classical music
section is vast; there's a booking office for Wembley pop
concerts; and even a café on the premises. Tower is open
till midnight.

Virgin Megastore, 14–16 Oxford St., W1N 9FL (tel. 631
1234). This is a vast and maze-like store, infinitely larger
than its relatively modest Oxford Street entrance suggests.
There's a huge range of records, compact discs, videos,
tapes, books, and comics. It's always crowded, but there's a
good café if you want to relax.

Knightsbridge, Kensington, and Chelsea

After the West End, this is London's other major shopping area and, like the West End, its shops run the gamut
from the extremely exclusive, such as the boutiques of

Beauchamp Place, to the less expensive shops of King's Road and Kensington High Street.

Knightsbridge is the home of Harrods, an ornate Edwardian structure fronting the Brompton Road, and attracting thousands of shoppers and sightseers every day. Harrods is worth visiting just to wander through its glitzy departments, although it's probably fair to say that it's lost the quality feel that gave it its worldwide reputation in bygone years. If you happen to be in London at sale time and can bear the hordes, then this is the place to pick up bargains.

Along the road, on the corner of Sloane Street, is Harvey Nichols, a small but equally revered Knightsbridge store, and one that, unlike Harrods, has managed to hang on to its classy image. Sloane Street itself is the hunting ground for designer fashion—it certainly isn't budget territory, but it is a delight for the window shopper. The stores bunch themselves at both ends of the street, with a long shopless stretch between. At the bottom end, a right turn takes you into King's Road, no longer the hippie haven and then bastion of punk fashion that it once was, but still worth wandering down for a taste of London street fashion. King's Road today has a mixture of shops ranging from antiques, through quality interior design fabrics and the clothes of young designers, to a myriad of denim shops.

Brompton Road and Fulham Road tend to sell fairly upmarket wares, while Kensington High Street falls into the more affordable category. At times it can feel like a scaled-down Oxford Street.

Clothing and Accessories

Fogal, 51 Brompton Rd., SW3 1DE (tel. 225 0472). The stock here is entirely made up of an amazing array of socks, pantyhose, and stockings in various materials—cotton, cashmere, silk, wool, and nylon—in almost every shade imaginable.

Tie Rack, Station Arcade, Kensington High St., W8 5SA (tel. 937 5168), and branches all over Central London. If you need something to put around your neck, or waist, or shoulders, these shops are a good place to look for reasonably priced ties, bow ties, scarves, shawls, cravats, and belts in all colors and patterns.

Department Stores

Harrods, 87–135 Brompton Rd., SW1X 7XL (tel. 730 1234). This must be the most famous store in London, with over 200 departments, each with a vast range of goods. The accessories counters are a good hunting ground for inexpensive treasures to take home, and the Food Hall is world-famous for Art Nouveau tiled walls and its fabulous displays of produce. It's always extremely busy so be prepared for some jostling.

Harvey Nichols, 11 Knightsbridge, SW1X 7RJ (tel. 235 5000). Harvey Nichols is considered by many to be London's most attractive department store, rivaled only perhaps by Liberty. It is relatively small and uncrowded, and has some of the most elegant clothes in town. This does put it right outside the budget range, but HN has an excellent policy of reducing ends of lines and items which sell slowly, all through the season, so you *might* be lucky and pick up a bargain. Other departments sell goods with the emphasis on quality rather than variety of choice, but the newly opened basement is the place for inexpensive accessories and gifts.

House of Fraser, 63 Kensington High St. (tel. 937 5432). Here's another recently remodeled store, complete with palms and a pianist, which give a pleasant, unhurried atmosphere. Again, you'll find high quality goods of all kinds here—the children's wear is particularly attractive.

Peter Jones, Sloane Sq., SW1W 8EL (tel. 730 3434). At the beginning of the King's Road, where it joins Sloane Square, this member of the John Lewis chain stocks a wide range of fabrics, china, and glass, all at reasonable prices. The coffee shop on the top floor is a pleasant watering hole after a foray into Chelsea.

Gifts

Brats, 281 King's Rd., SW3 5EW (tel. 351 7674); 624C Fulham Rd., SW6 5RS (tel. 731 6915). Just below the Cannon Cinema, this small shop sells all sorts of unusual and interesting gifts—nightshirts, colorful socks, lighters, books, sunglasses, watches, and jewelry. But you'll have to keep an eye on your budget.

General Trading Company, 144 Sloane St., SW1X 9LB (tel. 730 0411). Rather like New York's Hammacher Schlemmer, this store stocks all sorts of household goods, a delightful assortment of children's toys, posh-looking visitors' books, toiletries, china and glass, as well as bits and pieces from the Orient. It's definitely upscale, but—with goods pouring in from all over the world in great profusion—you're sure to find something to suit your pocket.

Specialist Shops

Bendicks, 195 Sloane St., SW1X 9QX (tel. 235 4749). There are some 30 different types of chocolate to choose from here, all of which come elegantly packaged. The bittermints are a perennial favorite.

Betjeman & Barton, 43 Elizabeth St., SW1W 9PP (tel. 730 5086). Here's an important stop for anyone interested in tea and how to make it. There are over 100 different types of tea in this tiny shop off Buckingham Palace Road, as well as all the necessary traditional equipment—teapots, strainers, and caddies.

Crabtree and Evelyn, 6 Kensington Church St., W8 4EP (tel. 937 9335). All the preparations here—soaps, cosmetics, toilet water, and bath oils—are beautifully packaged and make excellent, inexpensive gifts. The scents are all redolent of the English countryside and cottage garden.

L'Herbier de Provence, 341 Fulham Rd., SW10 9TW (tel. 352 0012). The herbs sold in this shop are all grown in the south of France, and are stacked in baskets and sacks around the floor. You can make your own selection from leaves and flowers for health-giving *tisanes,* special teas, bath oils, and essences. Naturally, the place has a glorious scent, like the granddaddy of all Provençal hillsides in bright sunshine.

Luxury Needlepoint, 36 Beauchamp Pl., SW3 1NU (tel. 581 5575). If you would like to reproduce an antique tapestry for a firescreen, for example, this is the place to look for a design. The shop uses patterns from old wallpaper and prints of different ages, as well as the work of modern designers.

Tree House, 237 Kensington High St., W8 6SA (tel.

937 7497). There are lots of cuddly bears and rabbits, games, books, and pocket-money toys in this delightful toy shop near the Commonwealth Institute. There are even gifts for children to buy for their parents—notepaper and executive marbles, for example.

Walton Street Stationery, 97 Walton St., SW3 2JX (tel. 589 0777). This stationer was established over 150 years ago and still sells cotton-fiber writing paper, tissue-lined envelopes, wrapping paper, and beautiful desk accessories. It's just south of Brompton Road.

Whittards, 111 Fulham Rd., SW3 6RL (tel. 589 2461). Whittards is one of London's more superior delicatessens, stocking wonderously fattening food of all kinds. It has been in business for over 100 years, and its specialties include teas and coffees.

Soho and Covent Garden

As we describe later on in our Exploring section, the 19th-century market of Covent Garden, once the home of London's fruit and vegetable trade, was elegantly restored several years ago. Now it houses small, high-fashion clothing and shoe stores, eateries, gift shops, and stalls selling mostly handcrafted items such as jewelry, knitwear (often expensive), pottery, and other crafty bits and pieces. The flea market in the lower part of the market is the place to look for old postcards, film memorabilia, books, and knickknacks of every sort. Covent Garden is an excellent place to wander around or to find a sidewalk café; window shopping or watching the street entertainment is just as much fun here as buying.

Soho is where you'll find London's Chinatown, centering on Gerrard Street. All kinds of intriguing Oriental shops are tucked into this area, but the food stores and supermarkets are perhaps the most interesting, stacked as they are with exotic vegetables and fruits, herbs and spices, remedies and medicines. Many of the shops and restaurants around here stay open late.

Books

Foyles, 119–125 Charing Cross Rd., WC2H 0EB (tel. 437 5660). This massive bookshop holds an incredible stock, but it is *very* difficult to find what you're looking for. Paying for your books can be another frustration—you may have to stand in line for up to 20 minutes. But Foyles is an essential, if irritating, part of London's book scene.

John Adrian, 14 Charing Cross Rd., WC2H 0HG (tel. 240 2337); 12 Cecil Ct., WC2N 4HE (tel. 836 2987). Both branches stock a wide range of books, none of which costs more than £2, so it's worth trying your luck here first.

Waterstone's, 121–125 Charing Cross Rd., WC2H 0EA (tel. 434 4291). Next door to Foyles, Waterstone's, a branch of a fairly new, adventurous chain, is a well-arranged bookshop, with an intelligently selected stock; there's classical music to put you in a relaxed frame of mind, and it's altogether quite the opposite to its neighbor.

Clothing and Accessories

The Button Box, 44 Bedford St., WC2E 9HA (tel. 240 2716). This fascinating little shop sells buttons of all kinds—little pearls, Scottie dogs, brilliantly colored wooden toggles—amounting to some 500 different varieties.

The Hat Shop, 58 Neal St., WC2H 9PA (tel. 836 6718). You'll find a hat for any occasion here: inexpensive caps and straw hats, Panamas and pith helmets, the traditional or adventurous.

Specialist Shops

Les Amis Gourmands, 30 James St., WC2E 8PA (tel. 836 4665). On a road leading down to Covent Garden, this shop sells a splendid selection of cheeses, croissants, cakes, ice creams, and many other tempting delicacies.

The Copper Shop, 48 Neal St., WC2H 9PA (tel. 836 2984). They've not only got copper ornaments here—pots and pans of every description hang from the ceiling and crowd the shelves.

Covent Garden General Store, 111 Long Acre, WC2E 9NT (tel. 240 0331). This is a knickknack shop on a grand scale: shelves and shelves of teapots with funny faces, jokey alarm clocks, china, bamboo and cane tables, fancy tights, socks, and a host of other pretty, wacky, and generally tasteless bits and pieces. There's a restaurant, too, if you get exhausted.

Culpepper, 8 The Market, WC2E 8RB (tel. 379 6698). There are herbal soaps and lotions, potted or dried herbs, and a host of other aromatic delights here, many available in trial sizes which will pack away neatly in your luggage.

Dobell's, 21 Tower St., WC2H 9NS (tel. 240 1354). This music store has a fine selection of new and secondhand jazz and blues records, tapes, and compact discs. It's also a good spot to look for deletions, obscure recordings, and jazz videos. Tower Street runs off Cambridge Circus.

The Doll's House, 29 The Market, WC2E 8RE (tel. 379 7243). This is the place for delightful miniature furnishings and fittings. The range is phenomenal—from Regency four-poster beds to microwave ovens.

Drury Tea and Coffee Co., 37 Drury Lane, WC2B 5SQ (tel. 836 2607). Over 100 varieties of tea are sold here, not including the many blends made up to order. If you are unsure of your favorite, you can buy small quantities to try. The shop also imports coffees from all over the world.

The Kite Store, 69 Neal St., WC2H 9PJ (tel. 836 1666). Hanging all over the shop, as if to try and make it airborne, are kites from many different countries, in all shapes and sizes, from the traditional box variety to the aerobatic.

Mysteries, 9 Monmouth St., WC2H 9DA (tel. 240 3688). This shop is one of the largest in the country, catering for the needs of those who dabble in the occult—everything from joss sticks to tarot cards, and crystal balls to Ouija boards.

Naturally British, 13 New Row, WC2N 4LF (tel. 240 0551). This shop specializes in handcrafted British goods: walking sticks, pottery, soft toys, Fair Isle woolens, traditional English fragrances, and many other lovely gift ideas.

Pollock's Toy Theater, 44 The Market, WC2E 8RF (tel. 379 7866). Models and reproductions of theaters from the Regency, Victorian, and Edwardian eras are the specialties here, but there is a selection of budget-priced toys as well. There is also a fascinating museum.

The Poster Shop, 28 James St., WC2E 8PA (tel. 244 2526). If you are looking for a chic (and large) picture for your wall, you'll find posters here from galleries in Paris, exhibitions in New York, etc. The Poster Shop will also frame your choice for you.

The Tea Shop, 15A Neal St., WC2H 9PU (tel. 240 7539). Downstairs at the Tea Shop they sell a wide range of teas, while upstairs you'll find all the accessories you'll ever need for making the perfect brew—novelty tea pots, infusers, and tea cosies.

Street Markets

The street markets of London are not only great places for bargains—or at least you can kid yourself that they are!—but full of genuine bedouin Londoners, from the Cockney stall holders—selling vegetables or antiques, their Jaguars parked in a nearby street—to the locals out buying their Sunday dinners. The markets are also a rich source of free entertainment, tasty snacks, and insights into the way London works. Naturally, there is a lot of rubbish on view, imported plastic from Hong Kong or cheesecloth shirts from Bombay, but there is also a seemingly endless supply of attractive plates and grubby, but delicately cut, glass, small Victorian jewel boxes, and brass candlesticks. Heaven alone knows where the stream of these items comes from, but the stalls that line the bustling streets never seem to be empty.

Even more colorful are the flower and vegetable sellers; increasingly exotic goods pile up on their barrows, as produce from Israel, Morocco, New Zealand, and—why not?—Tierra del Fuego pours in. Delicious imports that were unknown in Britain a decade ago are now everyday fare—kiwi fruits, guavas, and prickly pears. The language of the hucksters is even more colorful than their wares, with a line of badinage and friendly banter that will make you long for your tape recorder.

Street markets are mainly a weekend pastime. As many of them are open on Sunday mornings, they provide something to do on a day that can be extremely dull and dreary in London. A wander through one of the markets, followed by a good Sunday lunch, then an afternoon in a park or by the river, makes a classic London way of cheering up the sabbath.

Bermondsey, Tower Bridge Rd., SE1. Fri. 4:30 A.M.–

noon. Also known as the New Caledonian Market, this is one of London's largest market sites. There are hundreds of stalls selling a wealth of junk and treasures from Britain's attics. Note that the market is held on Fridays only—starting at the unearthly hour of 4 A.M.—and it's then that the really great buys will be snapped up. You should still be able to find a bargain or two if you turn up a bit later. To get there, take the 15 or 25 bus to Aldgate, then a number 42 over Tower Bridge to Bermondsey Square, or take the tube to London Bridge and walk.

Camden Lock (Dingwalls) Market, NW1. Shops Tues. to Sun. 9:30–5:30. This is just the place to pick up an unusual and inexpensive gift, besides being a picturesque and pleasant area to wander around, with its cobbled court-yards, and the attractive lock nearby. There's an open-air antiques market here on Sat. and Sun. though the individual craft shops are open during the week as well. It does get horribly crowded at weekends. You'll need to take the tube or no. 24 or 29 bus to Camden Town.

Camden Passage, Islington, N1. Wed. to Sat. 8:30–3. The endless rows of little antique shops here are the places to head for, particularly if you're interested in silverware and jewelry, though the market is by no means confined to these alone. Sat. is the big day for stalls; during the rest of the week only the shops are open. A 19 or 38 bus or tube to The Angel will get you there.

Greenwich Antiques Market, Greenwich High Rd., SE10. Antiques, crafts, and clothes Sat. and Sun. 9–5; fruit and vegetables Mon. to Fri. 9–5. If you're planning to visit Greenwich, then combine your trip with a wander around this open-air market near St. Alfege Church. You'll find the best selection of secondhand and antique clothes in London—good quality tweeds and overcoats can be amazing value. But, as in any self-respecting London market, you'll also find an enormous range of other items, ranging from the worthless to the wonderful. The market for antiques, etc. is open on Sat. and Sun. only, and to find it take a British Rail train to New Gate Cross and then a 117 bus, or a bus direct to Greenwich.

Leadenhall Market, EC3. Mon. to Fri. 7–3. The draw here is not so much what you can buy—plants and food mainly—as the building itself. It's a handsome late-Victorian structure, ornate and elaborate, with lashings of atmosphere. To get there you'll need to take the tube to Bank or Monument.

Leather Lane, Holborn, EC1. Mon. to Fri. noon–3. You won't find any great treasures here. This is a traditional, open-air London street market selling buckets and mops and spare parts for vacuum cleaners, rather than Victorian cut glass or Georgian silver. But it's not a bad place to browse through and there's still something of the atmosphere of genuine Cockney London that's all but disappeared elsewhere. The nearest tube is Chancery Lane.

Petticoat Lane, Middlesex St., E1. Sun. 9–2. Petticoat Lane doesn't actually appear on the map, but that is the commonly used name of this famous market on Middlesex Street. On Sun., it becomes Petticoat Lane, where you can pick up all sorts of bargains. Look out for good quality, budget-priced leather goods, dazzling knitwear, and cut-price fashions. There are also luxury goods such as cameras, videos, and stereos at exceptional prices. Liverpool Street, Aldgate, or Aldgate East tubes are the closest.

Portobello Market, Portobello Rd., W11. Fruit & vegetables Mon. to Wed., Fri., Sat. 8–5, Thurs. 8–1; antiques Fri. 5–3; both Sat. 8–5. This is no longer the place it once was for bargains, but Sat. is the best day to search the stalls for a not-quite-bargain-priced treasure in the way of silverware, curios, porcelain, and jewelry. Some of the clothes stalls are excellent value, selling well-known labels at knock-down prices. It's always crowded, there are street entertainers, an authentic hustle-and-bustle atmosphere, and, since it is firmly on the tourist route, you'll hear as much German or Texan as you will Cockney. It's open all week except Thurs. afternoon and you'll need to take a no. 52 bus or the tube to Ladbroke Grove or Notting Hill Gate.

Sports

SWIMMING. The weather in London is seldom good enough for swimming (though there are several indoor pools), but for those all-too-rare heat waves, two fairly decent swimming spots are worth mentioning. The Serpentine in Hyde

Park is the more central of the two, but it can be extremely crowded in hot weather. Those willing to travel a bit further afield might enjoy the so-called ponds on Parliament Hill, on the edge of Hampstead Heath.

TENNIS. Tennis in London means just one thing: Wimbledon. The championships are held in late June, but the rush for tickets starts many months earlier. To try and get hold of tickets, write to the All England Lawn Tennis Club, Church Rd., London SW19 5AE, enclosing a stamped, addressed envelope. You'll be sent an application form; tickets are then allocated by ballot and cost from £8 to £20.

If you want to take the chance, turn up and pay your £5 entry fee (less after 5). You won't get onto the center court, but in the first week the outer courts have some excellent games and big names. It can, however, get extremely crowded, and some of the subsidiary attractions are both expensive and tawdry. The nearest tube is Southfields, on the District line.

There are hundreds of public courts in London's parks for those who would rather play tennis than watch it. In most cases there is a charge of about £1.50 an hour.

Entertainment

WHAT'S ON. To find out what's on in London's entertainment world, consult *What's On, Time Out,* or *City Limits.* The evening papers, in particular the *Standard,* carry listings, as do the major Sunday papers and the daily *Independent.*

THEATER. The traditional theaters of the West End are around Piccadilly and Shaftesbury Avenue. These days, the emphasis seems to be on mediocre, middle-of-the-road musicals and sex comedies, but if you want something more serious you can always see what the Royal Shakespeare Company has in repertory at the Barbican Arts Center. The three auditoriums in the National Theater are also good for more classic plays.

Most theater tickets are a great buy, beginning at about £4. However, visit the **Society of West End Theater's** ticket booth in Leicester Square on the day of the performance, and you will find tickets on sale at half price (plus £1 service charge). The booth, on the west side of the square, is open Mon. through Sat. 12–2 for matinees, and 2:30–6:30 for evening performances. Students arriving at a theater a half hour before the show begins stand to get a student reduction of as much as half price.

There are many theatrical ticket agencies, of which Keith Prowse is probably the leader with around a dozen branches around the West End (look under *Keith* in the phone book—not *Prowse*). If you are coming from the States and want to book seats in advance, Keith Prowse has a New York branch—234 West 44th St., Suite 902, New York, NY 10036 (212–398–1430 or 800–223–4446).

Outside the West End there are all kinds of fringe theaters, with shows ranging from the avant-garde to Samuel Beckett revivals. Most fringe theaters stay afloat by having their shows transferred to the West End, so performance standard is high. The Donmar Warehouse, the Almeida, the King's Head, the Hampstead Theater, and the Orange Tree are usually worth going to.

The **Fringe Box Office,** in the Duke of York's Theater on St. Martin's Lane, WC2N 4BG (tel. 379 6002), handles bookings for some 40 fringe establishments, and can provide information on current productions. Credit cards are accepted, and the office is open Mon. through Sat. 10–6. A 50p booking charge covers *all* the seats you might require.

TV or radio fanatics can attend a live performance. Write in advance to **BBC Radio Ticket Unit,** BBC, London W1A 4WW; to **BBC Television Ticket Unit,** BBC, London W12 7SB; or to **Thames Television Ticket Office,** 149 Tottenham Court Rd., London W1P 9LL. Requests by phone are not accepted.

THEATER BOX OFFICES. Adelphi, Strand, WC2E 7NA (tel. 836 7611)

   Albery, St. Martin's Lane, WC2N 4AH (tel. 836 3878)
   Aldwych, Aldwych, WC2B 4DF (tel. 836 6404)
   Ambassadors, West St., WC2H 9ND (tel. 836 6111)
   Apollo, Shaftesbury Ave., W1V 7HD (tel. 437 2663)
   Apollo Victoria, Wilton Rd., SW1V 1LL (tel. 828 8665)
   Barbican Center, Silk St., EC2Y 8DS (concerts and Royal Shakespeare Company, tel. 628 8795, 638 8891)

Comedy, Panton St., SW1Y 4DN (tel. 930 2578)

Criterion, Piccadilly, W1V 9LB (tel. 930 3216)

Drury Lane (Theater Royal), Catherine St., WC2B 5JS (tel. 836 8108)

Duchess, Catherine St., WC2B 5LA (tel. 836 8243)

Duke of York's, St. Martin's Lane, WC2N 4BG (tel. 836 5122)

Fortune, Russell St., WC2B 5HH (tel. 836 2238)

Garrick, Charing Cross Rd., WC2H 0HH (tel. 379 6107)

Globe, Shaftesbury Ave., W1V 8AR (tel. 437 3667)

Haymarket, Haymarket, SW1Y 4HT (tel. 930 9832)

Her Majesty's, Haymarket, SW1Y 4QL (tel. 839 2244)

Lyric, Shaftesbury Ave., W1V 7HA (tel. 437 3686)

Lyric Hammersmith, Kings St., W6 0QL (tel. 741 2311)

Mayfair, Stratton St., W1X 5FD (tel. 629 3036)

Mermaid, Puddle Dock, EC4 3DB (day of performance tel. 236 5568, advance booking tel. 638 8891)

National Theater (Cottesloe, Lyttleton and Olivier), South Bank Arts Center, SE1 9PX (tel. 928 2252)

New London, Drury Lane, WC2B 5PW (tel. 405 0072)

Old Vic, Waterloo Rd., SE1 8NB (tel. 928 7616)

Palace, Shaftesbury Ave., W1V 8AY (tel. 434 0909)

Palladium, 8 Argyll St., W1A 3AB (tel. 437 7373)

Phoenix, Charing Cross Rd., WC2H 0JP (tel. 836 2294)

Piccadilly, Denman St., W1V 8DY (tel. 437 4506)

Prince Edward, Old Compton St., W1V 6HS (tel. 734 8951)

Prince of Wales, 31 Coventry St., W1V 8AS (tel. 839 5987)

Queen's, 51 Shaftesbury Ave., W1V 8BA (tel. 734 1166)

Regent's Park (open air), Inner Circle, Regent's Park, NW1 4NP (tel. 486 2431)

Royal Court, Sloane Sq., SW1W 8AS (tel. 730 1745)

St. John's, Smith Sq., SW1P 3HA (tel. 222 1061)

St. Martin's, West St., WC2H 9NH (tel. 836 1443)

Savoy, Strand, WC2R 0ET (tel. 836 8888)

Shaftesbury, Shaftesbury Ave., WC2H 8DP (tel. 379 5399)

Strand, Aldwych, WC2B 5LD (tel. 836 2660)

Theater Royal, Stratford, E15 1BN (tel. 534 0310)

Vaudeville, Strand, WC2R 0NH (tel. 836 9987)

Victoria Palace, Victoria St., SW1E 5EA (tel. 834 1317)

Westminster, 12 Palace St., SW1E 5JA (tel. 834 0283)

Whitehall, 14 Whitehall, SW1A 2DY (tel. 930 7765)

Wyndham's, Charing Cross Rd., WC2H 0DA (tel. 836 3028)

Fringe Theaters. The following are the main fringe theater venues:

Almeida, Almeida St., N1 1AT (tel. 359 4404)

Arts Theater, 6–7 Gt. Newport St., WC2H 7JB (tel. 836 2132)

Donmar Warehouse, 41 Earlham St., WC2H 9LD (tel. 240 8230)

Half Moon, 213 Mile End Rd., E1 4AA (tel. 790 4000)

Hampstead, Swiss Cottage Center, Avenue Rd., NW3 3EX (tel. 722 9301)

ICA Theater, The Mall, SW1Y 5AH (tel. 930 3647)

King's Head, Upper St., N1 1QN (tel. 226 8561)

Latchmere, 503 Battersea Park Rd., SW11 3BW (tel. 228 2620)

Orange Tree, 45 Kew Rd., Richmond, Middlesex TW9 2NQ (tel. 940 3633)

Riverside Studios, Crisp Rd., W6 9RL (tel. 748 3354)

Theater Upstairs, Royal Court, Sloane Sq., SW1W 8AS (tel. 730 2554)

Young Vic, 66 The Cut, SE1 8LZ (tel. 928 6363)

MUSIC. Classical. London has a number of symphony-sized orchestras, all of them giving regular concerts. The prestigious London Symphony Orchestra is resident at the Barbican Arts Center in the City, although other top-class orchestras, including the Philharmonia and the Royal Philharmonic, also play here from time to time. The Barbican also puts on chamber music concerts, featuring such celebrated groups as the Gabrielli String Quartet and the City of London Sinfonia.

The South Bank arts complex is another major venue. The Royal Festival Hall plays host to larger symphony orchestras, while the Queen Elizabeth Hall next door houses smaller groups. Concerts are held most nights of the week. Tickets range from £2.50 to £12, and most concerts featuring the big names are booked up well in advance. Go to the hall a half hour before the show for returns.

For less expensive concert-going, try the Royal Albert Hall during the famous Promenade Concerts season (July–Sept.). Line up outside for a special standing ("promenade") ticket, which usually costs half the regular price. During the summer there are concerts nightly, ranging from popular classics to contemporary avant-garde.

Open-air summer concerts in leafy Holland Park and Kenwood Park can be a real pleasure, assuming the weather behaves, that is. Check the listings, or the English Heritage Concert Line (tel. 734 1877).

For opera, the Royal Opera House in Covent Garden stands figuratively alongside La Scala of Milan and the New York Met—and can be just as expensive. Tickets start as low as £2 for seats up in the ceiling, but from here there is little chance of viewing the stage properly. As you come down, so the cost goes up: The most expensive tickets approach £50. English-language opera productions are staged at the English National Opera, at the Coliseum, St. Martin's Lane. Ticket prices start from an affordable £4.

Those who can't afford the expensive evening concerts in the major halls (although there are almost always reasonably inexpensive tickets available even for these), should look out for lunchtime concerts. These take place in smaller halls and picturesque churches all over London. They usually cost £1 (some are free), and feature string quartets or singers. One of the leading spots is St. John's, Smith Square—a converted 18th-century church near the Houses of Parliament.

MUSIC BOX OFFICES. Barbican Center, Silk St., EC2Y 8DS (tel. 628 8795, 638 8891)

Coliseum, St. Martin's Lane, WC2N 4ES (tel. 836 3161)

Royal Albert Hall, Kensington Gore, SW7 2AP (tel. 589 8212)

Royal Festival Hall, South Bank, SE1 8XX (tel. 928 3191)

Royal Opera House, Covent Garden, WC2E 9DD (tel. 240 1066)

Sadler's Wells, Rosebery Ave., EC1R 4TN (tel. 278 8916)

St. John's, Smith Sq., SW1P 3HA (tel. 222 1061)

Wigmore Hall, 36 Wigmore St., W1H 9DF (tel. 935 2141)

ROCK, FOLK, AND JAZZ. You'll find an exhaustive list of current venues in *Time Out* and *City Limits,* but here is a selection of the better known.

Camden Palace, 1A Camden High St., NW1 0JH (tel. 387 0428). There's a different theme each night at the Camden Palace, and you'll be charged £5 to get in. It's by Mornington Crescent tube, which is closed at the weekends.

Dingwalls, Camden Lock, Camden High St., NW1 8AF (tel. 267 4967). You'll find late-night rock here most of the week; this is a place strong on both visiting American artists as well as some of the great names from rock's heritage.

Electric Ballroom, 184 Camden High St., NW1 8QP (tel. 485 9006). This is just down the road from Dingwalls; some consider it's more than slightly run-down.

Hammersmith Odeon, Queen Charlotte St., W6 9QH (tel. 748 4081). This well-known venue is one of the two places where rock's megastars traditionally end their British tours.

Limelight, 136 Shaftesbury Ave., W1V 7DN (tel. 434 0572). There's live music several nights a week at this very central venue close to Leicester Square tube. It's often open till 3 A.M.

Marquee, 90 Wardour St., W1 3LE (tel. 437 6603). This famous name from the '60s is still going strong, albeit in the changed circumstances of Soho.

100 Club, 100 Oxford St., W1N 9FB (tel. 636 0933). The emphasis these days is more on rock, though you can catch some jazz here on a good night. It stays open late.

Pizza Express, 10 Dean St., W1V 5RL (tel. 439 8722). There's good jazz to be found down in the basement below the restaurant.

Rock Garden, 6–7 The Piazza, Covent Garden, WC2E 8RA (tel. 240 3961). This restaurant has a below-stairs club featuring all manner of rock and jazz.

Ronnie Scott's, 47 Frith St., W1V 5TE (tel. 439 0747).

By far and away the best jazz in town can be found here, in Soho. The food is expensive and mediocre, though.

Town & Country Club, 9–17 Highgate Rd., NW5 1JY (tel. 267 3334). This is a huge converted cinema up in Kentish Town that attracts many of rock and country's top names.

Wembley Arena, Empire Way, Wembley, Middlesex (tel. 903 1234). If a British tour doesn't end at the Hammersmith Odeon, then you're more than likely to find it here in this vast hall.

MOVIES. Despite the recession in moviegoing caused by the video revolution—videos have caught on in Britain in a really big way—West End cinemas continue to do good business. Most of the big houses are in the Leicester Square/Piccadilly Circus area; here tickets average £3.50 (though they can be up to nearly double that). On Mon. and at matinees, many cinemas have seats for £2.

Cinema clubs tend to show a more adventurous repertoire of classics, vintage movies, and Continental and underground films, as well as rare or underestimated masterpieces. They frequently have week-long seasons devoted to particular directors. Most charge a small membership fee of about £1, though sometimes you have to buy your membership card at least a half hour before the performance begins.

The National Film Theater on the South Bank (tel. 928 3232) is one of the best. Associated with the British Film Institute, the NFT runs a well-known film festival in the fall, as well as presenting visiting celebrities and holding lectures. It has an excellent bookshop and information center, and a bar/self-service cafeteria overlooking the Thames. You can easily get temporary membership for 80p a week. Getting tickets for a show might prove more difficult.

ROYAL
LONDON

◆

We have called this area "Royal London" partly because it is neatly bounded by the triangle of streets that make up the route that the Queen usually takes when processing from Buckingham Palace to the Abbey or to the Houses of Parliament on state occasions, and also because it contains so much that is historic and traditional in British life. The three points of this royal triangle are Trafalgar Square, Westminster, and Buckingham Palace, all of which appear below in our section on Major Attractions.

Naturally, in an area which regularly sees the pomp and pageantry of royal occasions, the streets are wide and the vistas long. With beautifully kept St. James's Park at the heart of the triangle, there is a feeling here of timeless dignity—flower beds bursting with color, long avenues of ancient trees framing classically proportioned buildings, constant glimpses of pinnacles and towers over the tree-tops, the distant throb of military bands on the march, the deep tones of Big Ben counting off the hours.

If you have time to visit only one part of London, undoubtedly this has to be that one. There is as much history in these few acres as in many whole cities, as the statues of kings, queens, soldiers, and statesmen that stand guard at every corner attest. The main drawback to

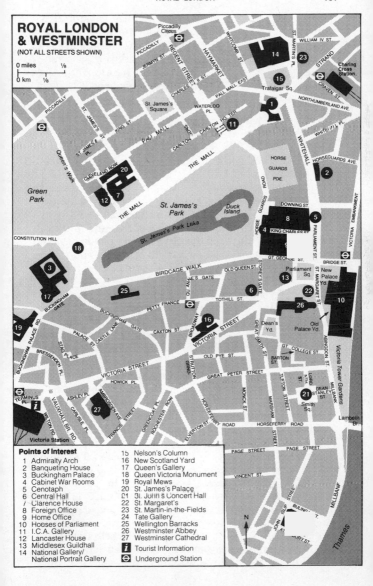

ROYAL LONDON & WESTMINSTER

(NOT ALL STREETS SHOWN)

0 miles ⅛
0 km ⅛

Points of Interest

1. Admiralty Arch
2. Banqueting House
3. Buckingham Palace
4. Cabinet War Rooms
5. Cenotaph
6. Central Hall
7. Clarence House
8. Foreign Office
9. Home Office
10. Houses of Parliament
11. I.C.A. Gallery
12. Lancaster House
13. Middlesex Guildhall
14. National Gallery/ National Portrait Gallery
15. Nelson's Column
16. New Scotland Yard
17. Queen's Gallery
18. Queen Victoria Monument
19. Royal Mews
20. St. James's Palace
21. St. John's Concert Hall
22. St. Margaret's
23. St. Martin-in-the-Fields
24. Tate Gallery
25. Wellington Barracks
26. Westminster Abbey
27. Westminster Cathedral

ℹ️ Tourist Information

Ⓔ Underground Station

sightseeing here is that half the world is doing it at the same time as you. So, even if you are feeling tired after a long day on your feet, try to come back in the evening, when the crowds have dispersed, and drink in the serenity of the trees and the buildings at your leisure. For a large part of the year a lot of Royal London is floodlit at night, adding to the theatricality of the experience.

Major Attractions

BUCKINGHAM PALACE, *The Mall, SW1A 1AA. Tubes: Green Park, Hyde Park Corner, Victoria. Changing of the Guard: Apr. to July, daily 11:30; Aug. to Mar., on alternate days. Note: state occasions and wet weather can lead to cancellation.* Buckingham Palace stands supreme among the symbols of London, indeed of Britain generally, and of the Royal Family. Its great gray bulk sums up the imperious splendor of so much of the city: stately, ponderous, and magnificent. There's every reason to believe—though there is no proof, of course—the claims that it is the most photographed building in the world.

Its setting is appropriately splendid. It is located at the west end of the Mall, the great tree-lined avenue that leads from Trafalgar Square. Directly in front of the palace are the leafy acres of St. James's Park; to the north is Green Park. Behind the palace are its 40 acres of *very* private gardens.

Buckingham Palace has been the principal residence of the monarch since Queen Victoria came to the throne in 1837. (Today, whenever the Queen is at home, her gorgeous personal standard is flown over the palace.) The building was originally a much more humble affair. It was built in the early 18th century for the Duke of Buckingham —hence its name—as his London home, and it stood on only three sides of a courtyard. It passed into royal hands in 1762, when George III bought it. In 1824 it was substantially rebuilt by John Nash, that tireless architect, for George IV, that tireless spendthrift. But, despite the money lavished on it, by the time Victoria came to the throne in 1837 it was in a sorry state. The bells didn't ring, the drains didn't work, many of the doors wouldn't close, and most of the windows wouldn't open. Queen Victoria and her husband, Prince Albert, rebuilt large parts of the palace, and added the east-facing front. This in turn was rebuilt at the beginning of this century to complete the building as it is today.

Despite its enduring popularity, Buckingham Palace remains resolutely shut to the public. It is, however, the site of one of the best free shows in the city—the **Changing of the Guard** (see above for times). It always draws substantial crowds, so get there early if you want a good view. The Queen Victoria Memorial, a mammoth monument in the traffic circle in front of the palace, makes an excellent perch from which to watch the show, as the guardsmen march in from their barracks, flags flying and bands playing.

The interior of the building is magnificent, though few get to see the sumptuous array of state rooms. These are where much of the business of royalty is played out—investitures, state banquets, receptions, lunch parties for the famous, and so on. Several times a year the Queen holds a garden party to which many more people are invited—though, even then, only on a very selective basis. Even on those occasions the lucky guests only get to see the garden and the facade of the palace that looks out over the lawns and is vaguely reminiscent of the White House in Washington. But there are two parts of the palace that are open to the general public: the **Queen's Gallery** and the **Royal Mews** (see below for details).

THE HOUSES OF PARLIAMENT, *Parliament Sq., Westminster, SW1. Tube: Victoria.* The Houses of Parliament stand by the banks of the river Thames overlooking Parliament Square. This is postcard London come to life. Parliament Square itself, permanently crowded and often choked with traffic, is also filled with statues. Prime ministers Peel, Palmerston, Disraeli, and Churchill are here. Abraham Lincoln is in front of the Middlesex Guildhall, a mock Renaissance courthouse on the west side of the square, while Richard Lionheart and Oliver Cromwell stand outside the Houses of Parliament, and King George V near the Jewel Tower. The whole of the south side of the square is taken up by Westminster Abbey (see below), and the north side by sturdy government buildings. But it is the Houses of Parliament that dominate.

Facing them you see, from left to right: **Big Ben,** the Houses of Parliament themselves, **Westminster Hall** (the oldest part of the complex), and the **Victoria Tower.** A thorough clean-up, completed in 1987, has restored the original honey-colored stone by removing the familiar layer of sooty grime. The most romantic view of the complex is from the opposite, south side of the river, a vista especially dramatic at night when the spires, pinnacles, and towers of the great buildings are floodlit green and gold.

The official title of the Houses of Parliament is the Palace of Westminster, a name that reflects accurately the institution's long and intimate connection with Britain's kings and queens. The first buildings here were put up by Edward the Confessor in the 10th century. William the Conqueror expanded the palace after 1066, and his son, William Rufus (assassinated while hunting by a courtier who "mistook" the king's red beard "for a squirrel"), added the 240-foot-long Westminster Hall. A great deal of rebuilding and expansion came in the following centuries, but, in 1834, a great fire swept through the buildings, reducing them overnight to a smoking ruin. Only Westminster Hall, the crypt of **St. Stephen's Chapel,** and the medieval **Jewel Tower** survived. Today's buildings are the work of two architects: Sir Charles Barry, who designed the structure, and Augustus Pugin, who presided over the decoration (including that of tiny details like hat stands and inkwells). Their brief had been to create a seat of government worthy of the most powerful nation in the world. The consensus of opinion was that they succeeded brilliantly, though Members of Parliament, the people who really have to use the buildings, have always complained of a chronic shortage of space. Nevertheless, the palace covers eight acres, has two miles of corridors, and more than one thousand rooms. There are two main debating chambers: the House of Commons, in the north of the building, and the House of Lords, in the south of the building.

At the southwest corner of the complex stands the Victoria Tower, at 336 feet the tallest square tower in the world. At the north end of the palace is the magnificent Clock Tower, "Big Ben," as it is always known, 316 feet high. The name is a misnomer, for strictly speaking "Big

Ben" is just the nickname of the largest bell in the tower, the bell on which the hours are struck. Weighing a mighty 13 tons, it takes its name from Sir Benjamin Hall, First Commissioner of Works when it was installed. When Parliament is in session, a flag flies from the Victoria Tower by day; at night a light burns at the summit of Big Ben.

The public is admitted to the Houses, but generally only after several hours of waiting, or if they have managed to secure a pass from their embassy or High Commission in London. Britons must contact their Member of Parliament for a similar pass. The effort is well worth making for anyone interested in politics, history, and/or mid-Victorian art. Entrance is also free, making this a tempting prospect for budgeteers.

THE MALL. *SW1. Tubes: Charing Cross, Green Park.* The Mall is not an indoor shopping center, but the stately tree-lined avenue that runs from Buckingham Palace to Trafalgar Square. It's one of the few really grand avenues in London, and the view down it to Buckingham Palace, especially in summer, when flags and banners line its length, is memorable. It was laid out in 1904 as part of the grandiose scheme that saw the construction of the **Queen Victoria Memorial** in front of Buckingham Palace, the refacing of Buckingham Palace itself, and the building of **Admiralty Arch,** the ponderous triumphal arch at the east end of The Mall. To the south of The Mall is **St. James's Park,** to the north are **St. James's Palace, Clarence House** (the Queen Mother's London home), and Carlton House Terrace.

Though it's a relatively new street, The Mall in fact follows the path of a much older thoroughfare. Like that of the similarly named Pall Mall a little to the north, The Mall's unusual name comes from the fact that this was a popular place to play "pell-mell," an early form of croquet. But it was also among London's most fashionable places to stroll, to see and be seen in. It remained fashionable, crowded from morning to night, until the end of the 18th century.

The largest building on The Mall is **Carlton House Terrace,** built by John Nash begun by 1827. It's a vast and princely structure, covered in cool, creamy stucco, with enormous and dominating classical pediments. Its splendor pales in comparison to that of the original buildings here, however. These were built from the end of the 18th century for the Prince Regent, later George IV, and were lavishly decorated even by that extravagant Prince's standards. The entire building was demolished in 1827, though the columns of the pediment were preserved. They were later used in the building of the National Gallery, where they form part of the portico.

At the base of Carlton House Terrace is the **Institute of Contemporary Arts** (tel. 930 3647 after noon). It's open daily noon–11 P.M., though the gallery closes at 8 P.M. This is London's premier showcase for the more bizarre forms of modern art. Admission is just 60p, making this a bargain for anyone looking for an inexpensive spot to pause while catching up on the latest developments in the world of contemporary art. It has also an excellent café and bar.

THE NATIONAL GALLERY, *Trafalgar Sq., WC2N 5DN (tel. 839 3321, recorded information 839 3526). Open Mon. to Sat. 10–6, Sun. 2–6. Admission free. Tubes: Charing Cross, Leicester Square.* The dignified bulk of the National Gallery stands on the north side of Trafalgar Square, in the very heart of London. It houses one of the world's great art collections, begun in 1824 when George IV encouraged his government to buy the collection of a recently deceased art lover. The Gallery itself was built between 1832 and 1838. From the nucleus of the original collection, the National Gallery's holdings grew rapidly throughout the 19th century, until, by 1900, they comprised one of the foremost picture collections in the world. Practically every European artist of significance from the 14th to the 19th centuries is represented here: Michelangelo, Raphael, Leonardo, Titian, Rubens, Rembrandt, Vermeer, Goya, David, Turner, and Monet, to name only some of the most famous.

Unlike some other state-owned museums in London, admission is absolutely free, making this one of the best bargains in the city. You won't be able to do justice to the collections in one visit, but the excellent plans at all the entrances make it easy to find your way to painters and periods that interest you especially. And of course the free admission encourages repeat visits. The Gallery also has the advantage, rare among the great museums of London, of being relatively easy to find your way around.

NATIONAL PORTRAIT GALLERY, *2 St. Martin's Pl., WC2H 0HE (tel. 930 1552). Open Mon. to Fri. 10–5, Sun. 2–6. Admission free, except for special exhibitions (usually about £2). Tubes: Charing Cross, Leicester Square.* This gallery is tucked around the corner from the National Gallery on Trafalgar Square, and should be a must for anyone interested in either the history or people of Britain. As its name implies, the National Portrait Gallery houses portraits of famous—or infamous—British faces down the ages. Not all items here are in the masterpiece class: They have been selected as records of the British character rather than as works of art, and this gives the place a wholly different interest from most galleries. The collection isn't limited to painted portraits; there are busts, photographs, even cartoons to help enrich the coverage of the British phizog. Writers, pop stars, politicians, soldiers, kings, queens, and ladies of easy virtue—they're all here. In recent years, the people who work on the display techniques of the gallery have shown a real theatrical flair, and many of the rooms almost have the effect of stage sets, with drapes, furniture, and other props to set the particular period. It helps if you can visit the place with a knowledgeable Brit, but if one isn't to hand, then there's lots of explanatory material about. There is an excellent shop for cards and books.

ST. JAMES'S PALACE, see page 128 .

ST. JAMES'S PARK, *SW1. Tubes: Charing Cross, St. James's Park. The bands in St. James's Park play late May through Aug., Mon. to Sat. 12:30–2 and 5:30–7, Sun. 3–4:30 and 6–7:30.* St. James's Park, bounded by the Mall to the north, Horse Guards Road to the east, Birdcage Walk to the south, and Buckingham Palace to the west, is probably the most beautiful of London's parks. It covers 93 acres, and was developed at different times by a series of monarchs, this having originally been the heart of the royal backyard when Britain's kings and queens lived in the great sprawl that was Whitehall Palace, now almost totally disappeared. Henry VIII was the first king to develop the Park, draining the marshes that had made it a handy hunting preserve.

Charles I took his last walk across the Park en route to his execution. But it was Charles II who began to convert it to its present shape. He employed Le Nôtre, a famous French landscape gardener who had worked for Louis XIV, and charged him with remodeling the Park. In 1829 John Nash relandscaped it again, for George IV, giving it the look it has today.

Although St. James's Park is an agreeable place to wander around during the day, with its superbly maintained flowerbeds, its lake, its exotic wildfowl, and its bands, it is particularly attractive after dark, especially in summer. Then the illuminated fountains in the lake are in full spate, and Westminster Abbey and the Houses of Parliament beyond the trees are floodlit.

THE TATE GALLERY, *Millbank, SW1P 4RG (tel. 821 1313). Open Mon. to Sat. 10–5:50, Sun. 2–5:50. Admission free, except for special exhibitions which are usually £2. Tube: Pimlico.* The Tate—everyone drops the word Gallery—overlooks the Thames, about 20 minutes' walk south from the Houses of Parliament. The tube is a quicker way of getting there, as it's only five minutes' walk from Pimlico station. It isn't easy to miss the impressive building, with tourist buses lining up outside, ice cream vendors doing a thriving trade, and plenty of people waiting for friends, or just enjoying the sun, on the steps.

Opened in 1897, the Tate houses two main collections: British painting from the 16th to the early 20th centuries (this includes a large number of Hogarths, Blakes, Constables, Turners, and Pre-Raphaelites); and an international modern collection, tracing the development of modern art through all its "-isms," from Impressionism to the most recent Post-Post Modernisms. The cream of European and American creativity—Picasso, Magritte, Giacometti, Dali, Warhol, Pollock, Rothko, to name just a very few artists—is well represented here. Apart from the permanent collections, the Tate lays on special single-artist shows, but it charges an entrance fee for these.

Also part of the Tate is the Clore Gallery, opened in 1987, where works by J.M.W. Turner—who lived and painted just a little way upriver—are on show. He bequeathed to the nation the works that remained in his studio at his death, with the stipulation that they should all be displayed in one place—and it took 136 years to meet the proviso! The bequest consisted of hundreds of oils, watercolors, and drawings, but many of his best works are in collections other than this. The Clore can be entered either from a newly laid out garden, or from one of the other galleries inside.

There is a good gallery shop for postcards, posters, books, and all the usual promotional material. In the basement you can get a cup of coffee and a snack at the very busy cafeteria. The main restaurant, though serving some unusual ancient English recipes, is certainly no great travel value.

TRAFALGAR SQUARE, *SW1. Tubes: Charing Cross, Leicester Square.* If Westminster is the modern center of London— "modern," that is, only when measured against the timespan of London as a whole—Trafalgar Square is its focus. It's a commanding open space, built on the grand scale demanded by its central position in the capital of an empire that reached to the farthest corners of the globe. The square's natural incline—it slopes down from north to south—was cleverly exploited by architect John Nash as a tier, a succession of high points from which to look down the imposing carriageways that run dramatically away from it towards the Thames, the Houses of Parliament, and Buckingham Palace. Nash began work here in 1829, but Trafalgar Square was completed only in 1841, some years after his death.

Today it's permanently alive with people, Londoners and tourists alike, and traffic roars around it. Marches, rallies, and political meetings are held here. Great events—New Years, royal weddings, elections, sporting triumphs—will always see the crowds gathering here. Every Christmas, a huge fir tree, a gift from the people of Norway to commemorate the help given them by Britain during the war, is put up.

Trafalgar Square takes its name from the Battle of Trafalgar, Nelson's great naval victory over the French in 1805. Appropriately, the dominant landmark here is **Nelson's Column,** a massive 185-foot column, topped by a 17-foot-high statue of the great admiral. Four huge lions,

modeled by the Victorian artist Sir Edwin Landseer, guard
its towering base. This in turn is decorated with four large
bronze panels, cast from the French guns captured in the
naval battles of St. Vincent, Aboukir Bay, Copenhagen,
and Trafalgar, and depicting scenes from the same battles.
The fountains on either side of the Column are modern;
the originals were sent as gifts to the Canadian government
just after World War II.

Along the north side of the square is the National
Gallery (see above), while the elegant, steepled church of
St. Martin in the Fields stands in the northeast corner. It
was built in the 1720s by James Gibbs and still carries out
its traditional role of caring for the poor (St. Martin of
Tours, after whom the church is named, is the patron saint
of the destitute). A number of famous Britons are buried
here, including Nell Gwynne, Charles II's mistress, and the
celebrated 18th-century furniture maker Thomas Chippen-
dale. But for most people, St. Martin in the Fields is best
known as the base of the Academy of St. Martin in the
Fields, one of the country's most prestigious small orchestras, which gives a regular series of candlelit concerts in the
church. You can often pick up half-price tickets on the day
of performances, though you may have to wait in line for
some time. The church, in spite of its rather fusty interior,
has a wonderful atmosphere for music making, but the
wooden benches can make it hard to give your undivided
attention to the music. The **London Brass Rubbing Center**
(tel. 871 5153) is now housed in the crypt. You can make
your own brass rubbings here from specially prepared
replicas of tombs.

WESTMINSTER ABBEY, *Broad Sanctuary, SW1 3BB (tel. 222
5752). Open daily 9–4; Sat. 9–2; closed to visitors during
services. The Pyx Chamber is open 10:30–4:30. Admission
free. Royal Chapels £1.60, children 40p (Royal Chapels free
Wed. 6–8 P.M.).* Tubes: St. James's Park, Westminster.
Westminster Abbey stands on the south side of Parliament
Square. Begun by Edward the Confessor in 1040, it is the
oldest and most important of London's great churches.
Most of England's kings and queens have been crowned
here, and many of them are buried here, too, along with
some of their more illustrious subjects.

Architecturally, the Abbey is a mixture. Edward the Confessor's original building was pulled down in the 12th century. The eastern part of today's church went up in the 13th century, while the nave was constructed in the 14th century. In the years 1503–09, Henry VII added his magnificent chapel to the east end. The last major building work—the erection of the two great west towers—was carried out in the mid-18th century.

Westminster Abbey ranks high among the most popular attractions of London, and it is rare to find it anything less than filled to the brim with visitors. The most meaningful way to experience the venerable building is to attend a service. But, failing this, try to visit as early in the day as you can, before the tourist buses start disgorging their daily freight.

Other than the mysterious gloom of the vast interior, the first thing to strike most people is the fantastic proliferation of monuments, statues, tombs, and commemorative tablets. In parts, the building seems more like a stonemason's yard than a place of worship. The **Tomb of the Unknown Warrior** and a **memorial to Sir Winston Churchill** are located immediately inside the main entrance. Churchill was not actually buried here; his resting place is his native village of Bladon, in Oxfordshire. The Tomb of the Unknown Warrior is one of the few floor-level tombs over which the countless thousands do not walk. A **Congressional Medal** is displayed on a pillar nearby, an echo of the Victoria Cross awarded by Britain to the Unknown Soldier in Washington. The most famous gathering of memorials is in **Poets' Corner,** in the south transept. Here, writers from Chaucer to the present day are commemorated: T.S. Eliot, Henry James, and Longfellow are remembered beside Shakespeare, Milton, and Tennyson.

Behind the magnificent choir stalls and the high altar lie two of the most imposing parts of the Abbey: the **chapel of Edward the Confessor** and of **Henry VII,** both crammed with sculptures of philosophers and saints, as well as monarchs and other lesser mortals. Though the rest of the Abbey is free, you must pay to see the Chapels (except on Wednesdays between 6 and 8 P.M.). Keep an eye open for St. Wilgefort, who was so concerned to protect her chastity that she prayed to God for help and woke up one morning with a full growth of beard. Here also are the tombs of Elizabeth I; Mary, Queen of Scots; and Henry II. Henry V is here, too. Originally his tomb had a solid silver head, but this was stolen during the Reformation. The head you see today is made of fiberglass. Queen Anne, who wore layer upon layer of leather petticoats at her coronation to keep out the Abbey's bitter damp, is also buried here, as are Richard II, who lies beside his wife, Queen Anne of Bohemia, and Edward III, his tumultuous life stilled to a figure of patriarchal peace. But the main feature of Edward the Confessor's Chapel is the **Coronation Chair.** This hastily made, uncomfortable chair was knocked together in about the year 1300, on the orders of Edward I. It encloses a lumpy-looking rock, the **Stone of Scone** (pronounced "Skoon"), or Stone of Destiny. It's long been a source of tension between the English and the Scots. It may not look like much, but the kings of Scotland were always crowned on it, including, in 1057, Macbeth's son, Malcolm III. The rampaging Edward I removed it from Scotland in 1296, with the inevitable result that the Stone became an even greater symbol of national pride to the Scots, then England's mortal enemies, and its removal a bitter blow. Centuries later, in 1950, a group of Scottish nationalists exacted revenge. They stole the Stone from the Abbey. But it didn't stay missing long. It was returned after only six months.

Henry VII's Chapel, built by the Tudor monarch between 1503 and 1519, is one of the architectural glories of Britain. The delicate fan vaulting, spreading out over the ceiling like a vast and intricate stone cobweb, is especially stunning, if sometimes hard to see; some of the finer details are lost in the darker corners of the building. Here, as so often when visiting old buildings, a pair of binoculars will come in very handy. Henry VII and his queen, Elizabeth of York, lie buried in the chapel. Their tomb was designed by an Italian sculptor, Torrigiano, otherwise best known for having broken Michelangelo's nose in a brawl in their native Florence.

To the south of the Abbey are the original monastic buildings, the most impressive of which are the **Chapter**

House and the **cloisters.** The Chapter House, originally the spot where the monks met to discuss the business of the Abbey, was also, from 1257, the meeting place of the King's Council and, later, Parliament. It is one of the great interiors of Europe, not least for its daring technical assurance, with a beautiful single column, like a frozen fountain, sustaining the roof. Off the cloisters are the Pyx Chamber—a new museum housing some of the Abbey's treasures—and the Undercroft Museum, with, among other items of historical interest, the effigies used in royal funeral processions.

WHITEHALL. *SW1. Tubes: Charing Cross, Westminster.* Whitehall is not a building, but a broad, slowly curving thoroughfare running from Trafalgar Square to Parliament Street. Walking up it, it's hard to realize that you are passing through the heart of Britain's bureaucracy. Practically every building here is a government office, as the faded and discreet brass plates by their doors indicate.

About one third of the way up Whitehall from Parliament Square is the **Cenotaph,** a simple white memorial to the dead of two world wars. It's the scene of a moving ceremony every year on Remembrance Day, November 11, when the Queen and other members of the Royal Family, along with the country's political leaders, lay wreaths on the memorial.

Just beyond the Cenotaph, as you head up Whitehall towards Trafalgar Square, there's a row of unassuming 18th-century town houses off to the left. This is **Downing Street.** Number 10 has been the official residence of the Prime Minister since 1732. The building was extended considerably some years ago, though there's still a sense of unreality that this modest dwelling should be the hub of government in Britain. Downing Street is unfortunately railed off these days. But you can often catch a glimpse of political comings and goings, as the official cars sweep backwards and forwards, and government ministers bustle past.

The next building of significance in Whitehall is the **Banqueting House,** built by Inigo Jones in 1625. *Open Tues. to Sat. 10–5, Sun. 2–5; closed Mon. Admission 70p.* It's on the opposite side of the street from Downing Street, and just a little farther up. It's all that remains of Whitehall Palace, an enormous and sprawling royal Tudor complex that covered the entire area between Whitehall and the Thames. It was the principal London residence of the monarch between the time of Henry VIII and the end of the 17th century, when the entire complex, other than the Banqueting House, was burned down. The fire was started by a Dutch washerwoman, who knocked a candle to the ground. A contemporary described the palace as "a glorious city of rose-tinted Tudor brick, green lawns, and shining marble statues."

The Banqueting House itself is a sturdy Renaissance building, much admired when it was built for its "pure and beautiful taste." The interior has magnificent, if overpowering, ceiling paintings by Rubens representing *The Apotheosis of James I* and *The Union of England and Scotland.* It was through this princely room in 1649 that Charles I, wearing two shirts to prevent him shivering from the cold of a dismal January morning, walked to the scaffold that had been put up outside one of the windows (nobody knows which) for his execution.

Almost opposite the Banqueting House is **Horse Guards,** a beautifully proportioned classical building with a handsome central arch surmounted by a clock tower. Here, the mounted Queen's Life Guards do sentry duty, resplendent in their glittering uniforms. There's a miniature version of the changing of the guards here every day at 11 (10 on Sundays).

Other Attractions

CABINET WAR ROOMS, *Clive Steps, King Charles St., SW1A 2AQ (tel. 930 6961/735 8922). Open daily 10–5:15. Admission £2.50. Tubes: Westminster, St. James's Park.* The Cabinet War Rooms are located at the eastern end of St. James's Park, just behind the bulk of the Foreign Office. They provide an enlightening—if distinctly overpriced—insight into the workings of Britain's government in World War II. It was from this maze of underground rooms, all now ingeniously restored, that Britain's wartime fortunes were directed. Among the most intriguing exhibits is the little room that housed the transatlantic telephone line to the White House. There's also a small suite of rooms prepared for Prime Minister Winston Churchill, complete with metal bed and government-issue furniture. The great man only slept here on a handful of occasions; he preferred the comfort of Downing Street, even at the height of the German blitz.

HORSE GUARDS PARADE, *SW1. Tube: Charing Cross.* Horse Guards Parade is a substantial open space, located just beyond the Cabinet War Rooms, facing St. James's Park. It's always had military overtones, having originally been the tiltyard of Whitehall Palace. Its name comes from the fact that there was a small guardhouse here. But today it's famous chiefly as the site of **Trooping the Color,** the great military parade that marks the Queen's official birthday in June (her real birthday is in April, but the monarch traditionally has a second, "official," birthday). It's the capital's most spectacular military occasion, with bands playing, flags fluttering, and massed ranks of soldiers, in scarlet coats and immense "busbies"—their curious, furry hats—marching up and down. It's practically impossible to get tickets for the parade, but it's always televised. You can watch it from the Mall, but you'll have to get there very early in the morning to get any kind of decent view.

QUEEN'S GALLERY, *adjoining Buckingham Palace, SW1A 1AA (tel. 930 4832). Open Tues. to Sat. 11–5; Sun. 2–5; closed Mon. Admission £1.10. Tubes: Green Park, Hyde Park Corner, Victoria.* This was formerly the chapel of the palace, bombed during World War II, and rebuilt in 1961. It now houses regular exhibitions of material selected from the riches of the royal collections, including such spectacular treasures as dozens of Leonardo drawings, or clutches of Fabergé eggs. To reach the gallery turn left past the front of the palace and follow the railings and wall.

ROYAL MEWS, *adjoining Buckingham Palace, SW1. Open Wed. and Thurs. 2–6; closed Ascot week (in June). Admission charge. Tubes: Green Park, Hyde Park Corner, Victoria.* These are the stables and coach houses of the palace, where the royal coaches are on view. Among them is the sumptuous State Coach, used at coronations. It's an elaborately carved and gilded affair, baroque in the extreme, that was built in 1761. Note that the Mews are open on only two afternoons a week.

ST. JOHN'S CONCERT HALL, *Smith Sq., SW1P 3HA (tel. 222 2168). Lunchtime concerts Mon. at 1, alternate Thurs. at 1:15, mid-Sept. to mid-July; closed rest of the year. Admission usually £2.50 Mon., £1.50 Thurs. Evening performances more expensive. Box office open Mon. to Fri. 10–5. Tube: Westminster.* St. John's, located a little south of the Houses of Parliament, was the grandest and most expensive of the 50 new London churches funded by an Act of Parliament in the early 18th century. It was bombed in the war, becoming a concert hall following its restoration. Its style is an exuberant, very un-English baroque, with four great towers. Dickens had rather a low opinion of the building, likening it to "some petrified monster, frightful and gigantic, on its back with its legs in the air." The lunchtime classical concerts are a not-to-be-missed bargain, and there's a very serviceable restaurant in the crypt.

VICTORIA TOWER GARDENS, *Millbank, SW1. Tube: Westminster.* These slightly gloomy public gardens beside the Houses of Parliament are an odd, almost forgotten spot, which make a very convenient place to escape from the crowds and noise of Westminster. They contain three monuments of interest: Rodin's *Burghers of Calais,* placed on a low plinth, as the sculptor wanted; a statue of Emmeline Pankhurst, a leader of the women's suffrage movement in England; and a lavishly ornate monument put up in 1865 to commemorate the ending of slavery in Britain's colonies in 1834.

WESTMINSTER CATHEDRAL, *Ashley Pl., SW1P 1QW (tel. 834 7452). Open daily, year round. Tower open Apr. through Sept. only, 10–5. Admission to tower 70p, senior citizens, students, and children 30p. Tube: Victoria.* Westminster Cathedral is the premier Roman Catholic church in Britain. It stands at the southern end of Victoria Street, a dreary, modern street leading from Westminster Abbey to Victoria Station. A few years ago, when Victoria Street was being rebuilt, the planners, with rare imagination, arranged for a small piazza to be left in front of the cathedral so that, for the first time ever, the facade could be seen from a distance.

The cathedral was erected between 1895 and 1903, yet the interior has never been finished, and, short of some unexpected and enormous windfall, is never likely to be. For all that, it's a striking and rather mysterious place, with golden mosaics gleaming in the darkness and smoke rising perpetually from the little pinpoints of light formed by the candles. The building is actually Byzantine in style, as foreign an architectural style as any in London. More than 100 different marbles were used to decorate it, including the facing for the dark green columns of the nave, which came from the same quarry that supplied the marble for the enormous cathedral of St. Sofia in Istanbul, built in the 6th century. The cathedral is lucky to have it at all; it was hijacked by the Turks when en route to London.

Lunch Spots

We have not graded our lunch spot suggestions; they all carry a range of dishes at various prices to suit your taste and pocket. The best-value budget bets are the pubs in the area; these often have the most atmosphere as well.

Carriages, 43 Buckingham Palace Rd., SW1W 0PP. Named with the Royal Mews, across the road, in mind, this attractive wine bar serves above-average French café food. There's classical music in the background. A separate restaurant has reasonable set meals.

Footstool Restaurant Gallery, St. John's Concert Hall, Smith Sq., SW1P 3HA. This bright and welcoming restaurant is in the beautiful crypt of St. John's church, behind Westminster Abbey. It serves fresh, crisp salads, game pie, quiches, and cheeses; there's the possibility of a concert, too.

Grandma Lee's, 2 Bridge St., SW1A 2JR. If hunger strikes while you're sightseeing around the Houses of Parliament, this offers a wide variety of sandwiches to take out. It can be frenzied at lunchtime, but you can quickly retire for a picnic in Victoria Tower Gardens, the Abbey Gardens, or St. James's Park.

Institute of Contemporary Arts, Carlton House Terr., SW1Y 5AF. The Institute itself will probably be on your itinerary anyway, but the wholesome Anglo-French food such as homemade soups, pâtés, quiches, salads, and outstanding puddings will tempt you in. It is self-service and you'll have to pay the 60p gallery entrance fee, but it faces right onto St. James's Park and is a much better bet than the park cafeteria.

Lyons Corner House, 450 The Strand, WC2R 0RG. This revived version of a very famous old London chain of eateries is sited immediately opposite Charing Cross station. Try upstairs for fast meals and snacks, downstairs for full lunches, teas, and dinners. It is excellently placed for sightseeing in the Trafalgar Square area.

Methuselah's, 29 Victoria St., SW1H 0EU. A very superior basement wine bar this, with exceptionally prepared food in a candlelit ambiance. Run by the same management as the perennial **Cork and Bottle** in Leicester Square, and always packed, it's highly recommended just the same. There's an impressive wine list, with plenty of selections by the glass.

National Gallery Restaurant, National Gallery, Trafalgar Sq., WC2N 5DN. If you need a break from touring the pictures, this is just the place for a quiet sit down and a snack. Cold meats, salads, quiches, and a choice of hot dishes are all on offer.

Tate Gallery Coffee Shop, Tate Gallery, Millbank, SW1P 4RG. The simple, basic snacks—ham rolls, quiches, omelets—available in the coffee shop are quite adequate for a short stop while visiting the gallery. The restaurant, famous for its wine list, British food, and murals, is expensive.

Wilkins Natural Foods, 61 Marsham St., SW1 4JZ. There are good-value lunchtime specials at this friendly vegetarian café, including pizzas, cracked-wheat casseroles, and a hot dish of the day. Interesting salads are available all day at budget prices.

GRACIOUS
LIVING THE
EASY WAY

◆

St. James's and Mayfair form the very core of London's West End, the city's smartest and most desirable central area—St. James's to the south of Piccadilly and north of the Mall, Mayfair to the north of Piccadilly and south of Oxford Street. Neither are any great shakes for regular sightseeing, though there is no shortage of history and fine architecture, but they *are* custom-built for window shopping and expansive strolling. Nor are they remotely budget areas. The shops, restaurants, hotels, homes, and offices crammed into this thriving, busy neighborhood are among the most expensive in London—which is saying something! Both St. James's and Mayfair epitomize so much of the flavor that is peculiarly London's, and that makes London special. The sense of being in a great, rich, (once) powerful city is almost palpable as you wander through the elegant streets and leafy squares.

St. James's is a rather masculine enclave, containing most of the capital's celebrated gentlemen's clubs (especially the classic Atheneum), long-established men's outfitters, and some interesting commercial art galleries and antique shops. In one corner is St. James's Palace, Tudor brick and marching sentries; in another is the Ritz hotel, refurbished to its original glittering dignity. The borders of St. James's are formed by two of London's great chain of parks, St. James's Park itself, with its lake floodlit at night, and its quiet air of a past age (for details see page 107); and Green Park, a verdant oasis, stretching away to Hyde Park Corner (see page 107).

Mayfair represents London's bid in the gracious living stakes, with an unmistakable air of wealth and leisure, even on busy days. It is easily located on the map, as it is bounded by four major thoroughfares—on the west by Park Lane, on the north by Oxford Street, on the east by Regent Street, and on the south by Piccadilly.

Major Attractions

BOND STREET, *W1. Tubes: Bond Street, Green Park.* Bond Street is probably the heart of modern Mayfair. So much of what makes Mayfair, Mayfair—fine buildings, a sense of history, plush and very expensive shops—is here. It runs north/south from Oxford Street to Piccadilly and is actually two streets, Old Bond Street and New Bond Street, the former at the southern end, the latter at the northern. There's no great difference between them, however, though a faint air of superiority still clings to the older partner (Old Bond Street was laid out 20 years before New Bond Street—in 1690, to be exact). Some of the most glamorous names in fashion are here, as well as a series of resolutely upmarket art galleries and jewelers: Gucci, Hermes, St. Laurent, Agnew's, Sotheby's, Cartier's. There's not the remotest chance of picking up a bargain, even during the sales. But it's hard to think of a better area for window shopping.

Toward the northern end of New Bond Street, Brook Street leads east to Hanover Square, site of the lovely 18th-century church of **St. George's,** still very much a top spot for society weddings. Farther down Bond Street, Clifford Street will lead you through to **Savile Row.** It's been the *only* place for the true English gent to have his suits made since at least as far back as the middle of the 19th century.

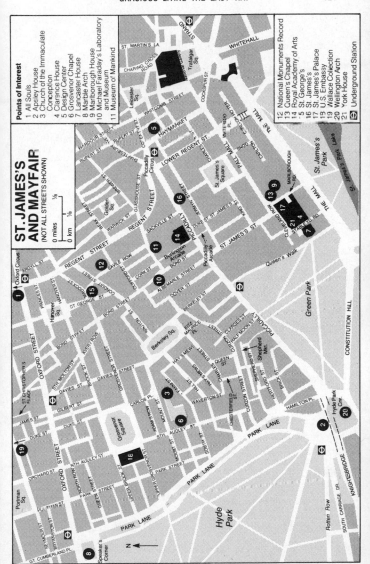

ST. JAMES'S AND MAYFAIR
(NOT ALL STREETS SHOWN)

0 miles   ⅛
0 km   ⅛

Points of Interest

1 All Souls
2 Apsley House
3 Church of the Immaculate Conception
4 Clarence House
5 Design Center
6 Grosvenor Chapel
7 Lancaster House
8 Marble Arch
9 Marlborough House
10 Michael Faraday's Laboratory and Museum
11 Museum of Mankind
12 National Monuments Record
13 Queen's Chapel
14 Royal Academy of Arts
15 St. George's
16 St. James's
17 St. James's Palace
18 U.S. Embassy
19 Wallace Collection
20 Wellington Arch
21 York House
Ⓤ Underground Station

OXFORD STREET, *W1. Tubes: Spaced out along the length of the street, west to east—Marble Arch, Bond Street, Oxford Circus, Tottenham Court Road.* Oxford Street is the northern boundary of Mayfair, but the sophistication and chic of Mayfair stops abruptly here. Yet Oxford Street can still fairly claim to be London's premier shopping street, an assertion more than borne out by the enormous numbers of shoppers who throng its length. Whether it's Christmas, the height of the tourist season, or the seasonal sales, you can guarantee that Oxford Street will be packed to bursting point and beyond. In truth, Oxford Street mostly offers cheap fashions at less than cheap prices, but there are one or two very reliable shops here nonetheless. Foremost among them are Selfridges, a giant department store at the west end of Oxford Street; two branches of Marks & Spencer, still Britain's most popular high street store; and John Lewis, whose quality and value-for money are unbeaten, especially where fabrics are concerned.

PALL MALL, *W1. Tube: Charing Cross.* Pall Mall's curious name derives from the "gentleman-like" ball game, similar to croquet, called "pell-mell," which used to be played here in the 17th century. As a sporting venue, Pall Mall was rendered less than ideal by the carriages that thundered past on their way to and from St. James's Palace just at the west end of the street, throwing up dust and interrupting play. So the pell-mell players sensibly took themselves off round the corner to where The Mall is now, and laid out a new course there. Then, in 1661, a new street—the present Pall Mall—was laid out.

Writers and artists flocked to Pall Mall in the 18th century: Swift, Sterne, Gainsborough, and Gibbon all lived here. It was figures like these who were partly responsible for the number of coffeehouses that were established in St. James's in the 18th century. These became a focal point for serious discussion (and idle gossip) in the capital, whether political, literary, or artistic. By the 19th century, the coffee-houses had become gentlemen's clubs, and a fair number are still going today, though their heyday is long since past. You can't actually go into any of them (unless you're a member, of course), but their stately, heavy facades add greatly to the rather dignified, time-honored atmosphere of Pall Mall and other parts of St. James's.

The exclusive **Reform Club** at 104 Pall Mall is still a favorite with writers and politicians. This was where Jules Verne's Phineas Fogg wagered he could travel round the world in 80 days. At the corner with Waterloo Place is the even more prestigious **Atheneum Club,** a handsome, cream colored neo-Classical building, with a frieze, copied from the Parthenon in Athens, running round the exterior (it's in better condition than the carpets inside).

Waterloo Place itself, at the eastern end of Pall Mall, contains more statues to the square yard than any other place in London. Among the frozen worthies here are: Florence Nightingale, the Lady with the Lamp and heroine of the Crimea; two luckless explorers, Sir John Franklin, who led an expedition to find the Northwest Passage in 1845 that ended with the death of every man under his command, and Captain Scott, who presided over another British polar fiasco, this one in the Antarctic in 1911–12; three monarchs, Victoria, Edward VII, and George VI; Sir John Burgoyne, son of the General Burgoyne who surrendered at Saratoga; Sir Colin Campbell, who led the relief of Lucknow in the terrible Indian Mutiny of 1851; and Lord Curzon, "the very superior person" who lived around the corner at 1 Carlton House Terrace.

PARK LANE, *W1. Tubes: Marble Arch, Hyde Park Corner.* Park Lane's evocative name can still summon up images of ladies twirling parasols, and strolling with gallant, bewhiskered gentlemen past gracious town houses with handsome rooms filled with flowers and the sounds of tinkling pianos. But times have changed for Park Lane. It's still an immensely wealthy street, but its fine Regency and Victorian houses have now mostly gone, to be replaced by hotels and offices, and other anonymous modern buildings. And, despite the name, it's hard to imagine any street less like a lane. There's a six-lane freeway here now, up and down which the traffic thunders permanently.

Park Lane forms the western edge of Mayfair and the eastern boundary of Hyde Park, hence the name. Its not a rewarding street to walk up and down, and it's impossible to cross (except by the underpasses at either end). But it is a convenient north/south route for anyone reluctant to take on the maze that makes up most of Mayfair. At its northern end is **Marble Arch,** a triumphal arch designed by John Nash for the forecourt of Buckingham Palace. It was never actually finished (which accounts for its forlorn aspect), and was moved here in 1851 when the east facade of Buckingham Palace was built. At the southern end of Park Lane is **Hyde Park Corner,** a veritable maelstrom of traffic at the junction of several major roads. There's a fine collection of statues here, but the centerpiece is the **Wellington Arch,** another triumphal arch, this one intended as a sort of monumental back gate to Buckingham Palace. It used to have a large statue of Wellington on it, a companion piece for Nelson on his column in Trafalgar Square. This is very much Wellington Country, for facing the arch is **Apsley House,** Wellington's London home (see *Other Attractions* for details).

Park Lane also makes a convenient place from which to find **Grosvenor Square,** site of the **US Embassy.** Take either Upper Grosvenor Street or Upper Brook Street—they both run east off Park Lane as you head toward Marble Arch. Grosvenor Square is large and elegant, surrounded by discreet and expensive apartment blocks. There's a garden in the center, with a statue of Franklin D. Roosevelt in the middle, put up in 1948. The embassy takes up the whole of the west side of the square. When the building first went up in the late '50s there were many wry comments about the huge gold eagle poised over the center of the facade, as if waiting to pounce on the London pigeons. John Adams, first U.S. ambassador to Britain and second president of the United States, had a house at the corner of Brook Street and Duke Street.

Another, rather more characterful, part of Mayfair is also easily reached from Park Lane (along Curzon Street). This is **Shepherd Market,** a network of narrow streets and alleys, which lies behind the Hilton. Its pubs and wine bars have long made it popular with visitors and Londoners alike. It's also a notorious, if reasonably discreet, red-light district. In fact even as far back as 1686, when the first May Fair was held here—an event that eventually gave its name to the whole district—the area had a dubious reputation.

The fair was regularly censured for "riotous and disorderly behavior."

PICCADILLY, *W1. Tubes: Piccadilly Circus, Green Park, Hyde Park Corner.* Piccadilly is not an area, but a street, the final section of the major route from the West Country to London. It extends from Hyde Park Corner to Piccadilly Circus, a busy, bustling thoroughfare, with traffic rumbling along and its sidewalks crowded with people. There are a number of fashionable shops here, as well as airline offices, learned societies, and several large and expensive hotels—the Ritz and the Piccadilly Meridien foremost among them. Again, this is an area to browse in and to stroll along rather than to sightsee in. There's also little here for anyone specifically watching their pennies, but the atmosphere makes it somewhere not to miss.

Heading down Piccadilly from Piccadilly Circus (see below), the first building to note is on the left, set back a little from the road. This is Wren's church of **St. James.** Built between 1676 and 1684, it reveals the architect's hand in every elegant line. It was damaged in the Blitz and subsequently much restored. The spire was replaced only in 1968, and is built of less than authentic fiberglass. There's a wealth of beautiful craftsmanship inside, including a reredos—an altar screen—carved by the Dutch master carver Grinling Gibbons. He was responsible for the intricate organ case and the font, too. There's a commemorative courtyard outside the church, ideal for a pause. A coffeehouse has been thoughtfully provided. A crafts market is held here several times a week.

Continuing west along Piccadilly you'll pass some famous shops, including Hatchards's, one of the best bookstores in London, and Fortnum and Mason, the Queen's grocer. Fortnum's, as it is commonly known, has three tea shops of varying degrees of elegance and price for mid-sightseeing snacks. But it's worth going in anyway just to catch a glimpse of the "beadles," the senior staff at Fortnum's, in their colorful liveries, or maybe to pick up a pot of "Gentleman's Relish," a curious English preserve made from anchovies—you'll find it an acquired taste—for the folks back home.

PICCADILLY CIRCUS, *W1. Tube: Piccadilly Circus.* Once the hub of the West End and a proud symbol of London worldwide, Piccadilly Circus—"circus" meaning circular intersection—had grown distinctly tacky recently. But there are, at long last, signs of rejuvenation, all the more welcome after some 40 years of abortive planning. The famous statue of **Eros** (not, in fact, Eros at all, but an allegory of Christian Charity), was brought back to Piccadilly Circus in 1986, clean and bright after much restoration. Tourists now sit on the relocated steps of the monument where, until World War II, "flower girls" (elderly Cockney women) sold their wares, and where, in the '60s and '70s, junkies sold theirs.

Among the versions of how Piccadilly got its name, the most likely one seems to be the tale of an upwardly mobile tailor called Robert Baker, who built a house in 1612 close to where the Circus is now. His snooty neighbors called the place "Pickadilly Hall," pickadills being a kind of collar that was then fashionable. It was not until the 19th century that the Circus was laid out in approximately its present form, and most of the surrounding buildings are Edwardian, dating from the turn of the century.

Whatever can be said against it—and there's a great deal—Piccadilly still pulls in the crowds, and not only of tourists. The new Trocadero entertainment complex, home of the Guinness World of Records, located just to the east of Eros, is popular with Londoners, while the Criterion Brasserie on the south side, with its original turn-of-the-century decor—admire the gold mosaic ceiling—is always bursting at the seams with "bright young things" in the evenings. It's surprisingly good value, too. Just across the Circus you can buy records, tapes, CDs, and videos at Tower Records until midnight, while national and international newspapers are sold from the newsstand at the Shaftesbury Avenue exit of the tube station long after other news vendors have packed up and gone home.

REGENT STREET, *W1. Tubes: Oxford Circus, Piccadilly Circus.* Regent Street connects Piccadilly Circus and Oxford Circus in one long sweeping curve. The street was originally conceived by architect John Nash in the 1810s as the central section of a triumphal way which would connect his patron's, the Prince Regent's, home, Carlton

House, with Regent's Park. The original grandiose plan was never more than half realized, and then only at vast expense and amid bitter public criticism. Very little of the original buildings survive, most of Nash's elegant houses having been swept away at the beginning of this century to be replaced by slablike and dreary blocks.

Regent Street is traditionally most famous for its festive Christmas lights. But it is also the locale of those airline offices not located on Piccadilly, and a series of good shops, of which the best are Hamley's toy shop, Dickins & Jones department store, Waterstone's bookstore, and Liberty, which sells fine silks and specially designed fabrics. Liberty's Regent Street frontage has an immense carved frieze depicting trade with the Orient. The spacious interior of the shop is strikingly furnished in dark wood, some of it taken from the gnarled timbers of old fighting ships. Liberty is by no means a place for the bargain hunter, but its appealingly chic atmosphere makes it a frontrunner among London's department stores. It's a great place for a splurge.

THE ROYAL ACADEMY OF ARTS, *Burlington House, Piccadilly, W1V 0DS (tel. 734–9052). Open daily (including Sun.) 10–6. Admission charge varies with the exhibition. Tubes: Green Park, Piccadilly.* Burlington House was long at the forefront of artistic life in London. It belonged originally to Lord Burlington, the champion in England in the early 18th century of Palladian architecture, a style that had an immense influence on the many stately homes of England. The Royal Academy itself was founded in 1768, with George III as its patron and Sir Joshua Reynolds as its first president. It was an immediate success, and all artists of stature in 18th- and 19th-century Britain belonged to it. The Academy moved into Burlington House in 1868, sharing the premises, as it still does, with the Geological Society, the Chemistry Society, the Linnean Society, the Society of Antiquaries, and the Royal Astronomical Society. The original buildings of Burlington House had by then been enlarged and partly rebuilt, though the centerpiece of Lord Burlington's house was left intact.

The Royal Academy of Arts—or RA as it is more commonly known—still actively carries on its teaching role, though it's doubtful whether it's been in the forefront of British artistic development for many a long year now. Its abiding appeal remains the series of exhibits that are held here, all of them also providing the opportunity to see the handsome, classical interiors of the main galleries. The most famous exhibit is the annual Summer Exhibition, a show of mixed amateur and professional work open to all comers. Opinions on the quality of the works shown have long been divided, but the exhibition has nonetheless successfully held onto its place in the affections of the English, and remains a highlight of the social calendar. There's less controversy about the RA's other exhibits, most of them of the highest quality. There'll nearly always be something unique here, so make a point of checking it out. The RA is also home to one of the great art treasures in London, Michelangelo's *Madonna Taddei,* a circular relief sculpture.

ST. JAMES'S PALACE. *SW1. Tubes: Charing Cross, Green Park.* St. James's Palace stands at the west end of Pall Mall. It's still a royal palace, but for 150 years or more it's taken a back seat in the affairs of the nation. Various court officials work here, and all foreign ambassadors to Britain are still officially accredited "to the Court of St. James's"; however, when they are received by the Queen, it is Buckingham Palace they visit.

The palace took its name from a leper hospital that stood here, built in the 11th century. In the 1530s, Henry VIII bought the hospital, and tore it down to build the palace. Even then, its role was largely secondary, the sprawling colossus of Whitehall Palace remaining the focus of the court. St. James's Palace regained a degree of royal favor after Whitehall Palace burned down in 1698, though by then it had also to compete with Kensington Palace and Hampton Court, both generally more popular with Britain's kings and queens in the 18th century. In 1837 Victoria finally put paid to St. James's when she moved into Buckingham Palace.

St. James's Palace is, for all that, still one of the most popular buildings in London among tourists, largely because of its Tudor gateway facing St. James's Street, with scarlet-coated guardsmen standing sentinel outside. Unfortunately, you can't visit the interior, but there are a series of picturesque courtyards and outbuildings that suggest something of the atmosphere that must have been here when St. James's was still the home of royalty. Walk around to the side of the building facing The Mall to admire Wren's 17th-century additions. They contrast well with the Tudor frontage on Pall Mall.

There are a series of other buildings and homes around St. James's Palace, all of them linked in one way or another with the Royal Family. Just to the east, on the other side of Marlborough Road, is the Queen's Chapel—open occasionally to the public for services (usually in early summer)—designed by the great Jacobean architect, Inigo Jones, in the 1620s. Behind the chapel is **Marlborough House,** built in 1709 for the Duke of Marlborough by Christopher Wren. Edward VII lived here for many years when he was Prince of Wales, turning the place into a byword for fast talk and high society. His widow, Queen Alexandra, beautiful, long-suffering, and virtually deaf, lived here for a further 15 lonely years after Edward's death in 1910. Her pets, including Benny the Bunny, are buried in the garden. Marlborough House is now the Commonwealth Center, and tours are possible when conferences are not in session.

On the opposite, west side of St. James's Palace, are **Clarence House,** London home of the Queen Mother, and **Lancaster House,** once the home of the Duke of York, second son of George III, and now used for government conferences.

WALLACE COLLECTION, *Hertford House, Manchester Sq., W1M 6BN (tel. 935 0687). Open Mon. to Sat. 10–5, Sun. 2–5. Admission free. Tubes: Bond Street, Marble Arch.* This is one of the best value museums in London. It isn't just because the place is free, and it isn't just because it's almost always deserted, too. It isn't even just because of the richness and diversity of the collections. Rather, it's a combination of all these factors; the works of art are housed in what, to all intents and purposes, is still a private house (and a pretty sumptuous one at that). They are displayed much as they were when the place still *was* a private house, which also makes this museum quite unlike any other in London. There's none of the intimidating formality of other great museums, there are no crowds jostling to see the pictures, and no hubbub from a busy shop selling postcards, posters, and reproductions. The atmosphere here is ideal for looking at pictures contemplatively and seriously, more as though one were a guest of the owner than just another tourist.

The collection was formed by the second, third, and fourth marquesses of Hertford, whose London home this was. Each was a born collector, with a shrewd eye for a bargain and a keen nose for quality. Many of the 18th-century French pictures in the collection, for example, were snapped up in Paris at the time of the French Revolution, when a suddenly impoverished—and endangered—aristocracy was desperate to raise cash. These in fact form the heart of the collection, but there are many other fine works, too. Rubens, Rembrandt, Poussin, Van Dyck, Frans Hals, and Canaletto are all well represented, while there are also many other excellent Dutch 17th- and 18th-century works. There is room upon room of magnificent furniture, porcelain, clocks, miniatures, arms and armor, and silver.

Other Attractions

APSLEY HOUSE, *Hyde Park Corner, W1V 9PA (tel. 499 5676). Open Tues. to Thurs. and Sat. 10–6, Mon. 2:30–6; closed Mon. and Fri. Admission 60p, children 30p. Tube: Hyde Park Corner.* Apsley House, today also known as the **Wellington Museum,** used to have the best address in London. It was, quite simply, Number 1, London. It may no longer enjoy this distinction, but it remains a stately and impressive building, a fact helped in no small measure by its prime location at the southern end of Park Lane, overlooking Hyde Park Corner.

The house was built in the 1770s by Robert Adam. In 1817 it was bought by the Duke of Wellington, the "Iron Duke," victor in 1815 of the battle of Waterloo. His heir, the seventh duke, presented it to the nation in 1947 (though sensibly retained the top floor for his own use). Then, in 1952 it officially became the Wellington Museum. The interior is still much as it was in the Iron Duke's day, full of heavy ornate pieces of furniture and decoration, much of it perhaps more impressive than beautiful. But there is a fine portrait of the Duke by Goya, painted during the Peninsular Campaign, and, in the hallway, a huge statue of "Boney," the Duke's mortal foe, Napoleon Bonaparte, by Italian sculptor Canova.

GUINNESS WORLD OF RECORDS, *Trocadero, Piccadilly Circus, W1V 7FD (tel. 439–7331). Open daily 10–10. Admission £2.80, children £1.80, senior citizens £2, group rates for parties of 10 or more. Tube; Piccadilly Circus.* Consistently popular despite the high admission prices, the Guinness World of Records is a diverting and slickly run exhibit housed in the purpose-built Trocadero leisure complex. It's located just to the east of Piccadilly Circus. You won't find much in the way of old London here, but anyone with a taste for giants and dwarfs, bearded ladies, and 700-pound men will enjoy it.

JERMYN STREET, *SW1. Tubes: Piccadilly Circus, Green Park.* Jermyn Street is to St. James's what Savile Row is to Mayfair. Having ordered his suit from Savile Row, your English gent will then make for Jermyn Street to buy his shirts (handmade, naturally), ties (silk, of course), and shoes (also handmade). Jermyn Street, which runs east/west from the Haymarket to St. James's Street, has a distinctly masculine flavor. Anyone who has lately come into a legacy and feels the need for the whole range of essential gentlemen's accessories—from ivory-backed hairbrushes to original Edwardian aftershaves—need look no farther.

But, in the middle of what will inevitably be a window-shopping street for the budget visitor, there are still some classic shops that could provide thoroughly affordable items. Chief among them is Floris (#88–89), a very old-established perfumier, with a big range of unique products, and Paxton and Whitfield (#93), one of London's leading cheese shops, with cheeses from all over England, indeed all over Europe—not, perhaps the sweetest smelling remembrance of Britain to carry home, but definitely a practical reminder of your trip.

ST. JAMES'S STREET, *SW1.* St. James's Street runs northwards from St. James's Palace uphill to Piccadilly. It's long been famous for its coffee shops, clubs, and exclusive stores. A good many famous figures lived here over the years, too, including Christopher Wren, Alexander Pope, Edward Gibbon, Charles James Fox, and Lord Byron. There are no coffeehouses left now, and only a few of the great clubs, but those that remain are among the oldest and most celebrated in London. There's something about their names that suggests the combination of grandeur and eccentricity that so distinguished the London clubs in their days of glory: White's, the oldest surviving club in London (founded in 1736), Boodle's, Brook's, Arthur's, the Constitutional, the Carlton, and last, but by no means least, the Savage. A similar air of dusty, time-honored charm is found in Lobb's, which has been making shoes at 9 St. James's Street since 1850, and Lock's, which has been making hats at #6 for even longer, since 1765 in fact. You won't pick up any bargains here, but there are few places in London where the sense of time standing still is more obvious or appealing.

Halfway up St. James's Street, King Street will take you into **St. James's Square,** with the imperious bulk of Christie's auction house on your left. St. James's Square was probably just about the most fashionable address in London when it was first laid out in 1670. By 1720 no less than seven dukes and seven earls had homes here. Bomb damage in the war put paid to a number of the original gracious houses, but enough remain to give a taste of the onetime plush and swank of this lovely locale. The rather cramped-looking building in the northwest corner of the square is the London Library, the most exclusive and probably the best lending library in London, more than a million volumes lining its creaking shelves.

MICHAEL FARADAY'S LABORATORY AND MUSEUM, *The Royal Institution of Great Britain, 21 Albemarle St., W1X 4BS (tel. 409 2992). Open Tues. and Thurs. 1–4; parties at other times by arrangement. Admission 40p, children 20p. Tubes: Green Park, Piccadilly.* Lurking in the heart of Mayfair in the basement of this weighty building, whose facade is almost hidden by a screen of giant columns, is a little museum devoted to the work of Michael Faraday. He was a self-taught chemist, who rose to be Fullerian Professor of Chemistry, and was a prodigious discoverer and inventor. His work in chemistry—he discovered benzene, invented several kinds of optical glass, liquefied gases, and worked on alloys of steel—was overshadowed by his work with electricity. His chief discovery was the induction of electrical currents. His was one of the fertile talents that most influenced the Industrial Revolution, and completely changed the face of England in the first half of the 19th century.

MUSEUM OF MANKIND, *6 Burlington Gdns., W1X 2EX (tel. 437 2224). Mon. to Fri. 10–5; Sun. 2:30–6. Admission free. Tube: Piccadilly Circus.* This is the British Museum's department of ethnography. The bottom end of Savile Row may seem an odd place to find so serious-minded a museum, but the collections here—on Aztec, Mayan, West African, Pacific Island, and North American peoples—are both imaginatively displayed and stimulating. The free admission is a bonus.

Lunch Spots

We have not graded our lunch spot suggestions; they all carry a range of dishes at various prices to suit your taste and pocket. The best-value budget bets are the pubs in the area; these often have the most atmosphere as well.

L'Artiste Musclé, 1 Shepherd Market, W1Y 7HS. Reasonably priced, one-dish French food is on offer in this popular wine bar/restaurant just off Piccadilly, but it can get very cramped.

Audley, 41 Mount St., W1Y 5RB. The chef presides over the long counter offering exceptional bar food in this Victorian pub. Avoid the restaurant upstairs if you're budget conscious.

Bubbles Wine Bar, 41 N. Audley St., W1Y 1WG. This pleasant bistro/wine bar serves interesting seafood salads, charcoal-grilled steaks, and an excellent choice of English and Continental cheeses. It's not far from Marble Arch.

Design Center Coffee Shop, 28 Haymarket, SW1Y 4SU. Open from breakfast time through to afternoon tea, this self-service restaurant serves good wholesome food and vegetarian dishes. It's above the Design Center, just down from Piccadilly Circus.

Downs Wine Bar, 5 Down St., W1Y 7DR. There is an outstanding wine list with over 80 varieties to choose from in this cosy wine bar—the food is good, too. Down Street is across Piccadilly from Green Park, near Hyde Park Corner.

Fino's Wine Cellar, 37 Duke St., W1M 5DF. Hot and cold dishes are served in this basement wine bar, but for a truly bargain lunch choose one of their filling sandwiches of hot salt beef or crab. There's also a **Fino's Wine Cellar** at 123 Mount St., W1Y 5HB. It's always crowded, so go early.

Granary, 38 Albemarle St., W1X 3FB. If you feel like a picnic in nearby Green Park you can buy take-away dishes from this busy self-service restaurant. The hot dishes and salads are delicious.

Green's Champagne Bar, 36 Duke St., SW1Y 6DF. This is a champagne and oyster bar, but the adjoining restaurant serves superior versions of traditional British favorites like bangers (sausages) and mash (potatoes), grills, and fish.

Justin de Blank, 54 Duke St., W1M 7QW. You'll find excellent freshly prepared Anglo-French food here: unusual salads, homemade bread, marvelous casseroles, and mouth-watering desserts. There is also a take-out service. It's between Grosvenor Square and Oxford Street.

Red Lion, 1 Waverton St., W1X 7FJ. Tucked away behind the Hilton in a tiny Mayfair street, the Red Lion almost has the atmosphere of a country pub. It serves real ale, and although the superior pub food is priced at about the going rate, the restaurant is very expensive.

The Wren at St. James's, 197 Piccadilly, W1V 9LF. Beside St. James's church and handy for Piccadilly shopping, this self-service coffee shop has a hot (vegetarian) dish of the day every lunchtime.

AT HOME ON THE SLOANE RANGE

◆

Even in these supposedly democratic days, you still sometimes hear people say that the *only* place to live in London is in the grand residential area of the Royal Borough of Kensington and Chelsea. Apart from the district's endless cavalcade of streets lined with splendid houses—many of which sport the consular flags or shields of nations represented in Britain's capital—there are hidden corners, too. It's full of small squares that seem to belong in a dozy cathedral city; delightful pubs tucked away in back lanes; and antique shops, their windows aglow with ancient, polished wood, and the rich colors of oil paintings. There are also several concentrations of top-level sightseeing interest, foremost among which is the South Kensington complex of museums, and the Albert Hall.

This is the territory of the Sloane Rangers, who take their name from Sloane Square and Sloane Street, the core of Chelsea—a quintessentially London type of gilded youth, a combination of yuppie, preppie, and social snob, who have upper-class accents that make English sound like a foreign language. The most common example is "yah" said with a drawl, and meaning "yes."

For the socially curious, the long, long shopping stretch of the King's Road will provide plenty of research opportunities, especially at weekends when it is the parade ground for the most outrageous purple-and-green punk hairdos. For those who prefer the peaceful seclusion of the past, a visit to Charles II's Royal Hospital is a must—though it becomes an unbelievably crowded spot when the Chelsea Flower Show is mounted there in May. Harrods, surrounded by streets of pricey shops all aiming at the same upmarket clientele, is hardly the place to find bargains, except in the hugely popular twice-yearly sales, but it is an excellent spot for a sightseeing wander and a cup of coffee or a snack in the middle of a crowded day.

The southern side of this varied area is bounded by the river Thames: A stroll along here (despite the sometimes heavy traffic) makes a relaxing counterbalance to the hectic bustle of the King's Road only a few blocks away. There are pretty bridges (at least one of them illuminated at night like a fairy-tale arch), and houseboats are moored along the western section. You will be especially lucky if you catch this reach of the Thames on a day when the light has that pearly quality that Turner and Whistler loved to paint, rare now that the London fogs are a thing of the past.

Major Attractions

HYDE PARK AND KENSINGTON GARDENS, *W2. Tubes: Spaced around the park's periphery, starting from Hyde Park Corner and working clockwise: Hyde Park Corner, Knightsbridge, High Street Kensington, Notting Hill Gate, Queensway, Bayswater, Lancaster Gate, Marble Arch.* The largest in the chain of royal parks, Hyde Park's 340 acres stretch from Park Lane in the east to Alexandra Gate in the west, and from the Bayswater Road in the north to Knightsbridge in the south. There are entrance gates all round the park, but the main, and most attractive one, is beside Apsley House (see above), where Park Lane joins Piccadilly. Just behind Apsley House is one of the park's finest statues, the 20-foot Achilles, a tribute to Wellington, subscribed for by the women of England. At the northeast

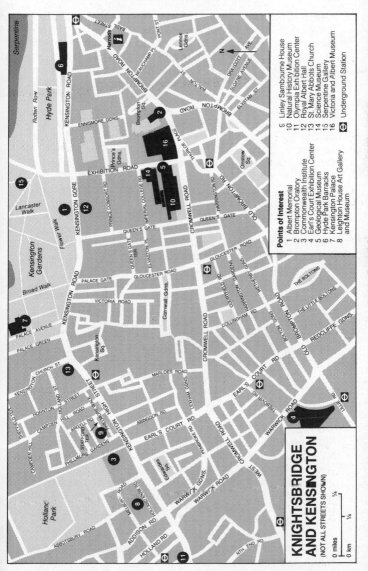

KNIGHTSBRIDGE AND KENSINGTON

(NOT ALL STREETS SHOWN)

0 miles   ¼

0 km   ¼

Points of Interest

1 Albert Memorial
2 Brompton Oratory
3 Commonwealth Institute
4 Earl's Court Exhibition Center
5 Geological Museum
6 Hyde Park Barracks
7 Kensington Palace
8 Leighton House Art Gallery and Museum
9 Linley Sambourne House
10 Natural History Museum
11 Olympia Exhibition Center
12 Royal Albert Hall
13 St. Mary Abbots Church
14 Science Museum
15 Serpentine Gallery
16 Victoria and Albert Museum

Ⓔ Underground Station

corner of the park, close to Marble Arch, is the area called
Speakers' Corner, where anyone with a compulsion to air
their views, however batty, can do so on a Sunday afternoon. This is one of the strangest free shows in town.

Along the south side of the park runs a long avenue,
Rotten Row, its sandy track now used for horse riding. The
odd name derives from the time when King George II lived
in Kensington Palace and took this route to and from
Whitehall—the *route du roi*. The long, crescent-shaped lake
that flows through the center of Hyde Park is called the
Serpentine until it reaches Kensington Gardens, when it
changes its name to the Long Water. Strolling along the
lakeside is one of the few rural pleasures that Central
London can still afford. At any season the lake has its own
special atmosphere, busy and crowded in summer, with an
air of gentle melancholy in fall and winter. There is a
bathing area, boats to be rented, and two cafés, the main
one beside the elegant bridge that divides the Serpentine
from the Long Water. Although it is perfectly safe in the
daytime, Hyde Park can be dangerous after dark.

Kensington Gardens—another 273 acres—have a different atmosphere from Hyde Park. They were once the
private grounds of Kensington Palace, and still keep the air
of a privileged park, with more trees to vary the wide
stretches of grassland. Beside the Long Water you'll find
Peter Pan's statue (he was supposed to live on an island
here, and his creator, J.M. Barrie, did live on the Bayswater
Road, just to the north of the park). The lake ends
romantically in a slightly decayed, Italianate paved garden
called the Fountains. Near the bridge is the Serpentine
Gallery, which houses temporary exhibitions of modern
art, while close by is the elaborate memorial to Victoria's
husband, Prince Albert. The long Flower Walk, bordered
by seasonally changed flowerbeds, runs from here towards
Kensington Palace, a lovely setting for a quiet stroll.

The hurricane in October 1987 did terrible damage to
the ancient trees all over the southeast of England. In
London, the damage is most obvious in the parks, where
many sections are devastated, and many of the trees left
standing have lost their tops. It will be decades before the
wooded areas of this part of Britain regain their former
status.

KENSINGTON GARDENS, see Hyde Park, above.

KENSINGTON PALACE, *W8 4PY (tel. 937 9561). Open Mon. to Sat. 9–5, Sun. 1–5 (last admission 4:15). Admission £2.20, children £1, covers both State apartments and Court Dress Collection. Tubes: Kensington High Street, Notting Hill Gate, Queensway (but all three involve a walk).* William III suffered from asthma and found the Thames mists in Whitehall trying, so in 1689 he bought a country manor, Nottingham House, as a rural retreat. Since it was now a royal residence and the village it stood in was called Kensington, naturally the place was renamed Kensington Palace. Over the centuries many famous architects had a hand in enlarging it—Wren, Hawksmoor, Vanbrugh, and William Kent, but the sprawling building remained comparatively modest, an attractive, comfortable, *big,* country house. It is remarkable in that it lies at one side of the public Kensington Gardens, with throngs of people, Londoners and visitors alike, close to its walls. It is still home to 14 members of the royal family, including the Prince and Princess of Wales, and Princess Margaret.

A visit to the palace falls into two parts: the State apartments, with memories of many generations of royalty, especially of Queen Victoria and Queen Mary (the present Queen's grandmother), both of whom were born here; and the Court Dress Collection of gowns and uniforms worn at court.

NATURAL HISTORY MUSEUM, *Cromwell Rd., SW7 5BD (tel. 589 6323). Open Mon. to Sat. 10–6, Sun. 2:30–6. Admission fee £2 adults, £1 children. Tube: South Kensington.* Although it doesn't have quite the space-age draw of the Science Museum, the Natural History Museum still has a great deal going for it in the way of fascination for kids of every age: vast prehistoric skeletons, a massive full-size model of a whale, and eight exciting exhibitions which together form a lively new way of looking at the whole story of natural history. This is another branch of the British Museum.

SCIENCE MUSEUM, *Exhibition Rd., SW7 2DD (tel. 589 3456). Open Mon. to Sat. 10–6, Sun. 2:30–6. Admission free. Tube: South Kensington.* The Science Museum has consistently proved itself one of London's most successful—especially with children. It is full of working models, imaginative displays, historical collections with items ranging from the almost microscopic to the huge, all coming right up to date with the latest developments in science, space research, and medicine—in fact, two whole floors are devoted to the Wellcome Museum of the History of Medicine. This is the ideal place to take youngsters, with plenty to see and do, and more than enough to keep their parents interested at the same time.

VICTORIA AND ALBERT MUSEUM, *Cromwell Rd., South Kensington, SW7 2RL (tel. 589 6371; recorded information 581 4894). Mon. to Sat. 10–5:50, Sun. 2:30–5:50. There is a "voluntary" charge for entry—about £2 seems to be what's expected. Tube: South Kensington.* Having two museums such as the British Museum and the V&A—as it's generally known—in the same city must appear rather odd, but they do serve different ends. The V&A was originally designed in the 1850s as a teaching museum of ornamental art, a very wide brief that really means that it is dedicated to the art of design from every age and from most of the world. It actually calls itself "The National Museum of Art and Design."

It's wise to arm yourself with a free floor plan when you go in, as the place is a bewildering maze. The collection is so rich and vast that it is difficult to pick out briefly the most exciting elements. The paintings of Constable would rank high on anyone's list; the jewel rooms, especially the cases containing the baroque gems, are always a draw; the delicate portrait miniatures, some of the best dating from the reign of Elizabeth I, towards the end of the 16th century, will give any visitor a series of intimate glimpses of the faces of those who formed British history. The medieval church art—carving, metalwork, painting, and embroidery—from all over Europe, leaves an indelible impression of the time when man devoted all his considerable talents to the service of God and was terrified by the fear of death. The Costume Hall displays clothes from many centuries, while the V&A's collection of musical instruments, finely crafted and of complex design, are frequently played in recitals that bring them back to life.

There are two great halls of plaster casts of architecture and sculpture, and this is where the teaching aspect of the museum asserts itself most. Japanese art is now housed in recently renovated rooms, which create exactly the right ambience for these fragile masterpieces. The list is endless.

There are always restoration works in progress, so one or two galleries will certainly be closed when you visit. The building as a whole is fairly decrepit, but the recent policy has been to upgrade as many rooms each year as possible, using the latest display techniques, with the result that a wander round the maze of corridors, stairs, and galleries will often bring a strikingly lit and decorated room into view, full of new treasures.

Regular exhibitions, major and minor, back up the permanent collections, and there is a daily round of lectures and guided tours that can help you understand some of the subject areas of the museum in greater depth. You can buy unusual presents in the crafts shop (though not many of them are in the budget range), and there is the usual spread of postcards, books, and posters available. The restaurant will provide a welcome break, with both hot and cold dishes at lunchtime.

Other Attractions

BELGRAVIA. To the southwest of Hyde Park Corner is the splendidly aristocratic area of Belgravia. The streets and squares were laid out in the mid-1800s by Thomas Cubitt, one of Britain's greatest entrepreneur architects, a man who had even more effect on the look of the capital than did Wren or Nash. If you start at the Hyde Park Corner tube, and take exit 5, you will be poised to plunge into Belgravia. Turn right down Grosvenor Crescent, and you will find yourself in Belgrave Square, ringed by imposing mansions that were once the houses of dukes and lords, and now mostly house embassies and discreet offices

Kitty-corner across the square, Belgrave Place will lead through to Eaton Square, the aptly chosen locale for *Upstairs, Downstairs.* It's no accident that this whole neighborhood of wealth and elegant splendor is grouped round the back of Buckingham Palace. In the days when the area was laid out, the bulk of the court had town houses here or hereabouts. Take a gentle stroll around Belgravia, looking into chic alleyways, called "mews" from the time when they housed horses and carriages. Nowadays a former stable can change hands at over three-quarters of a million pounds. Eaton Square also signals the beginning of a long, fairly straight, route westwards—here residential, but very soon, after it crosses Sloane Square, a bustling shopping area centered around the King's Road.

CHELSEA PHYSIC GARDEN, *Royal Hospital Rd., SW3 4HS (tel. 352 5646). Open Wed. and Sun. 2–5, from mid-Apr. to mid-Oct., closed rest of the year. Admission £1.50. Entrance from Swan Walk. Tube: Sloane Square.* This is a specialist garden, started by the Society of Apothecaries in 1673. It's full of unusual plants, and over the years it has kept a research link with the Royal Society, one of the most prestigious scientific bodies in the world. The great storm of October 1987 wrought terrible harm to the garden. At least 15 large trees were lost, with the result that the shelter they provided will certainly affect the microclimate, lowering winter temperatures, and endangering tender rare species.

CHEYNE WALK, *SW3.* This is one of the most interesting areas in London for the literary history maven. Cheyne Walk (pronounced "chainy") runs west from the Royal Hospital, and features a mixture of styles, the oldest houses dating back to the reign of Queen Anne, early 18th century, others dating from several later periods. These much-sought-after homes line one side of the street, while the other is formed by the embankment of the Thames, bordered by tall trees. This is Blue Plaque territory, called after the round, blue, ceramic memorials put up on the facades of buildings all over London to commemorate the fact that a house once had famous residents. To take a Cheyne Walk example: "GEORGE ELIOT, *Mary Ann Cross, née Evans,* (1819–1880), novelist, died here."

If you had walked down Cheyne Walk in the 19th or early 20th century, you could have seen any of the following writers and artists coming in or out of their homes: George Eliot the novelist; the artists J.M.W. Turner and James Whistler, both of whom were addicted to this stretch of the river; the American writer Henry James; the effete

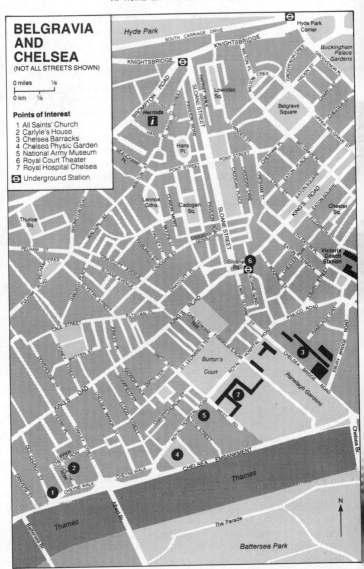

BELGRAVIA AND CHELSEA
(NOT ALL STREETS SHOWN)

0 miles   ⅛
0 km   ⅛

Points of Interest
1 All Saints' Church
2 Carlyle's House
3 Chelsea Barracks
4 Chelsea Physic Garden
5 National Army Museum
6 Royal Court Theater
7 Royal Hospital Chelsea
◎ Underground Station

Victorian poet Algernon Charles Swinburne; and Dante Gabriel Rossetti, leader of the Pre-Raphaelite Brotherhood, who revolutionized Victorian art. You couldn't have helped noticing the loud cries of the peacocks in Rossetti's gardens—his neighbors certainly complained about them. Turner painted Battersea Bridge from his window at #119, and he greatly valued the strange qualities of the light when the mists rose from the river. Whistler, too, made the river the subject of many of his most evocative works. Beyond Battersea Bridge is the Chelsea Basin, where deluxe houseboats jostle for space. All along Cheyne Walk you'll find interesting pieces of modern sculpture, such as the streamlined *Boy with the Dolphin* in bronze by David Wynne, or Epstein's sensuous relief of a nude girl.

COMMONWEALTH INSTITUTE, *Kensington High St., W8 6NQ (tel. 603 4535). Open Mon. to Sat. 10–5:30, Sun. 2–5. Admission free. Tubes: High Street Kensington, Olympia.* The huge, tentlike copper roof of the Commonwealth Institute stands back from the street at the foot of Holland Park. Although the Commonwealth concept which replaced the British Empire as a family of former colonies has slowly faded with the years, the Institute is flourishing as a London base for cultural links and international goodwill. It stages frequent exhibitions, film shows, concerts, and has a range of excellently displayed, permanent ethnic exhibits.

GEOLOGICAL MUSEUM, *Exhibition Rd., SW7 2DE (tel. 589 3444). Open Mon. to Sat. 10–6, Sun. 2:30–6. Admission £1 adults, 50p children, free after 4:30. Tube: South Kensington.* In comparison with the Science Museum, the Geological Museum is positively dull! It is another branch of the British Museum, the stone bit of natural history (see below). The displays set out to illustrate earth's history and the general principles of geological science, and for anyone interested in those areas it can be fascinating. Of much wider interest is the collection of gemstones.

HOLLAND PARK, *W8. Tube: High Street Kensington.* These 55 acres were once the grounds of Holland House, an Elizabethan mansion that was almost completely destroyed by bombing in 1941. They run up from the Commonwealth Institute on Kensington High Street, and are the venue for open-air theater performances and concerts in summer, and act as a public park all the year round. Where the house once stood there are now rose gardens, peacocks, and a former orangery which has become an expensive restaurant, boasting a list of 96 brands of malt Scotch whiskey (no way a great travel value!). Between 1773 and 1840 Holland House was the residence of the third Baron Holland and his wife, who was a dynamic hostess and attracted a brilliant circle to her soirées. She had been ostracized by the court for being a divorcée and, nothing daunted, created her own salon in revenge. All the elite from France and England (this was the time of the French Revolution and Napoleon) thronged to her lure—Byron; Talleyrand, the French politician who endlessly turned his coat; Sheridan, the Irish playwright; Dickens, at the height of his early fame; Palmerston, a brilliant politician and Prime Minister; and Macaulay, the best-selling historian of the age.

LINLEY SAMBOURNE HOUSE, *18 Stafford Terr., W8 7BH (tel. 622 6360, The Victorian Society). Open Wed. 10–4, Sun. 2–5; groups of 15 or more, by appointment only, can visit at other times—call above number. Admission £1.50. Tube: High Street Kensington.* This unusual museum lies in the network of streets to the east of Holland Park. It is a haven of Victoriana, a perfectly preserved late-19th-century "artistic" interior, now managed by the Victorian Society, which devotes itself to preserving the best from that prolific age. This survival was sold intact to the City of London by the Countess of Rosse, mother of Lord Snowdon. She was the granddaughter of Mr. Sambourne, the chief political cartoonist of *Punch* magazine, who built and furnished the place in the 1870s. For anyone interested in the atmosphere and character of Victorian England, this is a must.

NATIONAL ARMY MUSEUM, *Royal Hospital Rd., SW3 4HT (tel. 730 0717). Open Mon. to Sat. 10–5:30, Sun. 2–5:30. Admission free. Tube: Sloane Square.* The Army Museum stands beside the Royal Hospital—but is a fine example of "brutal modern" architecture, unlike the gracious home for old soldiers next door. The museum celebrates the exploits and achievements of the British Army from 1485 to 1982, and of the Indian Army until independence in 1947. It is a great place for an intelligent Rambo. Paintings, uniforms, weapons, regimental and personal mementos, and flags are all excellently displayed and provide a mine of information. Pity about the building!

ROYAL ALBERT HALL AND THE ALBERT MEMORIAL, *Kensington Gore, SW7 2AP.* The drumlike bulk of the Albert Hall rises on the south side of Kensington Gardens. It is the most northerly building in the great arts and science complex that stretches down to the V&A. Although the Hall is in use for a wild variety of events for most of the year—tennis matches, wrestling bouts, the commencement ceremonies of London University, rallies of every kind—it is with the BBC Promenade Concerts in the summer that the building really comes into its own. This is one of the most comprehensive music festivals anywhere in the world, with at least one concert every day for six weeks, and orchestras and soloists from every corner of the globe taking part. They really are promenade concerts, for the wide arena is stripped of seats so that students and other aficionados can stand, sit, walk around (if they can find the space), and generally rival the performers as the heart of the event.

The vast circular interior, resplendent in wine and gold, used to have an abominable echo, and it was said that visitors got two concerts for the price of one. It was a dandy place to hear Wagner in those days. But science came to the rescue and, after much experimentation, a fleet of flying saucers was parked in the big dome, thus improving the acoustics, if not the aesthetics, of the Hall.

If you can't get to a concert, walk round the outside armed with your binoculars, and look up at the frieze that encircles the building just below the dome. It sets forth the "Triumph of Arts and Letters" in true Victorian style.

Across the road, just inside the Gardens, is the **Albert Memorial.** This is even more of a Victorian temple than is the Albert Hall. It is like an immense Gothic space rocket, put up in the 1870s as a tribute to Prince Albert, Victoria's Prince Consort. He sits under an elaborate canopy, a 14-foot-high figure reading the catalog of the Great Exhibition of 1851—very much his brainchild—while all around the huge plinth are sculptures of the great artists, writers, and thinkers of the West. At each corner of the whole group are the four symbols of the Continents, complete with camels, elephants, and American Indians. The whole thing is a wonderful potpourri of marble, enamel, mosaic, stone, and bronze—and it's in terrible shape, corroded by pollution. There's no telling how much of it you'll be able to see. They are talking of covering it with a glass dome, rebuilding it, and generally treating it like a mini version of the Acropolis in Athens. It will almost certainly be shrouded in scaffolding and tarpaulins while the powers-that-be decide which course to take.

ROYAL HOSPITAL, CHELSEA, *Royal Hospital Rd., SW3 4SL (tel. 730 0160). Open Mon. to Sat. 10–12, 2–4, Sun. 2–4. Tube: Sloane Square.* This is a hospital in the antique meaning of the word, an almshouse or retirement home for old soldiers. It was founded in the late 17th century, built by Sir Christopher Wren, with the approval of Charles II. The king's statue stands in the grounds, and is decorated with oak leaves on May 29 each year, to commemorate his escape from Cromwell's Roundhead soldiers by hiding in an oak tree. The hospital, its bricks mellowing in the sun, is a very peaceful place, with the graciousness and elegance of a long lost age, worth visiting as a fine example of the work of a very great architect. There's a rather severe chapel, and a small museum dealing with the Hospital's history. The grounds are ideal for a quiet stroll, but with every spring they undergo an unbelievable change, for this is when the **Royal Horticultural Society's Chelsea Flower Show** comes to town. Then the wide stretch of grass disappears under huge tents, show gardens spring up from nowhere, complete with brick walls, fountains, even running streams. Thousands of people pour in for the few days the show is on—garden lovers are as ubiquitous in Britain as animal lovers, and even more obsessive. The show is always kicked off by the Royal Family; the first day is for RHS members only, and the last day sees the streets all around like Macbeth's walking wood, as people carry home the bushes, pots, and bundles of plants that they have bought at bargain prices.

The peaceful **Ranelagh Gardens** adjacent to the Hospital are all that's left of the now forgotten 18th-century pleasure gardens which used to boast a Chinese pavilion, a rococo rotunda, an ornamental lake, an orchestra stand (where Mozart once played), and booths for tea, wine, and smoking. At night it was lit by "a thousand golden lamps that emulate the noonday sun," and, according to the diarist Horace Walpole, it was so fashionable that you couldn't "set your foot without treading on a Prince, or a Duke of Cumberland."

Lunch Spots

We have not graded our lunch spot suggestions; they all carry a range of dishes at various prices to suit your taste and pocket. The best-value budget bets are the pubs in the area; these often have the most atmosphere as well.

Anglesey Arms, 15 Selwood Terr., SW7 3QG. The menu at this friendly Chelsea pub off Fulham Road ranges from a simple ploughman's lunch to classier chicken Maryland.

La Bersagliera, 372 King's Rd., SW3 5UZ. The delicious homemade pasta is inclined to run out at this busy, family-run Italian café. It's very noisy, but there's plenty of atmosphere.

Chelsea Kitchen, 98 King's Rd., SW3 4TZ. Basic, inexpensive, yet nourishing food tops the bill at this popular Chelsea haunt. Everything is fresh and homemade.

Chicago Rib Shack, 1 Raphael St., SW7 1DL. Hickory-smoked ribs, deep-fried potato skins, and onion rings are among the specialties served at this American-style spot off Knightsbridge. At lunchtime you can eat as many chicken wings as you like for £2.50.

Commonwealth Institute, Kensington High St., W8 6NQ. The coffee shop here is a pleasant place to rest after a walk around the exhibitions. It has a simple range of sandwiches, Danish pastries, and the like.

Dôme, 354 King's Rd., SW3 5UZ. Cocktails and French café-style food are served all day at this brasserie-inspired converted pub. It's a welcome place to stop while shopping in the King's Road.

L'Express, 16 Sloane St., SW1X 9BN. The latest food fads, from croissant breakfasts to sophisticated salads, are on offer here in the stylish basement of a smart—and pricey—dress boutique.

Grenadier, 18 Wilton Row, SW1X 7NR. The food counter at this pub above Belgrave Square has unusually good-value snacks, including quiche, ploughman's lunch, steak and kidney pie, and sandwiches.

Huffs, Chelsea Farmers' Market, 250 King's Rd., SW3 5UE. You'll find this spot right in the middle of a fresh produce market. The wonderful vegetarian and meat dishes it serves are cheap, fresh, and tasty.

Khun Akorn, 136 Brompton Rd., SW3 1HY. A delightful Thai restaurant that offers excellent-value set lunches in very attractive surroundings. It's just down the road from Harrods.

Natural History Museum, Cromwell Rd., SW7 5BD. When you need a break from the exhibits, both the snack bar and cafeteria are good value. Dinosaur burgers not available!

Pasta Mania, 390 King's Rd., SW3 5UZ. Eat as much freshly made pasta and sauce as you like for about £3 at this smart, modern restaurant, about halfway down King's Road.

The Roof Gardens, 99 Kensington High St., W8 5SA. The setting is the attraction here—it is supposedly the largest roof garden in Europe—while the main room indoors is just as attractive with its Art Deco theme. An all-in menu is available.

Victoria & Albert Museum, Cromwell Rd., SW7 2RL. There is so much to see in this museum that you will need to take a break. The spacious, reasonably priced restaurant serves a good selection of hot and cold dishes.

———————◆———————

S P L U R G E S

The Hyde Park Hotel, 66 Knightsbridge, SW1Y 7LA (tel. 235 4552). When you've fought your way through the corridor of Harrods, there's a lovely spot close by where you can sit and relax after a hectic day's shopping and sightseeing. The pastel-colored Park Room has huge windows that overlook leafy Hyde Park, and this is where they serve afternoon tea 3:45–6 on weekdays and 4–6 at weekends. The cost is £7.50 per person, and this includes service and tax. Make sure that you have a reservation.

LEGAL EAGLES AND THE LITERATI

The character of an area of London can change visibly from one street to the next. Nowhere is this so clear as in the contrast between fun-loving Soho and intellectual Bloomsbury, a mere 100 yards to the northeast, or between arty, trendy Covent Garden and—on the other side of Kingsway—sober Holborn. Both Bloomsbury and Holborn should be seen by day, when the leafy 17th- and 18th-century squares and the terraces of graceful houses can be best appreciated, and when the legal and academic institutions that are the principal residents here are bustling with serious-minded activity. By night the place is completely deserted, for, though there are plenty of people living here, they are not the kind to make the neighborhood hum.

Bloomsbury is the heart of literary and learned London. The University is here, so are the Law Courts, and the British Museum, with its amazing collection that would take several days to explore properly. Some of London's finest domestic architecture lines these streets, elegant houses which would have been familiar to Dr. Johnson and Dickens, whose own house can still be visited. The self-centered literary set which made the name of Bloomsbury famous has left hardly a trace, but these quiet 18th- and 19th-century squares have attracted publishers by the dozen, and they keep the bookish atmosphere going. Bedford Square is a case in point, its huge old trees almost completely surrounded by gentlemanly publishing houses that have found the commodious, late-1700s buildings very much to their taste. These row houses also convert well into small family hotels, and several of our budget selections are here.

Holborn is a different area again. Here the law contributes some magnificently ancient buildings to the district, and a lot of its atmosphere. The Inns of Court are the legal profession's colleges, union headquarters, office blocks, and licensing authorities all rolled into one. As they were founded as far back as medieval times, many of the buildings that house the Inns are worth visiting, even if you can only see them from the outside. Their setting among lawns and trees provides both the sense of a time warp and the chance to sit comfortably and contemplate the infinite. The sequence of Inns that runs down the west side of Holborn makes an attractive tour all by itself; it also gives you a chance to investigate the nearby streets and squares en route. It will also give you the chance to investigate the atmospheric pubs that line the way, almost every one with something of the timeworn hostelry about it. Not, you understand, that we are suggesting a pub crawl, simply that you might find them the best source of a delicious budget lunch.

Major Attractions

THE BRITISH MUSEUM AND THE BRITISH LIBRARY, *Great Russell St., WC1B 3DG (tel. 636 1555). Open Mon. to Sat. 10–5, Sun. 2:30–5. Admission free. Tubes: Holborn, Russell Square, Tottenham Court Road.* This huge, sooty, ponderously dignified building houses one of the world's greatest, and most extensive, museums. It was founded in 1753, but expanded at such a rate that it had to build itself new premises, which took from 1820 to 1847. There are blessedly no shiny modern giants in the immediate neighborhood, so the full majesty of this Greco-Victorian struc-

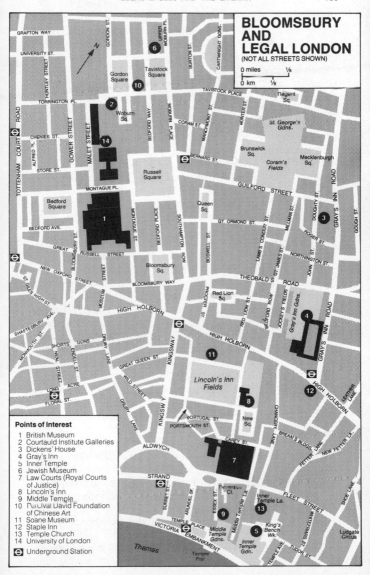

BLOOMSBURY AND LEGAL LONDON
(NOT ALL STREETS SHOWN)

0 miles ⅛
0 km ⅛

Points of Interest

1 British Museum
2 Courtauld Institute Galleries
3 Dickens' House
4 Gray's Inn
5 Inner Temple
6 Jewish Museum
7 Law Courts (Royal Courts of Justice)
8 Lincoln's Inn
9 Middle Temple
10 Percival David Foundation of Chinese Art
11 Soane Museum
12 Staple Inn
13 Temple Church
14 University of London

⊖ Underground Station

ture, with its facade like a great temple, comes over with full force. As at the V&A, you should arm yourself with a free floor plan directly as you go in—there is a second entrance on Montague Place—or they'll have to send out search parties to rescue you. The place is so vast and complex, and the collections so varied and fascinating, that a single visit will only scratch the surface of what's on offer.

Foremost among the countless treasures of the museum are the Elgin Marbles, an unrivaled collection of ancient Greek sculptures, housed in a purpose-built gallery donated initially by the art dealer Lord Duveen in 1938 but recently redecorated and dramatically relit. The sculptures date from around 450 B.C., the Golden Age of Athens, and were the work of Pheidias, greatest of all Greek sculptors. They originally decorated the Parthenon in Athens, from whence they were removed in 1811 by Lord Elgin, then the British Ambassador to Greece. Today, they are a bone of contention between Britain and Greece, whose government is lobbying fiercely for their return. It is unlikely, though, that they will leave London for many years to come.

Apart from these magnificent sculptures, the museum counts among its most prized possessions a superb collection of Ancient Egyptian relics, now displayed in an imaginative layout, which has given a fresh perspective to many of the huge figures. The Rosetta Stone, which helped archeologists to decipher Egyptian hieroglyphics, stands in pride of place at the beginning of the exhibition.

Upstairs, one of the most intriguing new displays is that of Roman Britain, including the Mildenhall treasure, a cache of Roman silver found in a Suffolk field in 1942. On this floor, too, are exhaustive displays of Greek and Roman art, some rather grisly remains from Egyptian tombs, and antiquities found on the site of Ur of the Chaldees—hometown of Abraham—by Sir Leonard Woolley in the 1920s. Seven new basement galleries display sculpture, mostly Greek and Roman again, which had been in storage from 1939–85, after being hidden from the bombs of World War II.

Further exploration of this vast treasure house reveals one of the original copies of the Magna Carta; a collection of drawings from virtually every European school of art since the 15th century; Renaissance displays of metalwork, jewelry, coins, pottery, and glass; exquisite Chinese ceramics from the Sung, Yuan, and Ming dynasties; Assyrian antiquities . . . in short, plunder of incalculable value and beauty from around the globe.

Just inside the Great Russell Street entrance to the museum is a shop selling postcards, transparencies, posters, books, and small reproduction pieces.

The British Museum also contains one of the world's great libraries, now called the **British Library,** and hived off from the museum proper to become a separate body. New premises are being built a few blocks to the north, between Euston and St. Pancras stations. Like the museum, the library's incomparable riches are greatly enhanced by its setting, especially the main Reading Room, beneath whose great copper dome some of the most famous scholars and thinkers of the world have worked, among whom probably the most unlikely were Marx and Lenin. While the average visitor won't be using the library for study purposes, the displays of manuscripts, bindings, and rare illuminated and printed books in the **King's Library,** the **Grenville Library,** and the **Crawford Room** are always fascinating. The library benefited from the gift of the then Royal Library by George II in 1757 to the fledgling museum. Along with the priceless volumes went the right to have a copy of every book published in Britain (technically it is known as a "copyright library"). The reference division alone has well over 10 million books, and they still flood in. There are guided tours of the Reading Room on the hour, every weekday from 11–4.

THE INNS OF COURT is the collective name for the four legal "colleges" that still contain the heart of British legal life. They lie spaced out from Holborn to the river, with Gray's Inn in the north, then Lincoln's Inn, and the Inner and Middle Temples by the Thames. It is perfectly possible to walk from one to another, savoring the delights of their ancient buildings, quiet gardens, and spacious lawns. When you leave the busy, noisy, surrounding streets, you will find yourself in an atmosphere very much like that of the Oxford or Cambridge colleges—not surprising, seeing that they are of much the same age.

Gray's Inn, *Gray's Inn Rd., WC1R 5EU (tel. 405 8164). Entrance to the Hall and Library by arrangement with the Treasury Office. Gardens open May to Sept., inclusive, but phone for times. Admission free. Tubes: Chancery Lane, Holborn.* Gray's Inn, the most northerly Inn, is also the least architecturally distinguished. Its great glory, though, is its garden, calm and broad. The Hall, where Shakespeare's *Comedy of Errors* was first performed in 1596, was bombed in World War II, though the fine Elizabethan oak screen escaped undamaged.

Lincoln's Inn, *Chancery Lane, WC2A 3TP (tel. 405 1393). Hall and Library open to individual visitors (as against parties), Mon. to Fri., closed for lunch; check precise times with the porter (tel. 405 6360). Gardens open to all, Mon. to Fri. 12–2:30, closed weekends. Admission free. Tubes: Chancery Lane, Holborn.* Lincoln's Inn is very easy to find as it lies between the wide sweep of Kingsway and narrow Chancery Lane, just southeast of Holborn tube station. The peaceful expanse of Lincoln's Inn Fields, full of trees, flowers, and seats, is bordered with lovely old buildings. On the north side is Sir John Soane's Museum (see below), on the south side the Royal College of Surgeons, and on the east the buildings and courtyards of the Inn, with the great Hall dominating them. There have been lawyers here at least as far back as 1292, maybe even longer, and though none of the buildings are that old, this certainly is one of the most evocatively ancient parts of London. It was mercifully spared bomb damage in World War II.

If you leave by the south gate, you'll be in Carey Street, facing the immense brick back of the **Royal Courts of Justice,** a magnificently opulent Victorian Gothic place, with an imposing Central Hall. This is where civil lay suits—fraud and other financial cases—are held. (Open Mon. to Sat. 10:30–4:30.)

Inner Temple. *Usually open mornings and afternoons, but before visiting write or call The Master, Inner Temple Church, Inner Temple, Fleet St., EC4Y 7HL (tel. 353 8462 for hours). Admission free. Tube: Blackfriars (there are stations at Aldwych and Temple, but they have limited operating times).* **Middle Temple,** *Fleet St., EC4Y 9AT (353 4355). Open Mon. to Fri. 10–11:30, 3–4; closed Sat.,*

*Sun., and Aug. It is best to check first, rather than just turn
up, especially for afternoon visiting. Tubes: as for Inner
Temple.* These two Inns of Court lie southeast of the Law
Courts, just across the Strand. Turn down Middle Temple
Lane. The "Temple" part of these names comes from the
Knights Templar, a crusading order, whose English headquarters this was in the 13th century. The two Inns
suffered extensive bomb damage in World War II, most of
it now skillfully restored. Two of the main points of interest
are the Temple Church, a rare, round church from the
1180s, with additions from about 50 years later, and the
Middle Temple Hall, Elizabethan (mid-1500s), badly
bombed but excellently restored, with a hammer beam roof
and carved screen, where Shakespeare is reputed to have
performed in his own play *Twelfth Night.*

Other Attractions

COURTAULD INSTITUTE GALLERIES, *Woburn Sq., WC1H
0AA (tel. 636 2095). Open Mon. to Sat. 10–5, Sun. 2–5.
Admission £1.50. Tubes: Euston Square, Goodge Street,
Russell Square.* These, the art galleries of the University of
London, house several prestigious collections that have
been gifted to the Institute. They are approached in a
typically academic way, up an elderly elevator, and are
housed in rather down-at-heel rooms. But the collections
themselves are superb, especially the French Impressionist
and post-Impressionist paintings (Monet, Manet, Degas,
Renoir, Cézanne, and so on). Check to make sure that all
the collection is on view, as a lot of the best works have
been on loan in the States.

DICKENS'S HOUSE, *48 Doughty St., WC1N 2LF (tel. 405
2127). Open Mon. to Sat. 10–4:30 (last admission), closed
Sun. Admission £1.50. Tube: Russell Square.* Dickens lived
here with his family from 1837–39, and so it is a shrine for
enthusiasts of his novels. The place is full of memorabilia
—manuscripts, furniture, autographs, portraits, and first
editions—and, as he finished writing *Pickwick Papers,* and
wrote *Oliver Twist* and *Nicholas Nickleby* here, the house is
also steeped in authenticity and atmosphere.

JEWISH MUSEUM, *Woburn House, Upper Woburn Pl.,
WC1H 0EP, entrance in Tavistock Sq. (tel. 388 4525). Open*

summer Tues. to Fri. 10–4, winter Tues. to Thurs. 10–4, Fri. 10–12:45; Sun. 10–12:45 all year. Admission free (but there's a voluntary contributions box). Tubes: Euston, Euston Square, King's Cross, Russell Square. This museum was founded over 50 years ago, and illustrates the long history of Jewry in Britain (dating back to the 13th century). The collection consists mainly of objects connected with the celebration of Jewish ritual, many of them precious antiques, survivals of the terrible times through which the Jews have lived over the centuries. There are manuscripts, embroidery, and silver, many of them of great intrinsic worth, and all of interest.

PERCIVAL DAVID FOUNDATION OF CHINESE ART, *53 Gordon Sq., WC1H 0PD (tel. 387 3909). Open Mon. 2–5, Tues. to Fri. 1:30–5, Sat. 10:30–1, closed Sun. Admission free. Tubes: Euston Square, Goodge Street, Russell Square.* This is another of the University of London's galleries, like the Courtauld (Woburn Square and Gordon Square are side by side), but this time attached to the School of Oriental and African Studies. The Foundation commemorates the presentation in 1950 by Sir Percival David of his fine collection of Chinese ceramics and his library of books dealing with Chinese culture. There are around 1,500 pieces from the Song, Yuan, Ming, and Qing dynasties. Part of the collection is displayed in a new gallery on the ground floor.

SIR JOHN SOANE'S MUSEUM, *13 Lincoln's Inn Fields, WC2A 3BP (tel. 405 2107). Open Tues. to Sat. 10–5, closed Sun. and Mon. Lecture tours Sat. at 2:30. Admission free. Tube: Holborn.* In the early 1800s this was the private home of Sir John Soane, an eccentric and brilliant architect. The collection it houses is as idiosyncratic and odd as the man himself—though he had a streak of genius both in his architecture and his collecting. His portrait hangs in the former dining room, and indeed the whole house retains the character of a private home of the period (the early years of the 19th century). As the place was not very large and he had grandiose ideas, he redesigned the interior to make the most of every inch. There are architectural relics everywhere, with plaster casts and original sculptures on every available surface. Among the treasures are a set of Hogarth's *The Rake's Progress,* on ingenious hinged walls, and the sarcophagus of the pharoah Seti I, which Soane bought after the British Museum had turned it down.

Lunch Spots

We have not graded our lunch spot suggestions; they all carry a range of dishes at various prices to suit your taste and pocket. The best-value budget bets are the pubs in the area; these often have the most atmosphere as well.

Museum Tavern, 49 Great Russell St., W1P 7FJ. Ploughman's lunches, pâtés, shepherd's pie, or steak and kidney pie are on offer at this real ale pub right opposite the British Museum. Tea is served from 3 in the afternoon.

Oodles, 42 New Oxford St., WC1A 1EP. Not far from the British Museum, this crowded little self-service café has a good selection of hot dishes and salads. There is seating outside in good summer weather.

Pizzeria Amalfi, 107 Southampton Row, WC1B 4HH. The ex-managers of the successful **San Frediano** restaurant in South Kensington offer great-value fresh pasta and pizza in these humble, busy surroundings.

Princess Louise, 208 High Holborn, WC1V 7BW. This is another real ale haunt, serving traditional pub fare—baked potatoes, maxi-sausages, salads, and the like.

Vats Wine Bar, 51 Lamb's Conduit St., WC1N 3NB. You'll find good-value wines (by the glass if you're feeling abstemious), and delicious homemade food at this above-average wine bar. It's sited not far from Dickens's house.

Winston's, 24 Coptic St., WC1A 1NT. There are marvelous casseroles and English puddings to be had at this wine bar and restaurant near the British Museum. It has plenty of atmosphere, but it's only a budget spot if you choose very carefully.

---◆---

S P L U R G E S

Bloomsbury Rare Books, 29 Museum St., WC1A 1LP. A charming and quite different keepsake to take home with you is an old print of London. Perhaps the best hunting ground for a print is in Museum Street, just south of the British Museum in Bloomsbury. Here you'll find mounted, yet unframed, prints from £6 upwards; the larger ones start at about £20. There are several shops in this street; others to look out for are Craddock & Barnard at #32, The Print Room at #37, and Weinreb Architectural Gallery at #34.

———————◆———————

THE
BORN-AGAIN
MARKET

◆

Soho and Covent Garden have always been colorful areas. Both of them used to be disreputable: Now only Soho is, though very much less so than only a few years back. It's not a question of trash on the sidewalks so much as of sin beckoning from behind neon-lit doorways, and of dealings of the shadiest kind. But don't let this prejudice you. Soho is London's most bohemian quarter, with lively street markets, plenty of theaters, the headquarters of the film industry, and numerous good-value ethnic restaurants.

It's conveniently bounded by Shaftesbury Avenue, Charing Cross Road, Oxford Street, and Regent Street—making a small, nearly square area, the geometry of which is emphasized by the grid pattern of the streets, or at least as near to a grid pattern as higgledy-piggledy London can come.

In not much more than a decade, Covent Garden—which lies just to the east of Soho—has gone from a time-honored fruit and vegetable market serving the whole of London, through a period of decline and near destruction, to its

present role as one of the busiest, most raffish, most
enjoyable parts of the city.

The streets leading off the superbly restored market building have received the kiss of life as well. Once
upon a time, the large buildings that rise on every hand
were fruit and vegetable warehouses, cavernous and grim.
Now they accommodate trendy design firms, chic boutiques, craftsmen's workshops, and commercial art galleries. The whole area pulses with a completely new, upbeat
way of life, that is slightly foreign to London. It is the
kind of excitement that you would expect to find in, say,
Paris or Rome. It is well worth spending some time wandering down the little alleys and lanes of the area, to see
exactly what is hidden there. You may not find much to
buy at budget prices, but you'll have a wonderful time
looking.

Major Attractions

COVENT GARDEN MARKET, *The Piazza, Covent Garden
WC2E 8RA. Tubes: Covent Garden, Leicester Square.* Covent Garden was once just that, the fruit and vegetable
garden for the 13th-century version of Westminster Abbey
(covent=convent, an all-purpose word for monastic). After
the Dissolution of the Monasteries in the mid-16th century, the Crown took over the lands, and in 1552 awarded
them to the first Earl of Bedford. In 1630 the fourth earl
commissioned Inigo Jones (court architect to both James I
and Charles I) to lay out a square on the site, with **St. Paul's**
(not the cathedral!) at one end, elegantly colonnaded
houses to the north and east, and the earl's town house (or
rather its garden wall) filling the south side. It was the first
of London's great squares, and it influenced the design of
many subsequent ones. Of the whole plan only the church
remains.

The market in the square gradually gained in importance, and, with the opening of Westminster Bridge, which
made transport to and from the market gardens south of
the city possible, it became one of the biggest and most
important in Europe. After World War II, as the market
expanded, it became clear that the streets round about
would not hold the traffic and, in 1974, operations were

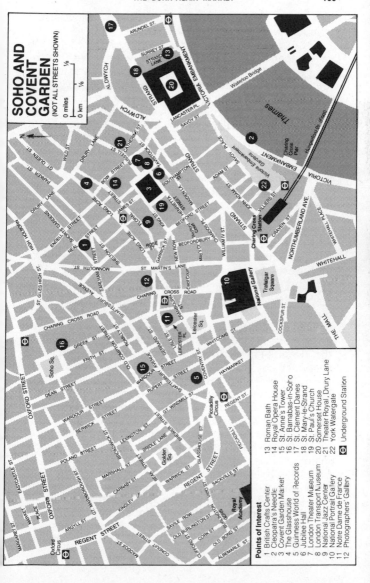

SOHO AND COVENT GARDEN
(NOT ALL STREETS SHOWN)

0 miles ⅛
0 km ⅛

Points of Interest

1 British Crafts Center
2 Cleopatra's Needle
3 Covent Garden Market
4 The Glasshouse
5 Guinness World of Records
6 Jubilee Hall
7 London Theater Museum
8 London Transport Museum
9 National Jazz Center
10 National Portrait Gallery
11 Notre Dame de France
12 Photographers' Gallery
13 Roman Bath
14 Royal Opera House
15 St. Anne's Tower
16 St. Barnabas-in-Soho
17 St. Clement Danes
18 St. Mary-le-Strand
19 St. Paul's Church
20 Somerset House
21 Theater Royal, Drury Lane
22 York Watergate
Ⓤ Underground Station

removed to Nine Elms, south of the Thames. The deserted buildings were ripe for redevelopment.

The main market building had been constructed in 1840 for the then Duke of Bedford, and it was realized that the layout of the buildings would be perfect for conversion to a modern shopping mall of quite remarkable period charm. A great deal of money and care was spent on refurbishing the central building, which now houses a multitude of stalls and small shops, where once there were mountains of fruit and forests of flowers. If you want to see the extent of the old cellarage where the vegetables were once stored, drop into *The Crusted Pipe* wine bar, and wander through its maze of small subterranean rooms.

Street entertainment flourishes here at every hour of the day, and often well into the night. Jugglers, acrobats, street theater groups, Punch and Judy shows, mime artists, itinerant musicians, classical quartets, even, on occasion, performances in the Opera House relayed to a huge outdoor screen—they are all here for free. For a positively un-English experience, Covent Garden is the place.

LEICESTER SQUARE, *W1. Tube: Leicester Square.* This is the big magnet for nightlife lovers, with movie theaters on three sides, buskers, occasional bagpipers, hordes of Londoners up for the evening, and even larger hordes of tourists. The Odeon, on the east side, is the venue for all the Royal Film Performances, and the movie theme is continued by a jaunty little statue of Charlie Chaplin in the opposite corner. Shakespeare sulks in the middle, remembering the days when the cinemas were live theaters—burlesque houses maybe, but live all the same. The booth of the Society of West End Theater is on the west side of the square, and is an essential goal for all visitors in search of great theater values. You can buy half-price tickets for many famous West End shows there on the day of performance—not, of course, the *most* popular ones, but a good cross section of what's on offer, all the same. There'll be a long line, so give yourself plenty of time.

Just off the northeast corner of the square is the Hippodrome, one of the most popular night spots in town. It's strictly for the young, and style is a must for getting in—it's the brainchild of entrepreneur Peter Stringfellow.

LONDON TRANSPORT MUSEUM, *Covent Garden, WC2E 7BB (tel. 379 6344). Open daily 10–6. Admission charge. Tubes: Covent Garden, Charing Cross.* For the adult nostalgia buff and any kid who's ever wanted to drive a trolley car, this museum gathers together examples of every kind of public transport that has plied the London streets in the last 150 years or so—horse buses, trolley buses, trams, even tube trains. A good port of call for the family exploring Covent Garden.

SOHO SQUARE, *WC2. Tube: Tottenham Court Road.* Soho Square makes a convenient starting place for exploring Soho in general. It's an attractive little square, with a small, cottagey toolshed in the middle of the trees, built in the 1880s and looking like something out of the Brothers Grimm. There's also a statue of Charles II, rather the worse for wear and pollution. Soho's cosmopolitan character dates from the 17th century, when thousands of Huguenot refugees (French Protestants) fled to England from religious persecution. Greek Christians moved here for similar reasons, and by the mid-18th century the foreign population predominated. Later came Germans, Swiss, Italians, Russians, and Poles (especially Polish Jews). As you wander up and down the streets, you'll see restaurants, ethnic delicatessens, cafés, and pâtisseries, all the panoply of international togetherness.

Famous people also gravitated here. Karl Marx lived at 28 Dean Street, Mozart played the piano at 21 Dean Street when only seven years old, Thomas Sheraton, the celebrated furniture maker, lived at 163 Wardour Street, while John Logie Baird first demonstrated television at 22 Frith Street.

Wander into any small side lane you can see, where often the best (if most decrepit) 18th-century architecture still lingers in neglect. Look, too, above street level at the upper floors of the houses, to see what they were like before the garish modern shop fronts were slapped on them. For a final taste of the Continent, drop into the French Pub on Dean Street, home away from home in London for the Free French during World War II and still exuding a distinctly Gallic flavor.

THEATER MUSEUM, *Old Flower Market, Covent Garden,*

WC2 (tel. 831 1227). Open Tues. to Sun. 11–7, closed Mon. Admission charge. Tubes: Covent Garden, Leicester Square. The theatrical treasures of the Victoria & Albert Museum were kept in storage for decades, lacking suitable display facilities, but on the anniversary of Shakespeare's birthday in 1987, this splendid showcase was at last opened for them. It is an attractively converted part of the old Covent Garden complex, the Flower Market, a large building which has been done over with the right stagey flair and style. Model sets, costumes, paintings, photographs, and all kinds of theatrical memorabilia bring to life the rich history of the British stage. Added attractions are a box office for tickets to current performances around town, a shop for souvenirs, and an elegant café.

Other Attractions

CHARING CROSS ROAD, *WC2. Tubes: Charing Cross, Leicester Square, Tottenham Court Road.* Book lovers will already know that this is London's book street—as will film buffs, since *84 Charing Cross Road* spread the fact worldwide. If you start at the bottom end of the road, just above Trafalgar Square, and gradually work your way north, taking side trips into the little lanes (or "courts") such as Cecil Court, you will be able to spend a blissful couple of hours browsing in and out of the secondhand—and new—bookshops. Near the top of the road you will come to the two big stores, Foyles and Waterstone's, to round off the safari. A couple of the courts have print shops, too, where you might find a bargain souvenir to help you remember your trip. By the way, 84 Charing Cross Road no longer sells books; it has reached the 20th century and now sells CDs.

CHINATOWN, *W1. Tubes: Leicester Square, Piccadilly Circus.* If you go by San Francisco standards, London's Chinatown should be called China village, since it's so small. It lies just below, and parallel to, Shaftesbury Avenue, east of Piccadilly Circus. The main village thoroughfare is Gerrard Street, supposedly a pedestrian precinct, but cars are always finding their way along it. Strenuous efforts have been made to give the area the right *Chinoiserie* feel—pagoda-style telephone booths, ornamental arches, even bilingual street signs. It all comes together when the Chinese New Year is celebrated, with all the colorful ceremony of dragons, fireworks, and dancing in the streets.

THE GLASSHOUSE, *65 Long Acre, WC2E 9JH (tel. 836 9785). Open Mon. to Fri. 10–5:30, Sat. 11–4:30, closed Sun. Admission free. Tubes: Covent Garden, Leicester Square, Holborn.* This commercial glass studio is open to the public, either to buy some of their hand-blown glass, or to watch the craftsmen at work.

NEAL STREET, *WC2. Tubes: Covent Garden, Leicester Square.* Neal Street is an excellent sample of what has been happening to the area around the reborn Covent Garden: It's a sassy, sophisticated street, pedestrian only in intent, lined with boutiques that seem to come and go like the tides on the Thames but which always have an air of the latest chic. On one corner (with Earlham Street) are the premises of **Contemporary Applied Arts** *(tel. 836 6993); open Mon. to Fri. 10–5:30, Sat. 11–5, closed Sun. Admission free.* Year-round exhibitions of contemporary crafts, most for sale though *not* inexpensive, are put on here, and they give a fair idea of trends in the British crafts field. Almost next door is the **Donmar Warehouse,** where exciting fringe theater is staged in the round.

ST. PAUL'S, *The Piazza, Covent Garden, WC2 (tel. 836 5221). (Main entrance from Bedford St.) Open Mon. to Fri. 9:30–4:30, closed Sat. and Sun., except for normal services. Tubes: Covent Garden, Leicester Square.* Designed by Inigo Jones, this church is the wrong way round. The striking pillared portico that faces the market is for decorative purposes only (it was the setting Bernard Shaw chose for the opening scene of his *Pygmalion,* and therefore of *My Fair Lady*). The real entrance is round the other side, reached through a small churchyard from Bedford Street. Inside, the church is full of memorials to theatrical personalities—it is known as the "Actors' Church"—and is worth exploring for that reason alone. Otherwise it is a rather stark though perfectly proportioned building.

VICTORIA EMBANKMENT GARDENS, *WC2 (tel. 798 2063).* South of Covent Garden, and across the Strand, lies a long, narrow park that follows the bank of the Thames. This is a quiet haven where many office workers have their lunch-time sandwiches in summer, and where people walk all the year round to get a breath of fresh air in the middle of the city's bustle. The flowerbeds here are regularly replanted, the shrubs and trees shield you from the traffic roaring along the embankment, and, hidden along the paths, there are some intriguing statues. Robert Burns sits on a tree stump at the mercy of his muse. Sir Arthur Sullivan (the partner of Gilbert, who reigned close by at the Savoy Theater) is memorialized, as are the blind statesman Henry Fawcett and Sir Wilfred Lawson, a temperance advocate, apparently caught in the middle of one of his fierce speeches.

Near the Charing Cross end of the gardens is the **York Watergate,** built in 1626, and the only remaining evidence of a house planned by the then Duke of Buckingham. It is interesting to note from the position of the gate just how high the tides used to reach before the Embankment was constructed in the 1860s. The Strand was, in fact, so named because it *was* the bank of the Thames.

On the other side of the roadway from the gardens, poised above the river, is **Cleopatra's Needle**—a weathered granite obelisk that has no connection whatever with Cleopatra. It was first erected at Heliopolis in Egypt around 1450 B.C., and was presented to Britain in 1819. It didn't arrive until 1878, to be placed in its present position. The two sphinxes at the base are pitted with shrapnel holes caused by a bomb in 1917. You will notice that the seats along this stretch of the Embankment carry on the Ancient Egyptian theme.

Lunch Spots

We have not graded our lunch spot suggestions; they all carry a range of dishes at various prices to suit your taste and pocket. The best-value budget bets are the pubs in the area; these often have the best atmosphere as well. The Covent Garden area, especially, has a proliferation of atmospheric pubs and wine bars.

Blake's Wine Bar, 34 Wellington St., WC2E 7BD. This is a good place to know about if you're around Covent

Garden. There's a cold buffet which includes savory pies and fresh salads, and also a hot dish of the day.

Boswell's Coffee House, 8 Russell St., WC2B 5HZ. You can get hot dishes and savory snacks here, as well as coffee. It's just off Covent Garden.

Cordon Brown, 32 Bedford St., WC2E 9ED. You'll find the hearty salt beef sandwiches here, hot and on rye. They also serve breakfasts, deli-bar specialties, and other sandwiches.

Cranks, 11 The Market, Covent Garden, WC2E 8RB. This small branch of the popular vegetarian chain serves whole-food fare in rustic surroundings.

Diana's Diner, 39 Endell St., WC2H 9BA. This is one of the best places in the area to sample generous portions of tasty English food at low prices. It's open from breakfast until the early evening.

L'Entrecôte Café, 12 Upper St. Martin's Lane, WC2H 3HA. The specialty of the house here is steak and frites at an all-in bargain price, or try the grilled fish of the day. It's handy for the Leicester Square area.

Food for Thought, 31 Neal St., WC2H 9PR. The menu changes daily at this simple, whitewashed vegetarian café. Good food and reasonable prices make it very popular at lunchtime.

Grahame's Seafare, 38 Poland St., W1V 3DA. Just off Oxford Street, this kosher fish restaurant serves wonderful fish-and-chips, and gefilte fish, all cooked to order and in generous portions. It's open at lunchtime but has rather odd evening hours.

Jade Garden, 15 Wardour St., W1V 3HD. This is a good place for Cantonese *dim sum.* All the lunchtime dishes are low priced and excellent value.

Jewel in the Ground, *27 St. Catherine St., WC2B 5JS.* This attractive wine bar is below the Indian restaurant, **Taste of India.** The stuffed pita bread makes a hearty snack for under £2. It's just off the Aldwych.

Nosh Bar, 42 Great Windmill St., W1V 7PA. This small Soho snack bar is noted for its salt beef, served on white bread or rye, with pickled cucumber or whatever else catches your eye.

Sandwich Scene, 155 Wardour St., W1V 3TB. You'll

have to stand in line to get your order here, but there is a vast array of freshly prepared sandwiches to take away. The nearest green space to sit down in is Soho Square, just a few blocks away.

Tony Roma's, 46 St. Martin's Lane, WC2N 4EJ. This large member of an American chain, Roma's serves ribs, steak, and salads. It also has daily specials.

◆

S P L U R G E S

Royal Opera House, Covent Garden, WC2E 7QA (box office tel. 240 1066). A night at the opera or ballet could be the splurge to end all splurges, as seats can go for as high as £75 a time. But, such is the splendor of the inside of Covent Garden Opera House, that you will certainly feel it is money well spent. Of course, £75 is the top, top price, and seats can be had for a tenth of that, though they won't be very good ones. The red and gold Victorian decor gives a very special feel to that hush which proceeds the start of a performance, and the bars, especially the Crush Bar, add opulence to the pastime of people-watching during an intermission. This is one splurge that you may have to think about ahead of time, as seats for the most popular productions are hard to get, even at these prices.

◆

WHERE IT ALL STARTED

◆

When an Englishman tells you that he works in the City, he isn't being vague. He's using the British equivalent of working on Wall Street. The City—or the "Square Mile"—extends eastwards from Temple Bar to the Tower of London, and north from the Thames to Chiswell Street. In this small area are sited most of London's banking, stockbroking, and insurance companies, as well as St. Paul's, one of the world's finest churches—a case of the money changers encompassing the temple!

It's no coincidence that the City should occupy this particular site. Commerce has always been London's *raison d'être,* right from Roman times to today. But it has not always been such an exclusively financial place. Until the 17th century, when people started to move westwards, this *was* London, with lively markets, churches and monasteries by the dozen, higgledy-piggledy houses, noise, dirt by the ton, and color in heraldic proportions. It was only to die as a community in the 19th century.

This is not to say that the City is lifeless. On the contrary, during the week it positively throbs with life. But visit in the evening or on weekends and you'll find it a ghost town. Fewer than 8,000 people actually live here now, less than one-fifth the population of Roman London at its height. During the week, though, you can instantly sense that you are surrounded by big business. Jobs here are highly paid and highly prized, even in the days following the crash of fall 1987. The traditional uniform of the City gent may have changed somewhat these days—you'll be lucky to see anyone wearing a bowler hat—but even in today's computerized world, where fortunes can be made and lost at the touch of a hi-tech button, and billions are sent round the world in an instant, some things never change. This is London, after all, where a member of the Stock Exchange here can be censured for wearing brown shoes.

It's this schizophrenic quality, swinging from hectic activity to near total silence, that accounts for much of the City's unique atmosphere. Where else do outsize skyscrapers tower over tiny parish churches? Where else does the Lord Mayor, clad in ceremonial robes and chain of office, and escorted by foot soldiers in 17th-century garb bearing pikes and muskets, ride in an 18th-century coach past buildings in which satellite communications have long since become routine?

Little remains of the Roman town of Londinium other than a few fragments of the original city wall and the foundations—little more than a heap of old stones really—of a Temple of Mithras. Charred debris near the Walbrook is all that's left of the London Queen Boudicca and her tribe burnt to the ground in A.D. 60, after Roman tax collectors not only confiscated her daughters' inheritance but rashly raped them as well. The 700 years or so between the departure of the Romans and the Norman conquest in 1066 left practically no trace. William the Conqueror's White Tower in the Tower of London, begun in about 1077, is the oldest building still standing in the City.

Records are more complete from about the 13th century, by which time the little walled city was becoming ever more crowded. It was also prone to devastating fires. A building act passed then decreed that more stone be used for construction, and that the use of thatch as a roofing material be limited. But it went largely unheeded. Even as late as the 15th century, the great cathedral of St. Paul's still had a wooden steeple. (It fell down in 1561.)

Throughout the Middle Ages the greatest buildings in the City were ecclesiastical. The first monks and friars to arrive were the Dominicans, in 1221. They established

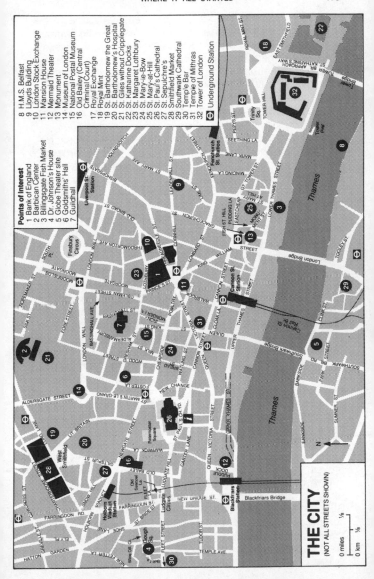

Points of Interest

1 Bank of England
2 Barbican Center
3 Billingsgate Fish Market
4 Dr. Johnson's House
5 Globe Theater site
6 Goldsmiths' Hall
7 Guildhall

8 H.M.S. Belfast
9 Lloyds Building
10 London Stock Exchange
11 Mansion House
12 Mermaid Theater
13 Monument
14 Museum of London
15 National Postal Museum
16 Old Bailey (Central Criminal Court)
17 Royal Exchange
18 Royal Mint
19 St. Bartholomew the Great
20 St. Bartholomew's Hospital
21 St. Giles without Cripplegate
22 St. Katharine Docks
23 St. Margaret Lothbury
24 St. Mary-ie-Bow
25 St. Mary-at-Hill
26 St. Paul's Cathedral
27 Sepulchre's
28 Smithfield Market
29 Southwark Cathedral
30 Temple Bar
31 Temple of Mithras
32 Tower of London
Ⓔ Underground Station

THE CITY
(NOT ALL STREETS SHOWN)

0 miles ⅛   ⅛
0 km

themselves by the Thames, in an area that came to be known as Blackfriars, after their black habits. The Franciscans, or Greyfriars, arrived soon afterwards, and it wasn't long before their churches were rivaling St. Paul's itself in size and splendor. It was around this time, too, that the City Livery Companies, or craft guilds, were formed, coming in time to control the mercantile and municipal life of the City. Most still exist, even though their crafts have long since declined.

In the 16th century Henry VIII dissolved the monasteries, grabbing their great wealth for himself. In the process, the way was paved for the further expansion of the Livery Companies. By the reign of Elizabeth I, at the end of the 16th century, a time of great mercantile wealth, their power and influence were at their height.

But Londoners were to pay for their wealth and consequent wickedness, in the eyes of the righteous, at least. The years 1665 and 1666 were the City's darkest, more devastating even than the Blitz in World War II. First, the Great Plague struck, killing one Londoner in four. The following year the Great Fire laid waste practically the whole area. Only nine people were actually killed by the fire, but practically the entire population was left homeless (see under **The Monument** for further details). The finest architectural phoenix born of the fire was the new St. Paul's Cathedral, the work of Sir Christopher Wren. But Wren also rebuilt 52 other churches, and these remain among the great treasures of the City, despite wartime damage to many.

Any remaining vestiges of the Middle Ages were lost in the 18th century, when the last city gates were pulled down, along with what was left of the Roman walls. The City suffered a further battering at the hands of the Victorians, who put up office blocks galore, and "improved" many of Wren's churches by tearing the fittings out, replacing them with interiors more suitable, they felt, for high-minded prayer. The devastation caused by the Blitz in 1940 and 1941—57 days and nights of near continuous bombing—led to further "improvements" after the war, much of it very ugly, and constituting a waste of a great opportunity for exciting redevelopment.

The City's colorful past can be hard to visualize among

today's gray reality, but there are clues. Wander through the maze of streets and alleys and you will come across ancient coats of arms representing the medieval trade guilds, and street names redolent of life in the Middle Ages: Ropemaker Street, Pudding Lane, Jewry Street, Poultry Street, Bread Street, and Fish Street. There are still great numbers of churches here, too, though many are no longer used. But they bear witness to the time when the City was a compact network of communities, each with its own parish church. Opening times of these churches are a problem for the visitor, though many are generally open for an hour or so at lunch. Don't be put off by the often unprepossessing exteriors. Wren especially concentrated his inventive energies on the interiors.

Major Attractions

BARBICAN CENTER FOR ARTS AND CONFERENCES, *Silk St., EC2Y 8DS (tel. 628 8795 for the booking office). While the building as a whole is open all day—until well after the last performance has finished—individual parts have their own closing times. For exhibition times call 638 4141. Tubes: Barbican, Moorgate, St. Paul's. (The route through the Barbican is best signposted from Moorgate.)* The Barbican is located in an ancient part of the City, with an equally ancient and evocative name. A "barbican" is a watchtower, and there used to be just such a tower here by the city walls for many years. Today, the Barbican is anything *but* historic and time-weathered. The area was mostly flattened during the Blitz, and the decision was taken after the war to make this a showcase for modern British architecture. As British architecture was going through a particularly bad patch at the time, the results were all too predictably disappointing. Deluxe high-rise apartment blocks—threaded through by a maze of passages, walkways, and bridges—tower over a central windswept piazza, with a shallow and murky lake and feeble fountains. To one side stands the rescued St. Giles-without-Cripplegate, one of the many historic City churches that was bombed during World War II.

But though the Barbican itself may be no great shakes architecturally, the Arts Center at its heart ranks among the best in Europe, and is a worthy rival to the South Bank complex. This is the London home of the Royal Shakespeare Company (the RSC), and the base for the London Symphony Orchestra. The two main auditoriums are housed in a building that is curiously turned in on itself, with some of the levels well buried, almost as if it were designed for well-heeled troglodytes. While the interior is lavishly decorated, there are very few windows to the outside, which, along with an extremely confusing system of stairways and elevators, makes it difficult for the first-time visitor to find the way around. But performances here, especially in the RSC's custom-designed auditorium, are well worth the trip. Prices, even for the best seats, are still relatively low—say £15 for the top price, and less than half that for the lowest—and the possibility of discounts makes it an even better prospect for the budget culture vulture. The RSC has a second, experimental, theater here, called The Pit, where plays are staged in the round. It is hidden in the bowels of the Center, beside a cinema which shows a mixture of current movies and classics. There is a good, recently refurbished cafeteria, and plenty of bars for coffee and drinks. At the top of the building, above the exhibition area and a branch of the local public library, is a big conservatory, about the only place in the Center where you can see greenery and sunlight.

Wandering the echoing, soulless expanses of the Barbican at night is not an experience to be recommended, so make sure you head for the tube with the crowds.

LLOYD'S OF LONDON, *Lime St., EC3M 7DQ (tel. 623 7100). Open daily 10–2:30. Admission free. Tubes: Bank, Monument.* The shiny new headquarters of Lloyd's, a company synonymous with the concept of insurance, can be found in Leadenhall Street, the continuation of Cornhill, just a short walk from the Bank tube station.

The extraordinary building was designed by Richard Rogers, architect of the Paris Pompidou Center, and it looks like something out of a science fiction movie. It is a sophisticated example of the let-it-all-hang-out high tech school of design, with transparent elevators whizzing soundlessly up and down outside, metal tubing everywhere, and a space-age atrium soaring up through the center of the building. Because it's still Lloyd's, and because it's still the home of sacred traditions, there are doormen in Dickensian red livery and top hats standing at the main entrance in Lime Street, ready to open your carriage (or limousine) door for you.

Just off Leadenhall Street, to the west of Lloyd's, is **Leadenhall Market,** a remarkable Victorian cream and maroon wrought-iron building containing a bustling weekday market. The site was the center of Roman London, and the remains of a basilica and other buildings were unearthed at the end of the last century.

MANSION HOUSE PLACE, *EC4. Tube: Bank.* This is the true hub of the City, site of three of its most important and historic institutions—the Bank of England, the Royal Exchange, and the Mansion House itself—and meeting place of seven streets: Poultry, Threadneedle, Princess, Queen Victoria, King William, Lombard, and Cornhill. In addition, there are dozens of other major financial institutions on and around Mansion House Place, among them the Stock Exchange.

The most striking building, and the most famous—even in these impecunious times its name still carries a splendid and weighty resonance—is the **Bank of England,** the Old Lady of Threadneedle Street. The bank can trace its origins back as far as 1694, and has been on this site since 1734. You can't actually go into it to see the huge and handsome 18th-century interiors, but the grand Classical exterior expresses much of the confidence and prestige that were once automatically associated with the phrase, in those days not even slightly ironic, "as solid as the pound sterling."

The **Mansion House** is opposite. This is the official residence of the Lord Mayor of London, though it's rarely used as such these days. The sumptuous State apartments, which are still sometimes used for official entertaining, are open to the public for guided tours Tues., Wed., and Thurs. at 11 and 2 (write The Principal Assistant, Mansion House, Mansion House Pl., London EC4N 8HH).

The strong room here guards all the gold and silver traditionally donated to the City by retiring Lord

Mayors—each serves for just one year—as well as the mayoral insignia; a crystal and gold scepter (part of which is believed to have been crafted in Saxon times); a gold and enamel collar dating from 1525; and the Mayor's mace and sword.

The ornate pediment of the building—it went up in about 1750—shows the City stamping on Envy while beckoning to Plenty, an appealing example of 18th-century allegory.

The third of this great trio of buildings is no less impressive. This is the **Royal Exchange,** an architectural Victorian paean to trade. Here, too, Commerce figures prominently among the jumble of heroic figures on the pediment. The building is no longer used as a meeting place for London's merchants and traders—it's actually the headquarters of an insurance company now—but its impressive and imperious Classical facade recalls its splendid heyday. It was opened in 1844 by a youthful Queen Victoria, nearly 300 years after Queen Elizabeth I had opened the first Royal Exchange. That original building was destroyed in the Great Fire, while its successor, the second Royal Exchange, also burned to the ground, in 1838.

MUSEUM OF LONDON, *London Wall, EC2Y 5HN (tel. 600 3699). Open Tues. to Sat. 10–6, Sun. 2–6. Admission free. Tubes: St. Paul's, Barbican, Moorgate.* If there's one place to get the history of London sorted out, it's here. More than 2,000 years unfold with the aid of reconstruction, relics, working models, costumes, weapons, background period music . . . everything to make the history of one of the world's greatest cities come alive. The museum is in a modern block, but capitalizes on its situation, with a long sloping window that looks out over a section of the ancient city wall still standing outside.

One of the highlights of the collection is the Lord Mayor's coach, resplendent in gold and red, which is still used in the Lord Mayor's Show, the procession held every November to celebrate the installation of a new Lord Mayor. There is a diorama of the Great Fire of 1666; audiovisual presentations; the Cheapside Hoard of Tudor jewelry, a collection that was possibly the stock of a 16th-century jeweler, which he had buried for safe keeping;

Oliver Cromwell's death mask; a 1780 doll's house, the miniature home of a wealthy household of the time; displays of the performing arts (some fine stage costumes), London in wartime, a 1932 BBC studio . . . in short the whole of London life crammed into one long chronological sequence.

You can either take the exhibits at a brisk pace, getting an overall view of the long development of London, or spend hours dwelling on the endless minutiae of the past that are on view. There is a good cafeteria handy for a coffee break. One word of warning. As the museum takes its role as a teaching facility very seriously, there are almost always parties of schoolchildren around, finding out about their own heritage, and ensuring that the place doesn't get too solemn.

ST. PAUL'S CATHEDRAL, *St. Paul's Churchyard, EC4M 8BU (tel. 284 2705). The cathedral itself is open for sightseeing daily to 6 in summer, to 5 in winter, except when in use for services. The ambulatory, crypt, and galleries are open Mon. to Fri. 10–4:15, Sat. from 11. Super Tours (so-called) lasting up to two hours and accompanied by a guide, take place Mon. to Sat. at 11, 11:30, and 2:30; charge is £3.25. Call for more information. There are admission charges to some areas. Tube: St. Paul's.* There had been a series of churches here for around 1,000 years before the Great Fire of London in 1666, the last being a Gothic cathedral which was almost totally destroyed, giving Sir Christopher Wren the chance to erect his masterwork. He is buried here, in the crypt, with one of the most telling epitaphs anywhere, *Lector, si monumentum requiris, circumspice*—Reader, if you seek his monument, look about you.

Despite its vast size, St. Paul's was built in just 35 years, finishing in 1710. This is an interior for state occasions, royal weddings, services of national thanksgiving or mourning—the great pageant of Nelson's funeral was held here, so was Churchill's. The huge dome is a technical triumph in itself, an elaborate brick cone built between inner and outer skins and strengthening both. The gallery that runs around the base is called the Whispering Gallery, where words breathed on one side can be heard on the other, 122 feet away. Unlike Westminster Abbey, St. Paul's has comparatively few memorials—Dr. Johnson's, John Donne's the poet and Dean Turner the painter, standing in his shroud, and a splendid one to the Duke of Wellington among them. The Jesus Chapel, behind the high altar, is dedicated to the 28,000 Americans stationed in Britain who lost their lives in World War II. There are yet more memorials in the crypt.

This is a most un-English cathedral which, despite its splendor and magnificent craftsmanship, lacks the atmosphere of many older English churches. There is a chill about it that seems to need the warmth of a Mediterranean sun to thaw its austere beauty. But there is no question that this is one of the world's great buildings. If only the same could be said for the huddle of badly designed, unimaginative boxes which crowd around its massive bulk, filling the gaps left by the bombs of the 1940s.

THE TOWER OF LONDON, *Tower Hill, EC3N 4AB (tel. 709 0765). Open Mon. to Sat. 9:30–5, Sun. 2–5, Mar. to Oct.; Mon. to Sat. 9:30–4, closed Sun. rest of the year. The Jewel House closes the whole of Feb. Admission £4, children £2. Tubes: Monument, Tower Hill.* Its unique architecture and turbulent, sinister history have made the Tower one of Britain's favorite tourist attractions, with the result that it gets very crowded, especially in summer. The most dramatic way to get there is by boat from Westminster pier, arriving in much the same way that condemned traitors did centuries ago. The more prosaic tube is only five minutes' walk away, though. However you arrive, it's wise to allow at least three hours for a visit. There's so much to see, and the lines can be so long.

The neatest way to explore the Tower, at any rate on the first visit, is to tag along on one of the free tours given by the Beefeaters—the Yeoman Warders of the Tower—who wear a distinctive Tudor costume, and start their tours every 15 minutes or so from the main entrance.

Built originally by William the Conqueror, starting in 1077, the Tower has been added to and extended numerous times over the centuries. It began life as a fortress—in which capacity it is still the home of the Crown Jewels— and as a palace, and it remains one of the royal palaces in name, though royalty hasn't lived here for centuries. At various times in its long history it has been the site of the Royal Mint, warehouse for the public records, location of the Royal Menagerie and the Royal Observatory, but, most famously, a prison and scene of countless executions.

The Tower straddles almost exactly the line of the old Roman city walls of London, fragments of which can still be seen. The **White Tower,** William's massive, brooding fortress, rises at the heart of the complex. When it was completed, in about 1097, it dominated the surrounding huddle of hovels, embodying the military might of the occupying Normans. The graceful cupolas on the four corner towers were largely the work of Wren in the 17th century and don't really soften the White Tower's imposing presence. Even though others apart from Wren have made changes to this tower, the building is still essentially Norman. The only part of the interior that is of major interest is the **Chapel of St. John,** the original Norman chapel, which is very simply designed, lacking in ornamentation, built in the characteristically weighty Norman style, but enormously impressive. It is one of London's foremost architectural treasures. The rest of the White Tower is used to display armor and weapons from many periods.

Surrounding the White Tower, the various buildings and fortifications vary in date from the 11th to the 19th century. If you start from the main entrance, **the moat** is the most striking feature, drained at the orders of the Duke of Wellington, hero of the Battle of Waterloo, in 1843. Until that time the moat was unbelievably polluted, and obstinately resisted all attempts to flush it out with water from the Thames. It was so foul that no prisoner ever succeeded in swimming the 128-foot width.

Across the moat a series of gateways, the **Middle Tower** and the **Byward Tower,** form the principal entrances on the landward side. You can't use them, though, and will have to follow the wharf, outside the Tower proper. Here stands **St. Thomas' Tower,** with **Traitors' Gate** beneath. This was once the main river entrance, by which the most important prisoners were delivered into durance vile. Immediately opposite Traitors' Gate is the **Wakefield Tower,** with the misleadingly named **Bloody Tower** next to it.

The Bloody Tower, built around 1380, was originally

known as the Garden Tower, and its present name can be traced back only as far as 1597. The tower's most celebrated inmates were the little princes, monstrously murdered on the orders of their uncle, Richard III, or so the story goes. Though nobody knows who was responsible for their deaths, it seems certain that they did die here. Sir Walter Raleigh was imprisoned here, too, between 1603 and 1616. He passed the time writing a history of the world. His wife lived here with him, and his son Carew was actually born in the Tower. His spacious rooms look much the same now as they did during his imprisonment. Sir Walter was released in 1616 to lead an expedition to El Dorado. The inevitable failure of his mission led to his execution in the Tower two years later. His widow used to carry his head in a velvet bag and ask people if they had met her husband.

The Wakefield Tower is a ponderous circular structure. For a brief period in the 14th century the national archives were kept here, and Henry VI was allegedly murdered here, one among the thousands of victims of the Wars of the Roses, England's bloody medieval civil war.

Inside the inner wall, or ward, you will find the sinister-looking ravens, long a feature of the Tower. Legend has it that the disappearance of these ill-omened birds will signal the disintegration of the kingdom. They have been known to attack visitors, so keep your eye on them.

Running the length of the inner compound on the east side are a series of buildings dating from the 17th to the 19th centuries—the **New Armories,** the **Hospital,** and the **Museum of the Royal Fuseliers.** The gloomy 19th-century bulk of the **Waterloo Barracks** takes up the north side. They house an interesting Oriental Gallery, and the Heralds' Museum, quite a recent addition, which is very informative on the recherché subject of heraldry.

Every visitor to the Tower wants to see the **Crown Jewels,** with the result that the waiting line is almost always a long one. Perhaps the most startling part of the Royal Regalia are the Royal Scepter, containing the largest cut diamond in the world, an incredible 530 carats, and the Imperial State Crown, made for the coronation of Queen Victoria in 1838, and inlaid with some 3,000 precious stones, mainly diamonds and pearls, including the second-largest cut diamond in the world which, like the one in the scepter, was cut from the Cullinan Diamond—the Star of Africa. In the crown made for the coronation of Queen Elizabeth (now the Queen Mother) in 1937 is the immense Koh-i-noor diamond.

To the west of the Waterloo Barracks is the little chapel of **St. Peter ad Vincula,** a parish church that was swallowed when the Tower walls were extended in the 1240s. This is the site of the burial over the years of some 2,000 prisoners, whose corpses were dumped under the flagstones after execution. It is also the resting place for some more celebrated victims of the executioner, among them Anne Boleyn, who had also been married to Henry VIII here in the Tower; Sir Thomas More; and Elizabeth's favorite, the Earl of Essex.

Directly outside the chapel is **Tower Green,** used both as an overflow burial ground when the chapel was full, and as the site of the very small number of private executions carried out in the Tower. There is a bronze tablet to mark the supposed place where the block stood. Most people were dispatched on nearby Tower Hill, where the thousands who flocked to watch could be accommodated.

To the west of Tower Green is the **Beauchamp** (pronounced Beecham) **Tower,** dating mainly from the reign of Henry VIII and used to house prisoners of importance. It is here, as much as anywhere in the Tower, that the eerie sense of the centuries rolling away is most vivid. The walls are liberally covered with graffiti and inscriptions (some actually brought here from other parts of the Tower), carved by despairing prisoners. A good many are in Latin—including the one that has traditionally been assumed to refer to Lady Jane Grey, who lost her head in 1554 in a failed attempt to gain the crown.

To the south of the Beauchamp Tower is an L-shaped row of black-and-white Tudor houses, the center one known as the **Queens House.** It dates from 1530. Here Anne Boleyn was imprisoned before her execution, and here the conspirators in the Gunpowder Plot of 1605 were interrogated and tortured.

Finally, you can get an excellent overview of the Tower from the battlements. There is a **walkway** along the walls of the inner ward, from the Wakefield Tower round to the

Martin Tower, with the possibility of further stretches being opened in future. It makes a fitting climax to the visit to gaze across the site where so much of the pomp, violence, and brutality of England's history has been enacted.

TOWER BRIDGE, *Tower Hill, EC3 (tel. 407 0922). Open daily 10–6:30, Apr. to Oct.; 10–4:45 Nov. to Mar. Admission £2. Tube: Tower Hill.* Tower Bridge is one of the popular symbols of London, along with Big Ben and the Beefeaters, even though it is a comparative newcomer to the London scene, dating only from the late 1880s. As it stands so close to the Tower, it was designed in a Gothic style, to harmonize with that ancient fortress, and now seems to have stood there always. It's an unusual bridge, in that the lower span can be opened to let tall ships pass through, though the days of regular heavy traffic on the Thames are over, and the bascules, as the raising sections are called, open only irregularly, some weeks four or five times, some not at all. In the end towers there are exhibitions related to the bridge and to the Thames in general, while from the second level you can get magnificent views up and downriver—a great place for the camera buff.

Other Attractions

DR. JOHNSON'S HOUSE, *17 Gough Sq., EC4A 3DE (tel. 353 3745). Open Mon. to Sat. 11–5:30, May to Sept.; 11–5, Oct. to Apr.; closed Sun. Admission £1.30. Tube: Blackfriars.* This was Dr. Johnson's home from 1749–59, and it was here that he compiled his dictionary. You can reach it by turning off Fleet Street at narrow Bolt Lane and following the winding alley into Gough Square. It is an appropriately 17th-century house, exactly the kind of place you would expect the Great Bear, as Johnson was nicknamed, to live in, the rooms now containing displays of relics of his period there, and of his friends and enemies. Round the corner in Wine Office Court is the Old Cheshire Cheese pub, with historic beams and ancient fireplaces, once Johnson and Boswell's favorite watering hole.

GUILDHALL, *King St., Cheapside, EC2P 2EJ (tel. 606 3030). Great Hall open Mon. to Fri. 9:30–5, unless a function is*

*taking place; Library open Mon. to Sat. 9:30–5; Clock
Museum open Mon. to Fri. 9:30–4:45; Art Gallery closed for
rebuilding. Admission free. Tubes: Bank, Moorgate, St.
Paul's.* The Guildhall was the center for the medieval trade
unions—the guilds—and is still the main focus for the
ceremonial life of the City. The building dates from around
1410, but has had more than its share of disasters, fires,
bombs, and alterations during its long life. Indeed only the
porch and one 15th-century window remain from the
original structure. It was severely damaged in the Great
Fire of 1666, was rebuilt, updated during the 18th and 19th
centuries, and nearly destroyed again by the Germans in
1940. But it is still an impressive structure, and a fitting
setting for the big civic events that are held here—the
election of the Lord Mayor and other City officers, banquets for visiting heads of state, celebrations of such
national days of rejoicing as the Silver Jubilee of the
Queen. The City of London records are housed here at
the Guildhall, and include documents going back nine
centuries.

Many City companies have their own guild halls around
here (mostly called livery halls): the Haberdashers, Wax
Chandlers, Pewterers, Brewers, Girdlers, Armorers and
Braziers, Grocers, Mercers, and, of course, the Goldsmiths,
whose magnificent collection of gold and silver plate is
sometimes on view to the public (in Goldsmiths' Hall at
the corner of Foster Lane and Gresham Street).

THE MONUMENT AND LONDON BRIDGE, *Monument St.,
EC3R 8AH (tel. 626 2717). Open Mon. to Fri. 9–6, Sat. and
Sun. 2–6, Apr. to Sept.; Mon. to Sat. 9–4, rest of the year;
closed Sun. Admission 50p. Tube: Monument.* This is a
massive Doric column of white stone, put up in 1667—
designed, of course, by Wren—to commemorate the Great
Fire of London. It stands 202 feet high, with its base
exactly 202 feet from the small bakery in Pudding Lane
where the fire started. The fire began at 2 A.M. on September 2, burned for three days and two nights, and during its
holocaust 89 churches and 13,200 houses were destroyed,
over an area of 400 acres. The amazing thing was that only
nine people lost their lives.

It's quite a climb to the top, 311 steps, but there's a

magnificent view from up there, just below the symbolic gilt urn with flames leaping from it.

Between the Monument and the Thames is the site of the former **Billingsgate Fish Market,** which was moved downriver to the Isle of Dogs in 1982. There has been a settlement here for well over 2,000 years—it was a Roman wharf, and the site has served a similar purpose for succeeding centuries. When the market was transplanted, archeologists moved in to excavate the area, but their complete findings are not yet known.

Next door is the **Custom House** *(Lower Thames St., EC3)*. The present building dates from 1852, but the first Custom House was built hereabouts in the 1380s. Downstream are the **Sugar Quay,** home of the sugar company, Tate and Lyle, and **Tower Pier,** where you can catch a boat to Greenwich or Westminster.

To the right is **London Bridge.** There has been a succession of London Bridges—wooden ones until 1176, when the first stone one was erected. It had such small arches, 19 of them, that the dammed-up water poured through in a dangerous torrent, and "shooting the bridge" became a daredevil sport. The bridge was also used to display the severed heads of traitors—Sir Thomas More among them.

This totally impractical structure somehow lasted until the 1820s, when it was pulled down to make way for a more elegant one. This, too, was replaced in 1967, when it could no longer cope with the volume of traffic, and the dismantled bridge was sold to the McCulloch Oil Corporation of California, and reconstructed in a corner of the Arizona desert, at Lake Havasu City. The popular myth in London is that the company thought it were buying the much more spectacular Tower Bridge and only found their mistake when they began to unpack it.

OLD BAILEY (CENTRAL CRIMINAL COURT), *Old Bailey, EC4M 7EH (tel. 248 3277). Public Gallery open 10–1, 2–4 (stand on line at the Newgate St. entrance). Tube: St. Paul's.* The Old Bailey, the place where all the headline-catching trials take place, stands on the site of one of London's grisliest jails, Newgate. This is a modern building, opened in 1907 and then considerably extended in 1971, which carries its famous symbol on top of its dome, a gilt statue of Justice, blindfolded and carrying her scales and sword.

Check the day's hearings on the sign outside, where the happenings in courts 1–19 are listed, then join the lines at the Public Gallery Entrance. There's always a rush when the doors are opened. Seats in the old courts 1–3 (much the most atmospheric) are keenly sought, for those are the ones where the more newsworthy trials are usually held. Courts 4–19, the more modern ones, have a restricted view of the courtroom from all but the front seats. You can move from court to court, within reason, to find a case that's to your taste.

ST. BARTHOLOMEW THE GREAT, *West Smithfield, EC1A 7JQ (tel. 606 5171). Tube: St. Paul's.* This is the second-oldest church in London, and was founded—like its neighbor, the hospital, next door—by the Normans in 1123. More specifically, it was founded by Rahere, the court jester to Henry I, following a dream in which St. Bartholomew appeared to him. Rahere became the prior of his own Augustinian priory, and is buried in a fine tomb in the choir. The story has all the elements of a popular medieval folk tale, although it is unquestionably true. The church is approached through an Elizabethan gateway, whose timbers were revealed as a result of a World War I bomb. Inside there is architecture from several periods, but far and away the most striking area is the choir, the only part left of the Norman building. Its round arches and massive pillars show quite clearly how the Normans adapted their skills as builders of castles to the job of building for God. The church is often used for concerts, and makes a wonderfully peaceful port of call at lunchtime, especially if they are playing Bach or Handel.

Next door is **Smithfield,** the main meat market for London, which makes an unusual, and very photogenic, stop on a walking tour through the City. Restaurants in the neighborhood naturally serve excellent meat dishes!

ST. KATHARINE'S DOCK, *E1. Tube: Tower Hill.* An echo of the Port of London's once thriving docklands can be found here, close to the Tower and past the Tower Hotel and David Wynne's delightful statue of a girl with a dolphin. St. Katharine's, just like London's other docks, was once the goal for cargoes from all over the world, but as trade died away, so the whole area of the docks fell into disrepair and decay. Unlike many of the others, though, St. Katharine's has found a new purpose in life. Part of the dock is now a marina for small craft, and a last port of call for some smaller historic boats. One of the old warehouses, the **Ivory House,** which indeed was once a storehouse for ivory tusks, has been converted into a fine set of imaginative apartments, cleverly using the features of the building. There is a series of shops and bars here, and, across the dock, the **Dickens Inn,** a completely reborn building—the whole structure has even been moved—which hosts evenings of rather rowdy Dickens-inspired and tourist-oriented entertainment. For a relaxing hour after visiting the Tower, drop by St. Katharine's Dock.

THE STOCK EXCHANGE, *Old Broad St., EC2N 1HP (tel. 588 2355). Open Mon. to Fri. 9:45–3:15. Guided tours at regular intervals. Admission free. Tube: Bank.* Although it no longer has the bustle and drama that it had before the days of the computerized "Big Bang," a visit to the Stock Exchange is still a thoroughly instructive experience. The guided tours and the accompanying films that illustrate how the system works go a long way to explaining just why the City of London is still the international financial powerhouse that it is—even after the disastrous 19th of October, 1987.

Lunch Spots

We have not graded our lunch spot suggestions; they all carry a range of dishes at various prices to suit your taste and pocket. The best-value budget bets are the pubs in the area; these often have the most atmosphere as well.

Balls Brothers, 42 Threadneedle St., EC2R 8AR. The cozy, wood-paneled bar with its interesting wine list, delicious sandwiches, and cheeses is much favored by City gents. There are other branches in the City.

Barbican Arts Complex, Barbican Center, Silk St., EC2Y 8DS. While there is a carvery-type restaurant—indigestibly decorated in pink and purple—there's also a very adequate self-service cafeteria, recently redecorated, and always busy. On fine days you can eat outside by the water.

Food for Health, 15 Blackfriars Lane, EC4V 6ER. A popular self-service, vegetarian restaurant, Food for Health serves good casseroles, pasta, omelets, and salads—the menu changes daily. It's very handy for St. Paul's.

Magpie and Stump, 18 Old Bailey, EC4M 7EP. You can get reasonably priced pub food in this hostelry, notable chiefly for its clientele, who spill over from the Central Criminal Court across the road. In the days when Britain still had the death penalty, the public hangman used to have his breakfast here.

Mother Bunches, Arches F & G, Old Seacoal Lane, EC4M 7LR. Just down the hill from St. Paul's, in a little street off Ludgate Hill, this eatery is high on decibels, strives for atmosphere (with sawdust on the floor), but generally makes for a lively lunch.

Vic Naylor's Bar and Grill, 38–40 St. John St., EC1M 4QJ. You'll find this interesting spot in a converted woodyard in Smithfield, with a varied menu offering grills, sausage and mash, and inventive salads.

Whittington's Wine Bar, 21 College Hill, EC4R 2RP. As the name suggests, this vaulted cellar is reputed to have been owned by Dick Whittington, a medieval Lord Mayor of London, and a character in popular Christmas shows. There is buffet food at the bar, or you can lunch in the small restaurant.

A PERCH FOR CULTURE VULTURES

◆

To Londoners, the South Bank means the riverside stretch between Waterloo Bridge and Hungerford Bridge which, since the 1950s, has been taken over by Culture with a capital and emphatically illuminated C. It was here, in 1951, that the nation finally threw off the dreary cares of wartime and staged the huge Festival of Britain which not only gave everyone a brighter outlook on life, but also launched a new school of design, bringing a different look to the country that led up to the Swinging Sixties. The year 1951 was chosen as it was the anniversary of the 1851 Great Exhibition which had been held in Hyde Park and gave a focus to the inventiveness of the industrial Victorian age. The only part of the festival site that remains today is the Royal Festival Hall, now a dowager among modern concert halls. It forms the nucleus of the South Bank Arts Complex.

It is fitting that so much of London's artistic life should be centered here on the South Bank, for Shakespeare's original Globe Theater stood just a short distance downstream. A new Globe is being planned on approximately the

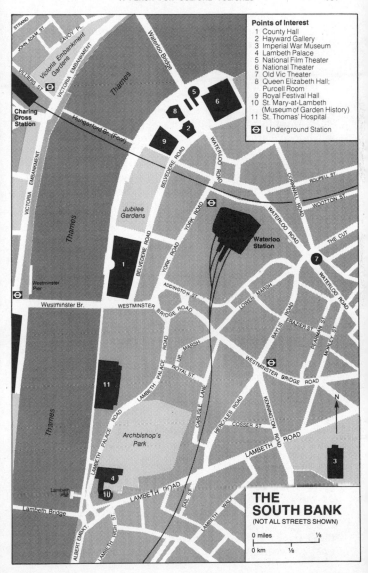

Points of Interest
1 County Hall
2 Hayward Gallery
3 Imperial War Museum
4 Lambeth Palace
5 National Film Theater
6 National Theater
7 Old Vic Theater
8 Queen Elizabeth Hall;
  Purcell Room
9 Royal Festival Hall
10 St. Mary-at-Lambeth
  (Museum of Garden History)
11 St. Thomas' Hospital

Ⓔ Underground Station

**THE
SOUTH BANK**
(NOT ALL STREETS SHOWN)

0 miles   ⅛
0 km   ⅛

same spot, where it is hoped to stage Shakespeare's plays much as the first Elizabethans would have seen them. The fund-raising drive is headed by the American actor Sam Wanamaker.

The most obvious way of getting to the South Bank is either by tube to Waterloo, and from there simply following the signs, or—and much more interestingly—by getting off the tube at the Embankment station and walking over the Hungerford footbridge, which runs immediately beside the rail bridge carrying trains to Charing Cross station. The second route has several advantages: first, there are often good musicians busking somewhere along the bridge; second, you have an exceptional view eastwards over London's skyline, with the dome of St. Paul's standing out among the skyscrapers; and third, you're much less likely to get lost that way—all you have to do is walk across the bridge with the Festival Hall in full view the whole time. Steer clear of this route at rush hour, though, because crowds of commuters tear across it to reach Waterloo and their trains home.

Beyond the Arts Complex—all of whose component parts are among the attractions listed below—lies the wilderness of Lambeth, a fairly depressed area, but with one or two outstanding points of interest (especially the Old Vic Theater).

To the western end of the South Bank lies Lambeth Palace, the London residence of the Archbishop of Canterbury, with the Imperial War Museum tucked away in the hinterland behind. It is possible to walk all the way along the river from the palace, past the Arts Complex, almost as far as Blackfriars Bridge. From the end of the walk you can strike inland again to find Southwark Cathedral, with its Harvard Chapel.

Major Attractions

SILVER JUBILEE WALKWAY. *Tubes: Waterloo, Lambeth North (at the Lambeth Palace end).* This long riverside walk is named for the 1977 Silver Jubilee of Queen Elizabeth II. It was an imaginative scheme, which opened up vistas over the Thames that, in some cases, hadn't been seen for at least 200 years. Although, to be accurate, the Silver Jubilee

Walkway covers just the stretch along the South Bank, it is actually possible to start further upstream, at **Lambeth Palace.** From here you can stroll downstream, looking across the obsidian waters of the river at the Victoria Tower Gardens and the whole majestic bulk of the Houses of Parliament. You'll pass on your left the old and new buildings of **St. Thomas's Hospital,** one of London's best teaching hospitals, badly damaged during World War II.

Cross over the end of **Westminster Bridge** (with a sally onto the bridge for better views of the Houses of Parliament), and you are on the **Albert Embankment,** in front of the curving, classical front of **County Hall.** This is where the Greater London Council (the governing body for the whole of London except the City) used to have its offices. The Council has been disbanded, and no use has yet been found for this vast 1922 building. On the other side of the river are the Victoria Embankment and the looming shapes of government offices, with Whitehall behind them. Next on the Walkway come the **Jubilee Gardens,** then you will be passing under **Hungerford Bridge.**

You have now reached the **South Bank Arts Complex.** Stay on the embankment level and walk under **Waterloo Bridge.** There are usually several bookstalls selling both new and secondhand books here, as well as outdoor seating if you want to drop into the national Film Theater's cafeteria for coffee and a bite to eat. You will have noticed the tall, ornate lamp standards most of the way along, with entwined dolphins at their base; some are original Victorian pieces, the others good recent copies. There are also several modern sculptures along the way, and some unusual garden designs, like the curved stone walls enclosing narrow steps, immediately in front of the lowest level of the Festival Hall.

Once past Waterloo Bridge, you are onto the newest stretch of the Silver Jubilee Walkway, opened in October '87. From this section you'll have a magnificent view of the opposite bank, dominated by skyscrapers, and the cupolas and massy dome of St. Paul's. Halfway along, there is a plan to help you identify all the buildings that you can see. The walkway here is cantilevered out over the river to make a better viewing platform, in one place by as much as

35 yards. There are plans to open up even more of this bank, and a part of the extension may even be ready by early 1988. Eventually it might be possible to walk all the way along the Thames from its distant source right down to the Thames Barrier.

Since so much of London is floodlit at night, this walk can be even more exciting then, especially as it gives the opportunity to see the Houses of Parliament and St. Paul's in, literally, a new light.

THE SOUTH BANK ARTS COMPLEX, *SE1. Tubes: Embankment, Waterloo.* As we have said above, the South Bank Arts Complex had its genesis on this site in 1951, when the Festival of Britain was staged on a stretch of the riverbank devastated by bomb damage. The Festival Hall was remarkable for its time, born in a period of austerity when Britain was still reeling from the traumas of war. The Festival Hall stands elegantly foursquare, as a testament to the hope of that epoch. Trains thunder past its side—the soundproofing copes with that problem extremely well— while its wide glass facade airily fronts the river. It wears its years with surprising lightness.

The rest of the buildings in the complex have not weathered their fewer years as well. They group themselves around—and indeed *under*—Waterloo Bridge like huge fortresses, with their concrete sides black-streaked by London's notoriously dirty weather. Here are the other concert halls, the Queen Elizabeth Hall and the Purcell Room, both in the same building—the one the most comfortable auditorium on the South Bank, used mainly for music that demands smaller resources, chamber pieces, and small choral works; the other a cozy recital room.

Next comes the National Film Theater (NFT), an essential mecca for every movie maven. One of the NFT's auditoriums (there are two) is actually located in an arch of Waterloo Bridge. Beside it is being built the Museum of the Moving Image, due to open some time in 1988. Dominating the complex at the rear is the Hayward Gallery, with a tall neon sculpture on its roof whose racing lights are governed by the speed of the wind funneling through an anemometer.

On the other side of Waterloo Bridge is the National

Theater, the last part of the complex to be built. Already the trees around it are maturing, helping to soften some of its harshness of line. A lighted, moving sign, high up on the river facade, tells the world on both sides of the Thames, and those crossing the bridge, what's on, and any other handy information.

And there is quite a lot going on on the South Bank all day: foyer performances in the National Theater, afternoon events in the concert halls, and Hayward Gallery exhibitions to see. There are also about 10 cafeterias for the visitor who wants to sit down and, if he chooses the right one, to enjoy the view. Of course, the place comes into its own in the evening, when all the auditoriums are going full tilt.

Hayward Gallery, *Belvedere Rd., SE1 8XZ (tel. 928 5708). Open Mon. to Wed. 10–8, Thurs. to Sat. 10–6, Sun. 12–6. Admission £3 (half price Mon., and after 6 Tues. and Wed.). Tubes: Waterloo, Embankment.* Major exhibitions, often of internationally celebrated artists, come here as part of the capital city circuit, including such places as Paris, New York, and so on.

National Film Theater, *South Bank, SE1 8XT (tel. 928 3232). Weekly membership, available from the box office at 80p, a better bet than a monthly one for visiting film buffs.* The Theater shows a vast range of films, some impossible to see anywhere else, many from its huge library.

National Theater, *Upper Ground, SE1 9PX (tel. 928 2252 for box office, 928 8126 for 24-hour recorded booking information).* Three auditoriums, the Olivier, the Lyttleton, and Cottesloe, range in size from the huge to the intimate. Plays are performed in repertory and none, however popular, for too long—so planning ahead is not easy. There are frequent transfers, however, to the West End. The National has several cafeterias, a good restaurant, and a very good drama bookshop.

Royal Festival Hall, Queen Elizabeth Hall, Purcell Room, *Belvedere Rd., SE1 8XX (tel. 928 3191 for box office). Tubes: Waterloo, Embankment.* These three concert halls are run together, though in two buildings. They, like the National Theater's, range down in size from the large to the intimate, and each specializes in concerts of music suitable to their capacity. There are always exhibitions in the Festival Hall, plus a large music-orientated bookshop, and a small record store. There are cafeterias on both the lower level and the main floor—though they are very busy just before concert time.

SOUTHWARK CATHEDRAL, *Borough High St., SE1 (tel. 407 2939). Tube: London Bridge.* Across the river from St. Paul's, and several centuries older, Southwark Cathedral is one of the finest Gothic buildings in London. For American visitors the highlight of a visit will be the Harvard Chapel, which commemorates John Harvard, founder of the university in Massachusetts, who was baptised here in 1607.

Other Attractions

HMS BELFAST, *Symon's Wharf, Vine Lane, Tooley St., SE1 2JH (tel. 407 6434). Open daily, 11–5:50 in summer, 11–4:30 in winter. Admission £3, children £1.50. Tubes: London Bridge, Tower Hill (then ferry from Tower Pier). HMS Belfast* is moored directly opposite the Tower of London, and can be reached either by boat from the jetty at the Tower, or by walking across Tower Bridge and turning right at the south end to reach Symon's Wharf. At 11,000 tons, she is the largest cruiser ever built for the Royal Navy and saw action in many parts of the world, including the Far East during the Korean War. She was permanently moored here in 1971.

IMPERIAL WAR MUSEUM, *Lambeth Rd., SE1 6HZ (tel. 735 8922). Open Mon. to Sat. 10–5:50, Sun. 2–5:50. Admission free (but contributions welcomed). Tubes: Lambeth North, Elephant and Castle.* The museum contains a Commonwealth (despite its name) collection of photographs, paintings, memorabilia, uniforms, and so on, illustrating the history of British and Commonwealth military operations, in particular the two World Wars. It lies a little south (inland) from Lambeth Palace.

LAMBETH PALACE, *Lambeth Palace Rd., SE1 7JU (tel. 928 8282). Open to groups by appointment only; write to the Palace Secretary. Tube: Lambeth North.* Lambeth Palace has been the official residence of the Archbishop of

Canterbury (head of the Church of England, after the Queen) for almost eight centuries—which is why it's open to members of the public by appointment only. It is, however, such an atmospheric piece of English history that we are including it in the hope that you will be able to get inside. The palace buildings date from a variety of periods; the main structure is early 19th-century Gothic Revival, and the arched gatehouse late-15th-century Tudor. It is an island of deep peace in the middle of a turbulent surge of modern traffic, but it was not always so. Heretics were tried here, the first prayer book in English was written here in the 1540s, Archbishop Cranmer arranged Henry VIII's marriages and divorces here, and angry crowds (such as Wat Tyler's in 1382 and the Gordon rioters in 1780) stormed the walls, burning everything they could lay their hands on, and, on one or two memorable occasions, causing the archbishop to flee.

LONDON DUNGEON, *28 Tooley St., SE1 2SZ (tel. 403 0606). Admission £3.50 (£2 for children under 14). Tube: London Bridge.* A waxworks show celebrating the more gruesome aspects of British history—and there are plenty of them! This is ideal for children of a gory disposition, but at these prices, you'll have to weigh gore against filthy lucre.

MUSEUM OF GARDEN HISTORY, *St. Mary-at-Lambeth Palace Rd., SE1 7JU (tel. 261 1891). Open from 1st Sun. in Mar. to 2nd Sun. in Dec., Mon. to Fri. 11–3, Sun. 10:30–5; closed rest of year, and all day Sat. Admission free. Tube: Lambeth North.* Right under the Archbishop's nose is a church that has outlived its religious usefulness and has been deconsecrated. But, in common with many such churches in Britain, it has found a new role. Its name is something of a misnomer, as it is really a museum dedicated to the work of two Tradescants, father and son, who lived in the 17th century and traveled widely (as far afield as Russia and North America), bringing back cuttings and seeds which later became standard British plants. The part of the church that is not dedicated to the Tradescants has a villagey air to it, tea and cakes in one corner, stalls selling lavender bags and corn dollies in another. The cemetery outside—where the Tradescants are buried, alongside Captain Bligh, of *Mutiny on the Bounty* fame—is laid out as a 17th-century garden, using, among others, plants discovered by the two intrepid gardeners themselves.

THE OLD VIC THEATER, *Waterloo Rd., SE1 8NB (tel. 928 7616 for booking office). Tube: Waterloo.* Many of the recent developments in Britain's theater started in this Victorian building. The National Theater, the Royal Ballet, and the English National Opera all began life here under the eagle eye of Lilian Baylis at the beginning of the century, though under different names. With the move of the National Theater to its new home on the river close by, the Old Vic was without a role to play for the first time in decades. At last a Canadian businessman, Ed Mervish, came to the rescue. He had the internal accretions of pointless walls ripped out, and restored the interior of the building to its original Victorian looks—with the added benefit of new stage machinery, and a series of dove grey foyers linked by a curving staircase. A new company under the direction of Jonathon Miller, whose productions have been startling the critical establishment for a decade or more, will start performing a mixture of classics and new plays early in 1988. It will be welcomed at the Old Vic as the start of a new chapter in the life of a very old and much loved theater. Try for a performance.

Lunch Spots

We have not graded our lunch spot suggestions; they all carry a range of dishes at various prices to suit your taste and pocket. The best-value budget bets are the pubs in the area; these often have the most atmosphere as well.

Archduke, Arch 153, Concert Hall Approach, SE1 8XU. Two railway arches are the unlikely setting for this useful spot by the Festival Hall Arts Complex. Try it for interesting food; the house specialty is international sausage dishes.

La Barca, 81–83 Lower Marsh, SE1 7AB. Reliable, homemade pasta served with classic Italian sauces is served in this thespian haunt—note the souvenir photograph-lined walls. Watch what you're ordering if you want to stay in the budget range.

Café de la Gare, 19 York Rd., SE1 7NJ. Inside Waterloo rail station, you'll find this interesting French-style café in what used to be a WC. The delicious soups, salads, and desserts are served in either the restaurant or the bar.

Dining Room, Winchester Walk, SE1. In a basement close to Southwark Cathedral, this interesting spot serves good, international vegetarian food at reasonable prices.

National Film Theater, Belvedere Rd., South Bank, SE1 8XT. On a terrace under an arch of Waterloo Bridge, this inexpensive restaurant serves the usual in the way of quiches, salads, and sandwiches.

National Theater, Upper Ground, South Bank, SE1 9PX. Only the Lyttleton Buffet is open at lunchtime. The menu offers the standard quiche and salad fare; it's not as good as the Festival Hall or the NFT, but it is somewhere to have a coffee or a drink.

Royal Festival Hall, Belvedere Rd., South Bank, SE1 8XX. The newly refurbished cafeteria on the lower floor offers excellent food at reasonable prices. On the upper floor there is a buffet with salads, pizza, and salt beef sandwiches. There's pleasant outdoor eating in summer, as well as a coffee bar and snack bar—sometimes with live classical music.

South of the Border, 8 Joan St., SE1 8DA. This is one of the few restaurants near the Old Vic theater that is good for pre- or post-theater dining as well as lunch. It's in a converted bed factory with English, country-kitchen-style decor; there's also an upper gallery room. The menu offers an interesting selection of international food—some of it quite exotic. This is another eatery where you'd be wise to watch what you're ordering, to stay in a budget range.

Green Acres

Visitors to the Regents Park area have at hand the Zoo, the park itself, with its summer display of prize roses in Queen Mary's Gardens, and, just down the Marylebone (pronounced "Mar-le-bun") Road, Madame Tussaud's. The fictitious address of the fictitious Sherlock Holmes can also be tracked down at 221B Baker Street—the number of the Abbey National Building Society. A walk around the perimeters of the park will give devotees of Classical architecture a thrill, for John Nash's long and lovely terraces are among the finest sections of inspired town planning anywhere.

If Regent's Park is really a summer destination, especially for anyone who wants to end their day with a performance at the Open Air Theater, Hampstead is even more so. Lying further north than the park, the village of Hampstead—and it is still recognizably a village—has always had the reputation of being a place apart from the rest of the capital. This is partly geographical, of course, but the almost countrified atmosphere of the neighborhood has exerted a special attraction over the years for literati, radical politicians and thinkers, musicians, and indeed for anyone wanting to combine the pleasures of country life with the excitement of being close in to the center of things. "Hampstead" is a synonym for free thinking, liberal, a bit oddball—rather the same as "Village" in New York, but perhaps more upscale.

The discovery of mineral springs in the 18th century turned Hampstead from a place of refuge in time of pestilence or disaster to a decidedly fashionable place to live, with the result that there are plenty of small streets of extremely attractive period houses, which now command extremely modern prices. We briefly describe a walk round the area under **Flask Walk** below. It is a fine way of spending a day out of the center of town—if your vacation allows you so much leeway.

Major Attractions

KENWOOD HOUSE, *Hampstead Lane, NW3 7JR (tel. 348 1286). Open daily 10–7 in summer; 10–5 Feb., Mar., and Oct.; 10–4 Nov. to Jan. Admission free. Tubes: Archway, Golders Green; then bus 210.* This, the principal sight on Hampstead Heath, is a fine country house standing in spacious landscaped grounds that were united with the Heath proper when the house was opened to the public in 1924. The original 17th-century building was substantially remodeled by John Adam at the end of the 18th century. He refaced much of the exterior, and created the handsome neo-Classical Library, a gorgeously colored and gilded room with unusual curved ends. The chief treasures of

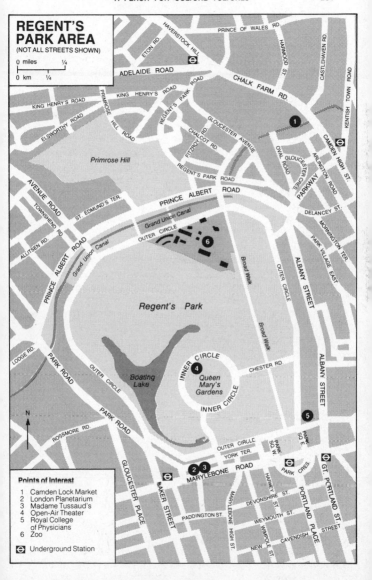

REGENT'S PARK AREA
(NOT ALL STREETS SHOWN)

0 miles   ¼
0 km   ¼

Primrose Hill

Regent's Park

Grand Union Canal

Boating Lake

Inner Circle

Queen Mary's Gardens

Inner Circle

Broad Walk

Prince Albert Road

Marylebone Road

Points of Interest

1 Camden Lock Market
2 London Planetarium
3 Madame Tussaud's
4 Open-Air Theater
5 Royal College of Physicians
6 Zoo

⊖ Underground Station

N

Kenwood, though, are the pictures. They belonged to the Earl of Iveagh, who gave them to the nation in 1927. (The place's proper name is "The Iveagh Bequest.") Like the Wallace collection in Manchester Square—and indeed, the Frick in New York—this magnificent collection is greatly enhanced by being displayed not in the formal surroundings of a museum, but in the kind of grand house for which most of the works would originally have been painted. This is particularly true of the superb portraits by Reynolds, Lawrence, Van Dyck, and Gainsborough, though there are also magnificent works here by Rembrandt, Vermeer, Guardi, and Turner, among others. Upstairs is a small collection of jewelry and such accessories as antique shoe clips and buckles.

The lawns in front of the house run down to a small lake crossed by a charming fake bridge, just the sort of stage scenery that the 18th-century upper class delighted in. The lake itself is the setting for some of London's celebrated open-air summer orchestral concerts, many including a spectacular fireworks finale. There's a very useful restaurant housed in one of the outbuildings. This is a great place to spend a happy summer afternoon, seeing the house and its treasures, and then strolling under the trees and over the wide lawns. And all of it free!

LONDON PLANETARIUM, *Marylebone Rd., NW1 5LR (tel. 486 1121). Star shows seven days a week 11–4. Admission £2.20, children £1.40, senior citizens £1.70. Laser shows most evenings from 6 (tel. 486 2242 for details). Admission £3.25, £2.25 for children, £2.75 for students (but check as prices may have risen by 1988). See Madame Tussaud's below for the price of a Combined Ticket.* The Planetarium, adjoining Madame Tussaud's, is in many ways more interesting. The night sky of both hemispheres is vividly brought to life, taking you on a thrilling journey through time and space. In addition, there are excellent lectures and displays of holography. Educational the Planetarium undoubtedly is, but it's the kind of instruction that is extremely easy to take.

MADAME TUSSAUD'S, *Marylebone Rd., NW1 5LR (tel. 935 6861). Open Mon. to Fri. 10–5:30, Sat. and Sun. 9:30–5:30. Admission £3.95, children £2.50, senior citizens*

£2.95. Tube: Baker Street. This is not exactly a bargain spot, especially if you are taking the family along. It is, however, possible to get a Combined Ticket to Madame Tussaud's and the London Planetarium, £5.50 for adults, £3.10 for children, £3.80 for senior citizens, which does represent quite a saving. Madame Tussaud's is one of the most sought-after halts on the tourist map of London. There are almost always long lines waiting to get in—despite the fact that it is not the cheapest place in the world. If an ever-changing parade of famous faces from the past and present is your cup of tea, this is the place for you. Madame Tussaud herself originally made her reputation at the court of Louis XVI in France. Swept up by the tumult of the French Revolution, she continued her art by making casts of guillotined heads—which must be one of the grisliest ways of making a living! She arrived in London in 1802, and a number of her original heads are still on view here.

The present-day management of the waxworks are great showmen, as the way they have handled their acquisition of Warwick Castle proves. So the theatricality of the exhibits in the Marylebone Road is assured. What is sometimes in doubt is the fact that the blander a famous face is in real life, the less convincing the model will be. The Queen, whose face is most characterful when in movement, is not a good likeness, while someone whose face is closer to an unmade bed—like Picasso, say—is immediately recognizable.

REGENT'S PARK, *NW1 (tel. 486 7905). Open daily to around dusk, all year. Bands play during the summer, 12:30–2 and 5:30–7 Mon. to Sat., 3–4:30 and 6–7:30 Sun. and Bank Holidays. Tubes: Baker Street, Great Portland Street, Regent's Park.* Regent's Park—named in honor of the Prince Regent—is the youngest of London's great parks, laid out in 1812 by Nash. His plans were both innovative and ambitious, calling for a series of magnificent terraced houses overlooking the park as though they were country houses overlooking their landscaped grounds. The country-loving English gentry and aristocracy—the People of Quality—for whom these stately buildings were intended would thus have London homes that as nearly as possible resembled their country homes. The park is still fringed with many of Nash's lovely stucco marvels, grandiose, florid, and unique designs that flowed unstoppably from Nash's busy pen.

Enter the park by the gate at the top of Park Square East, just across the road from the Royal College of Physicians, a strange structure designed by Denys Lasun (who also conceived the new National Theater). It could easily be taken for a temple of some dark cult. The flowerbeds between this gate and Chester Road, which crosses the park, are all formal ones. Like those in other London parks, they are regularly restocked as the seasons pass, and you will be able to see some quite stunning displays of, for example, fuschias if you are there at the right time of year. The park also contains a semipermanent display of large pieces of sculpture by British artists. The main avenue is called the Broad Walk and, geographically, it is a long, leafy continuation of Portland Place.

When you reach Chester Road, turn left and walk towards the Inner Circle. This road is lined with cherry trees which are magnificent for a few weeks in spring. Arriving at the Inner Circle you will be opposite the wrought-iron gates to Queen Mary's Gardens. The gardens are not all that large, but within their spherical boundary they contain an incredible variety. Their chief glory comes in May to July when the endless beds of roses are at their peak. The scent and the shadings of color are enough to send the most casual visitor into a Persian dream. Evergreens, heathers, azaleas, and much more beside keep the interest going the year round. On an island in a little lake is a Japanese garden, where all sorts of small plants are delicately tended.

The delights of this part of the park are not ended there. Hidden behind a high hedge is the Open Air Theater, where Shakespeare is performed in the middle months of summer. It is a magical setting for the plays, especially those like *A Midsummer Night's Dream* which have an open-air theme. As the sun sets and the stage lights take over, the sense of being transported to a place of magic is strong. But the evenings can be chill, so go prepared.

A section in the north of the park is occupied by the Zoo (see below).

THE ZOO, *Regent's Park, NW1 4RY (tel. 722 3333). Open daily 9–6 in summer, 10–dusk in winter. Admission £3.60, children £1.80 (under 5, free); Dec. through Feb. £3.20, children £1.60. Tubes: Camden Town, Great Portland Street.* As you will see from these prices, a visit to the Zoo (its correct name is the Gardens of the Royal Zoological Society) is not much in the way of a great travel value if you're expecting to take the kids along. The reason for the fairly stiff price of admission is that the Zoological Gardens are privately operated by the Zoological Society, which is a serious scientific body. The costs of running the enterprise escalate every year—think of the food bill alone for all those hungry beasts—and the expenditure has to be reflected in the entrance fees. However, there *is* a lot to see there, and children are especially well catered for.

The Zoo has been going for over 150 years, absorbing, en route, such collections as that of the royal menagerie, which used to be housed in the Tower of London. The Zoo itself is one of the busiest mazes in the world. Focal points are: firstly the Mappin Terraces, which were originally built some 70 years ago as an early experiment in trying to create fairly natural, cageless conditions for such animals as goats, pigs, and bears; the Children's Zoo, where children can play with the smaller animals; the Snowdon Aviary, designed by Lord Snowdon in 1965 (this lies across the Regent's Park Canal); the Lion Terraces; the Elephant and Rhino Pavilion (an oddly delicate name for such a massive castle); the Small Bird House; and the Tropical House with its darting hummingbirds. One fascinating and unique exhibit is the Moonlight World, on the lower floor of the Charles Clore Pavilion. Here nighttime conditions are simulated so that nocturnal animals are busily leading their night lives during the outside world's daytime, with the process reversed at night, when the lighting in the cages grows bright and the animals progress to their daytime activities.

Other Attractions

FLASK WALK, *NW3. Tube: Hampstead.* We are using Flask Walk as the central point for a suggested tour of Hampstead. You'll arrive at the Hampstead tube, which is the deepest in London (the elevator goes down 181 feet), and can start wandering as soon as you surface. Flask Walk is on your left, after you have turned left out of the station, and you can stroll down it past the secondhand bookshops, to find a network of pretty streets lined with attractive houses from all periods—fine 18th-century ones, or interesting modern constructions—all of them dripping flowers and shaded by trees.

After ambling round the little lanes here, walk across the tube station to explore the area opposite, starting down Holly Hill. Then go up Heath Street, following Spaniards Road until you arrive at the Spaniards pub, which, especially in summer, is a great place for lunch and a drink out in the fresh air. You could then continue either across the Heath itself, or continue walking along the road (Hampstead Lane) until you reach Kenwood (see below).

FREUD MUSEUM, *20 Maresfield Gdns., NW3 5FS (tel. 435 2002). Open Wed. to Sun. 12–5. Admission £2, £1 students. Guided tours available for groups of 10 or more, 48 hours notice needed. Tube: Finchley Road.* There are now at least two meccas for dedicated followers of Freud to visit: his flat in Vienna, and this house in London. Freud lived here for the last year of his life (he died in 1939, having fled from Vienna in 1938). Ill though he was, he was able to supervise the decoration of his new home, and to install his bizarre collection of statues, photographs, and pictures, but most of all his books and his celebrated couch. Here they all are, lovingly preserved as they were when he died. This tends to give the place a somewhat sanctified and mummified air, naturally, but it is fascinating for all that. The life and work of Freud's daughter, Anna, are also commemorated here, as she continued to live on in the house until her own death in 1982.

HIGHGATE CEMETERY, *Swains Lane, N6 (tel. 340 1834). Western section open seven days a week, 10–3, for tours only (every hour on the hour). Eastern side open 10–5, 10–4 in winter. Tube: Archway.* To the east of Hampstead, and also topping a hill, is Highgate, a genuine village if ever there were one, filled with fine houses and attractive pubs. But it is the Cemetery for which Highgate is chiefly known.

The cemetery is divided into two sections, the eastern side (the "new" cemetery), and the western side (the "old" cemetery). In the new cemetery are buried some famous literary figures, novelists George Eliot and John Galsworthy among them; Friese-Green, the English inventor of cinematography (one among several to claim the honor); William Foyle, founder of Foyle's bookshop on Charing Cross Road; and—the most popular grave in the place—Karl Marx. His tomb is the goal of parties of visiting Russian and Chinese dignitaries and such-minded folks who are very fond of posing in front of the large, clumsy bust that tops the tomb, to show their comrades back home that they have made the Communist equivalent of the pilgrimage to Mecca.

For anyone interested in social history—or who is just plain morbid—it's the western side, the old cemetery, that'll be most interesting. This is a showplace of ornate and enormous Victorian tombs, scattered through overgrown and slightly sinister acres. It has been used countless times as a location for horror movies, usually involving Dracula in one of his many manifestations. It is being restored by a society—the Friends of Highgate Cemetery —that organizes hourly tours (see above), for which they ask a donation (£1 is suggested) that goes towards their very worthwhile work.

KEATS' HOUSE, *Keats Grove, NW3 2RR (tel. 435 2062). Open Mon. to Sat. 10–1 and 2–6. Sun. 2–5. The shop selling "Keatsiana" in the basement is open same hours, but closes 15 minutes earlier). Admission free. Tubes: Belsize Park. Hampstead.* Keats' life was a short one, and most of his creative years were spent in this attractive Regency house. It was here that he met and fell in love with Fanny Brawne, and the place is full of mementos of them both. His books, furniture of the period, and a small garden, where the poet wrote *Ode to a Nightingale,* all make this a place of pilgrimage for anyone who loves poetry.

Lunch Spots

We have not graded our lunch spot suggestions; they all carry a range of dishes at various prices to suit your taste and pocket. The best-value budget bets are the pubs in the area; these often have the most atmosphere as well.

Camden Brasserie, 216 Camden High St., NW1 8QR. Booking is advisable here for the good quality French regional food and daily specialties. Everything is home-made and at the weekend there's a special brunch menu.

Maxwell's, 76 Heath St., NW3 1DN. A bistro-style spot for hamburgers, steaks, kebabs, salads, and yummy desserts—with a separate games room, bar, and garden for outdoor eating in summer. Hampstead Heath is just up the road.

Nontas, 16 Camden High St., NW1 0JH. Not too far from the north side of Regent's Park, this Greek restaurant serves good national specialties, including an excellent *mezze.*

Regent's Park, NW1. There is a very adequate cafeteria tucked away among the roses in Queen Mary's Gardens, with plenty of open-air tables for summer lunching. The **Open-Air Theater** also has a lot of light food on offer if you are heading for a performance and need to fuel up first.

Spaniards Inn, Spaniards Rd., NW3 7JJ. Historic pub, hard by Hampstead Heath, which is often crowded, especially at weekends, but always good value. It's atmospheric, with reasonably priced food, and outdoor eating in summer.

◆

S P L U R G E S

Camden Boat Cruises, 250 Camden High St., NW1 8QS (tel. 485 4433/6210). Waterbuses and barges ply the Regent Canal between Camden Lock (Camden Town tube) and Little Venice (Warwick Avenue tube) and this can be a real break for those tired of seeing the city on foot. You can either take a cruise or, if you want to splash out, a cruise with a meal included. The floating restaurant "My Fair Lady" operates all year round, and offers dinner at £16.95 and Sunday lunch at £10.75. These prices include everything apart from drinks. Book in advance from the above address.

◆

CAPITAL DAYS OUT

◆

There's no shortage of places to visit and things to do inside London, but if you're there for more than just a few days, you may well want to get out and about to see what else is on offer nearby. You can, of course, do that by taking a fast train to visit, say, Bath (just over an hour), Canterbury (one hour 20 minutes), or even York, far to the north (three hours, and quite possible for the day—if you get up early enough!) Oxford, Cambridge, Brighton, Norwich—the list of possibles is long. If you have a BritRail Card or one of the other available budget tickets you can do a series of such days, using London as your home base. Or you can book one of the many bus tours and see several places in one day (Bath, Stonehenge, and Stratford-upon-Avon, for example), though, of course, you will only get a very short time at each destination. The London Tourist Board office at Victoria Station can give you the latest fare prices for all the possibilities in the south, along with comprehensive details of how to make the trip.

If you do not want to take up so much of your vacation, but still want to see some locales outside London, then here are a few that are easy to reach, and can almost be described as integral parts of London itself.

London has been Britain's power center for centuries, so it is only natural that many visitable places, intimately associated with royalty and the ruling establishment, should be found close to the capital. For this section we have selected only four of the most famous—Greenwich, Kew, Hampton Court, and Windsor. The factor that links them together is the River Thames, as they all lie on its banks and can be explored by boat from the center of town. The trip to Windsor is the longest, taking around four hours to follow the sinuous course of the river, but on a sunny day it is a marvelous way of relaxing and watching London and the surrounding countryside drift by. Naturally, you'd only take the river one way, preferably going there, and then return by train.

GREENWICH

Greenwich (pronounced Gren-itch) Palace was built downriver of London (to the east) for Henry VII, the first of the Tudors, around 1430. It became one of the palaces most favored by that family, and the place for births, marriages, and deaths, with Henry VIII responsible for a fair number of each—especially the last two! Since about 1700, the days of William III, who preferred Hampton Court to Greenwich, it has been closely associated with the sea and ships. It is now the location of the Royal Naval College and the Maritime Museum. As you will see below, it is easily reached by boat from the center of town, and this is by far the best means of getting there—you arrive by water, passing as you go the speedy developments along the river's banks, where upmarket apartment blocks are replacing the decaying hulks of disused warehouses.

The buildings of Greenwich are among the most splendid in Britain, spreading both grandly and elegantly beside the river, the colonnades and pediments seeming to be part of a complex of Grecian temples, transported to the Thames. Some of England's best architects of the age worked here—among them Wren and two of his assistants, Hawksmoor and Vanburgh, each of whom became famous in his own right. The College's dining hall, the Painted Hall, is one of the most impressive pieces of illusionistic decor that you're likely to see anywhere. It was the work of James Thornhill from 1707–17.

The Maritime Museum traces Britain's naval history with paintings, models, maps, uniforms . . . the panoply of a long and illustrious struggle to conquer the oceans of the world and to gain the upper hand over other seagoing nations. Some of the collection is on view in the Queen's House, an older part of the site, built in 1616 by Inigo Jones for the wife of James I, Anne of Denmark, and subsequently the home of her daughter-in-law, Henrietta Maria, the wife of Charles I. Though simple in the extreme —not much more than a perfect rectangle, with a Cube Room at its heart—it is usually cited as the first genuinely Classical building in the country. It is linked to the rest of the museum by an arcade.

Near the College are two ships, the *Cutty Sark,* the sole survivor of the fleets of clipper ships that used to race with their cargoes across the world's oceans in the 19th century, and the tiny *Gipsy Moth IV,* in which Sir Francis Chichester sailed single-handed round the world in 1966.

Up the hill behind the College in Greenwich Park, overlooking the river, is the old Royal Observatory, with antique telescopes, imaginatively displayed, and the prime meridian—zero of longitude—which runs through the courtyard.

If you can stay for the evening, there's a good local theater, which often has well-known names on its cast lists.

Getting to Greenwich

By Train. *Twice-hourly service from both London Bridge and Charing Cross. Trip takes approximately seven and 14 minutes respectively. Tel. 928 5100 for times and fares.*

By Bus. *53, 177, 188.*

By Boat. *Year-round service from Westminster and Tower piers; 45 and 35 minutes respectively. Tel. 930 4097 and 930 0344 for times and fares.*

Main Attractions

NATIONAL MARITIME MUSEUM, *Romney Rd., SE10 9NF (tel. 858 4422). Open Easter through mid-Oct., Mon. to Sat. 10–6, Sun. 2–5:30; rest of the year, Mon. to Fri. 10–5, Sat. 10–5:30, Sun. 2–5. Admission £1.20.*

OLD ROYAL OBSERVATORY *(tel. 858 4422). Same hours and*

admission as the Maritime Museum. Combined ticket covering both, £1.80.

ROYAL NAVAL COLLEGE, *including Painted Hall and Chapel (tel. 858 2154). Open daily 2:30–5; closed Thurs. Admission free.*

Other Attractions

CUTTY SARK *Greenwich Pier, SE10 9HT (tel. 858 3445). Open Apr. through Sept., Mon. to Sat. 10:30–5:30, Sun. 12–5:30. Oct. through Mar., Mon. to Sat. 10:30–4:30, Sun. 12–4:30. Admission £1.20*

GIPSY MOTH IV, *Greenwich Pier, SE10 9HT (tel. 858 3445). Same hours as* Cutty Sark. *Admission 20p.*

Lunch Spots

Colonel Jasper's, 161 Greenwich High Rd., SE10 8JA. There's an olde worlde atmosphere to this cellar bar and dining room where you'll find homey British food such as steak and kidney pie, Stilton cheese, and treacle tart.

Cutty Sark, Ballast Quay, Ladsell St., SE10 9PD. This Georgian pub overlooks the river and wharves close to where the Cutty Sark herself is docked. The fish suppers are delicious.

Davy's Wine Vaults, 165 Greenwich High Rd., SE10 8JA. Good food and fine wines are on the menu of this wine bar in a candlelit Victorian cellar. The cold buffet offers inexpensive dishes.

Gachons, 269 Creek St., SE10 8NB. Snacks, salads, and pastries as well as good hot French dishes make up the fare on offer in this quaint coffeehouse. It's open 10:30–5 every day except Tues., and 7–10:30 P.M. from Thurs. to Sat.

KEW

Kew itself is an attractive village—swamped, of course, by the sprawl of the London suburbs—with fine 18th-century houses surrounding the Green, a trim, grassy open space, much loved by local cricketers. Kew church is the last resting place for some notable people, with the painters Gainsborough and Zoffany leading names. There's a quite distinct atmosphere around Kew. It's very popular as a convenient commuting area, preserving its village feel, but at the same time being definitely upscale as an address.

Kew is known chiefly for the Royal Botanical Gardens (or Kew Gardens, as they are usually called). It's the country's leading botanical institute, and a substantial public garden covering 300 acres and containing more than 25,000 varieties of plant life. Until 1841, when the Gardens were handed over to the nation, they had been the grounds of two royal residences—the White House, or the original Kew Palace, and the Old Dutch House, which is known as Kew Palace today. It was Frederick, the Prince of Wales—George II's eldest son, who died before he could succeed to the throne—who moved here first, living from 1730 in the White House. Following his death, his wife Princess Augusta began to develop the gardens. Under the official directorship of the celebrated botanist Sir Joseph Banks, and with the talents of the great landscaper Capability Brown, Kew developed rapidly as both a beautifully laid out garden, and as an important center for study and research. The architect Sir William Chambers also did a lot of work here, building a series of pretty temples and follies, as well as his most unusual work, the Chinese Pagoda, built in 1751. It's a splendidly eccentric 18th-century tower that can still be seen for miles around.

In 1803, George III, who had spent most of his childhood here and loved the area, knocked down the White House, intending to rebuild it on a more lavish scale. While the work progressed, he and his queen lived in the comparatively small Old Dutch House nearby. But as poor George slowly descended into madness, work on the new palace first slowed down, then halted altogether. It is one of the sadder and more bizarre periods of the history of the British monarchy, and descriptions of the mad old king wandering around the gardens appear in several diaries of the time. Following George's death in 1820, his son George IV, formerly the Prince Regent, ordered the destruction of his father's stillborn palace. Nonetheless, the Old Dutch House remains a charmingly domestic place, quite unlike a royal palace, even though it did assume the name of one. It has been carefully restored and furnished in the right period style. The little formal gardens to its side and rear have been redeveloped as a 17th-century herbal garden, wih trim hedges, statues, and carefully planned beds, close above the bank of the river.

To some extent the real architectural glories of Kew Gardens are the 19th-century buildings, in particular the two giant greenhouses, the Palm House and the Temperate House. These were both built in mid-century by Decimus Burton to house the rapidly expanding collection of exotic species. Time and the weather have taken their toll of these buildings, and their preservation is now a very serious matter. The Palm House is the more famous of the two, but both represent the daring of Victorian engineering and taste. Along the front of the Palm House stands a row of massive heraldic animals, the Queen's beasts, created to decorate Westminster Abbey for the coronation of the present queen.

There is an interesting example of ultramodern techniques on show in the brand new Princess of Wales Conservatory, opened in 1987, where a very wide variety of plants is cultivated in controlled climates, changing almost from one moment to the next, and from one adjacent area to another.

The terrible storm of October '87 did maximum damage to the ancient and extremely rare trees of Kew; altogether about 1,000 were destroyed or badly damaged.

As you will see from the data below, Kew represents one of the very best travel bargains around London.

Getting to Kew

By Tube. *Underground to Kew Gardens on the District Line, and then a 10 minute walk.*

By Train. *Every half hour from Waterloo to Kew Bridge. Trip takes around 20 minutes. For fares and times, tel. 928 5100.*

By Boat. *From Westminster Pier (en route for Hampton Court). Apr. through Oct. only, four sailings a day. For further information tel. 930 2062.*

Main Attraction

KEW GARDENS (THE ROYAL BOTANIC GARDENS), *Kew Rd., Richmond, Surrey TW9 3AB (tel. 940 1171). Gardens open*

*year-round (except Christmas Day and New Year's Day),
9:30 to dusk. Kew Palace daily 11–5:30, Apr. to Sept.; Queen
Charlotte's Cottage Sat., Sun., and Bank Holiday Mons.
only 11–5:30. Admission 50p (gardens), 80p (palace), and
40p (cottage).*

Lunch Spots

There is an acceptable Refreshment Pavilion quite close
to the Chinese Pagoda, for snacks, coffee, and such.

Original Maids of Honour Shop, *288 Kew Rd., Kew
Gardens (tel. 940 2752). Open 10–5:30 Tues. to Sat., Mon.
10–1, closed Sun. This very long-established bakery has a
tearoom serving its namesake pastries, plus savory pies and
pasties.*

HAMPTON COURT PALACE

If it's historic atmosphere you're after, then head for
Hampton Court Palace. It's a combination of mellow
Tudor brick and classically cool Wren proportions, with
magnificent gardens, a park alive with sheep and dappled
deer, great wrought-iron screens closing in the views of the
river lazing by, and a maze of rooms, furnished with
paintings and furniture which recreate the aura of the past
ages of power and pomp that characterized life in this
favorite residence of earlier monarchs.

Hampton Court lies some 20 miles from London, on a
loop in the Thames, and is easily reached by train or bus,
and less easily, but with more fun, by boat. The palace was
begun in 1514 by Cardinal Wolsey, Henry VIII's ambitious
and worldly Chancellor, who intended that it would sur-
pass in size and splendor all other private residences. It did,
with the result that Henry decided that his minister was
getting far too big for his purple shoes. He dismissed
Wolsey (who died a year later), took possession of Hampton Court, added a great hall and a chapel, and lived most
of the rest of his monstrous life there. The ghosts of two of
his unfortunate wives, Jane Seymour and Catherine How-
ard, are said to haunt the place (the first died in childbirth,
the second was beheaded).

It continued as a favorite royal residence for decades,

but, by the end of the 17th century, was beginning to be rather run-down. Plans were drawn up by the joint rulers William III and Mary II to demolish the buildings and replace them with a more splendid structure, in conscious emulation of Versailles in France. However, the cost was clearly too great, and it was decided to keep the existing palace, but extend it with a new complex at the rear. The ever-ready Wren got the job, and his graceful design resulted in one of the loveliest buildings in England. William and Mary, especially Mary, were very happy here, and much of their life is still in evidence—collections of Delftware and other porcelain, for instance.

The Royal Family has not lived there since the death of George II in 1760, but parts of the palace are still inhabited. There are private quarters in several areas, called "grace and favor apartments," where pensioners of the crown—former civil servants, and the wives of high-ranking military officers, for example—live out their last years in atmospheric retirement. It was in one of the grace and favor apartments that a serious fire started at Easter 1986, when a candle, by the light of which a general's widow was reading, was knocked over. The conflagration spread to the state rooms below, and she died in the fire. Restoration was put in hand straight away, and it is expected that most of the damage will have been repaired by late 1988.

To wander through the palace is to walk through a couple of centuries of English history, taking in the changes in architectural fashions as you go. Claustrophobic Tudor rooms, lined with dark wooden paneling, give way to the airy spaciousness of Wren's additions. There is a long succession of stately rooms, hung with paintings and tapestries; rooms with four-poster beds like great plumed catafalques; cobblestoned courtyards and cavernous kitchens; the Great Hall, with its minstrels' gallery and stained glass windows; and staircases with soaring frescoes.

The gardens are magnificently maintained, varying from a formal Elizabethan patterned one (a knot garden), to the long, multicolored herbaceous borders, and the sweeping lawns that border the Long Water (a decorative canal). There is an ancient vine, still producing grapes after 220 years; a court for playing Real Tennis, the original form of the game; a maze that has been puzzling people for 270 years; and a cafeteria, hidden in the walled gardens, for the ideal summer lunch (though it's the surroundings that are ideal rather than the food).

Getting to Hampton Court

By Train. *Twice an hour from Waterloo. Trip approximately 32 minutes. Tel. 928 5100 for times and fares.*

By Bus. *Greenline hourly from Eccleston Bridge, Victoria, SW1. Trip approximately 40 minutes. Tel. 668 7261 for times and fares.*

By Boat. *From Westminster Pier, Apr. through Oct. only. Four sailings a day. Trip three to four hours. Tel. 930 2062.*

Main Attraction

HAMPTON COURT PALACE, *Hampton Court, East Molesey, KT8 9AU (tel. 977 8441). Open Apr. through Sept., Mon. to Sat. 9:30–6, Sun. 11–6; Oct. through Mar., Mon. to Sat., 9:30–5, Sun. 2–5. Admission £2.80. The gardens are open every day, free of charge, until dusk.*

Lunch Spots

Cardinal Wolsey, The Green, Hampton Court Rd., East Molesey, KT8 9BW. This charming inn offers a three-course set menu with a wide choice of dishes. It's open 12:30–3 and 7–10:30.

Etoile Bistro, 41 Bridge Rd., Hampton, KT8 9ER. You'll find home cooking at its best, and very friendly service, in this excellent-value, bistro-type restaurant.

Hampton Court Palace. There's a cafeteria in the gardens (by the Tiltyard Gardens and the Wilderness) which is open 12:00–4 and 7–10:00.

WINDSOR CASTLE

Windsor, 21 miles west of London, close to Heathrow airport, is an essential day out for any visitor. The principal attraction here is the castle, high on its bluff above the Thames, but the town, too, is interesting, with its narrow streets and ancient buildings, huddling round the castle's gray walls.

Windsor Castle was started by William the Conqueror in the 11th century, though none of his buildings remains. It was transformed by Edward III in the mid-1300s, when he greatly extended it, with the huge round tower among his improvements. The chapel was begun by Edward IV (early 1400s) and finished by Henry VII and Henry VIII; Elizabeth I and Charles I both made additions, but the final seal was set by George IV, who, between 1824 and 1837—with the aid of the architect Wyatville—transformed what was essentially a medieval castle into the royal palace you can see today. This means that work on the castle was spread over more than eight centuries, with most of the kings and queens of England showing their attachment to this building that holds a quintessential place in the life of the realm.

You'll be able to visit the State Apartments when the Queen is not in residence. She uses the castle far more than any of her predecessors, and it has become a kind of weekend country home, close—but not too close—to London, with the space and security for the Royal Family to relax in private. It is, incidentally, the largest inhabited castle in the world.

Here, more than in any other royal residence that the public can visit, you will realize the immense wealth of treasures that the Queen owns. There are pictures, furniture, porcelain, armor, tapestries, just about everything that's collectible—even postage stamps! Apart from the State Apartments themselves, other attractions you should be sure to see are: Queen Mary's Doll's House, a perfect palace-within-a-palace, with lights that work, running water, even a library of lilliputian books especially written by famous authors of Queen Mary's day; an exhibition of drawings from the Queen's collection (she owns a large part of the known drawings by da Vinci, plus 87 Holbein portraits; and the Royal Mews, with carriages, coaches, and resplendent red-and-gold harness.

Architecturally, the most impressive building is St. George's Chapel, one of the noblest structures in England. It is over 230 feet long, with two tiers of great windows, and hundreds of gargoyles, buttresses, and pinnacles. Light floods in through the stained glass onto the dark oak of the stalls, above which hang the banners, swords, and helmets of the Knights of the Order of the Garter, the most venerable heraldic order in Britain, and whose base is here at Windsor. Many of the most famous kings of England lie buried here, from Henry VI, Charles I, Henry VIII, and others, up to George VI, the father of the present Queen.

The walls of the castle itself enclose only 13 acres of land, but beyond the battlements are the 4,800 acres of Windsor Great Park. The ancient trees here suffered severely in the great storm of October '87.

In part of Windsor rail station, Madame Tussaud's has set up an exhibition to commemorate Queen Victoria's Diamond Jubilee in 1897, called "Royalty and Empire."

Across the river lies Eton College, Britain's leading public (that is, extremely private!) school, which has a fine 15th-century chapel.

Two miles to the southwest is the Windsor Safari Park, with a drive-in lion reserve, a children's farm, and a dolphinarium.

Getting to Windsor

By Train. *From Waterloo station every half hour; trip takes approximately 50 minutes. Tel. 928 5100 for train times and fares.*

By Bus. *Three Greenline buses an hour from Eccleston Bridge, Victoria, SW1; trip takes approximately an hour. Tel. 668 7261 for times and fares.*

Excursions. *Evan Evans Tours, 27 Cockspur St., SW1Y 5BT (tel. 930 2377—line open 24 hours a day), takes in Windsor in its escorted, whole-day, bus-and-boat tour, which also visits Hampton Court and includes a Thames cruise. Available mid-Apr. to mid-Oct., daily.*

Frames Rickards, 11 Herbrand St., WC1N 1EX (tel. 837 3111). Afternoon (morning in winter) escorted bus tour, daily Apr. to Oct., taking in Windsor and Runnymede (an alternative tour also includes Hampton Court and Stoke Poges); price includes all admission charges, lunch, too, on whole-day tours.

London Regional Transport Guided Tours, 55 Broadway, SW1H 0BD (tel. 222 1234). Whole-day escorted bus tour, taking in Windsor and Hampton Court (an alternative tour does Windsor only, afternoons only); price of former includes lunch and all admission charges. Check for '88 program.

Main Attraction

WINDSOR CASTLE, *Windsor (tel. 0753 868286).* **Castle Precincts.** *Open daily Apr. and Sept. to late Oct., 10–5:15; May through Aug. 10–7:15; late Oct. through Mar. 10–4:15. Admission free.*

State Apartments. *Opening times are very complicated and change often. Basically, open Mon. to Sat. in winter (but closed for royal occupation most of Dec.); and daily during the summer. Phone for exact details. Admission £1.60*

Queen Mary's Doll's House, Exhibition of Drawings, Royal Mews. *Similar times to the State Apartments, but it's best to check ahead (tel. above). Admission 70p.*

St. George's Chapel. *May through Oct., Mon. to Sat. 10:45–4, Sun. 2–4; Nov. through Apr., Mon. to Sat. 10:45–3:45, Sun. 2–3:45. Admission £1.50.*

Other Attractions

ETON COLLEGE, *Eton (tel. 0753 863593). School yard, College Chapel, Cloister Court, and Museum of Eton Life all open daily (with a couple of exceptions—check) end Mar. to start Oct. 10:30–5 during school vacations, 2–5 during term time; last admission 4:30. Admission £1.50. Hour-long guided tour 2:15 and 3:15. (Specialist tours available, contact College.)*

MADAME TUSSAUD'S "ROYALTY AND EMPIRE" EXHIBITION, *Windsor and Eton Central Railway Station, Thames St., Windsor, SL4 1PT (tel. 0753 857837), opposite Windsor Castle. Open daily 9:30–5:30 (4:30 in winter). Admission £2.65, children 5 to 15 £1.85, senior citizens £2.20.*

WINDSOR SAFARI PARK, *Winkfield Rd., Windsor, SL4 4AY, (tel. 0753 869847). Open from 10 daily, year-round, but closing time varies considerably, depending on when night falls. It's around 6 in summer (7 at weekends), and 3:30 in winter (4:30 weekends)—no, we know that dusk isn't later on Sats. and Suns.! Admission £6, children and citizens £5 (£4 and £3 respectively in winter). The Greenline*

Coach #700 runs from Central London direct to the Safari Park throughout the summer. Tel. 668 7261 for times and fares.

Lunch Spots

The Christopher Hotel, 110A High St., Eton, SL4 6AN. Once a famous coaching inn, this civilized place offers quiches and a generous ploughman's lunch, as well as hot dishes.

Drury House, 4 Church St., Windsor, SL4 1PE. You'll find good English cooking at this 17th-century house close to the castle. It's open Tues. to Sun. 12–5:30.

The Eton Buttery, 73 High St., Eton, SL4 6BT. This charming restaurant, overlooking the Thames, has a mouth-watering selection of pastries and cakes to accompany your morning coffee or afternoon tea. Lunches range from quiches and salads to lasagne and roasts. It is open all day.

The Royal Oak, Datchet Rd., Windsor, SL4 1QD. Opposite the train station and close to the castle, this 15th-century pub has a good selection of hot and cold dishes.

The Three Tuns, 8 Market St., Windsor, SL4 1PB. Originally The Guildhall, the Three Tuns was built in 1518. Soft lighting and wrought-iron furniture create a period atmosphere. The lunchtime food is excellent.

INDEX

Map page numbers appear in **boldface**

FODOR'S TRAVEL GUIDES

Here is a complete list of Fodor's Travel Guides, available in current editions; most are also available in a British edition published by Hodder & Stoughton.

U.S. GUIDES

Alaska
American Cities (Great Travel Values)
Arizona including the Grand Canyon
Atlantic City & the New Jersey Shore
Boston
California
Cape Cod & the Islands of Martha's Vineyard & Nantucket
Carolinas & the Georgia Coast
Chesapeake
Chicago
Colorado
Dallas/Fort Worth
Disney World & the Orlando Area (Fun in)
Far West
Florida
Fort Worth (see Dallas)
Galveston (see Houston)
Georgia (see Carolinas)
Grand Canyon (see Arizona)
Greater Miami & the Gold Coast
Hawaii
Hawaii (Great Travel Values)
Houston & Galveston
I-10: California to Florida
I-55: Chicago to New Orleans
I-75: Michigan to Florida
I-80: San Francisco to New York
I-95: Maine to Miami
Jamestown (see Williamsburg)
Las Vegas including Reno & Lake Tahoe (Fun in)
Los Angeles & Nearby Attractions
Martha's Vineyard (see Cape Cod)
Maui (Fun in)
Nantucket (see Cape Cod)
New England
New Jersey (see Atlantic City)
New Mexico
New Orleans
New Orleans (Fun in)
New York City
New York City (Fun in)
New York State
Orlando (see Disney World)
Pacific North Coast
Philadelphia
Reno (see Las Vegas)
Rockies
San Diego & Nearby Attractions
San Francisco (Fun in)
San Francisco plus Marin County & the Wine Country
The South
Texas
U.S.A.

Virgin Islands (U.S. & British)
Virginia
Waikiki (Fun in)
Washington, D.C.
Williamsburg, Jamestown & Yorktown

FOREIGN GUIDES

Acapulco (see Mexico City)
Acapulco (Fun in)
Amsterdam
Australia, New Zealand & the South Pacific
Austria
The Bahamas
The Bahamas (Fun in)
Barbados (Fun in)
Beijing, Guangzhou & Shanghai
Belgium & Luxembourg
Bermuda
Brazil
Britain (Great Travel Values)
Canada
Canada (Great Travel Values)
Canada's Maritime Provinces plus Newfoundland & Labrador
Cancún, Cozumel, Mérida & the Yucatán
Caribbean
Caribbean (Great Travel Values)
Central America
Copenhagen (see Stockholm)
Cozumel (see Cancún)
Eastern Europe
Egypt
Europe
Europe (Budget)
France
France (Great Travel Values)
Germany: East & West
Germany (Great Travel Values)
Great Britain
Greece
Guangzhou (see Beijing)
Helsinki (see Stockholm)
Holland
Hong Kong & Macau
Hungary
India, Nepal & Sri Lanka
Ireland
Israel
Italy
Italy (Great Travel Values)
Jamaica (Fun in)
Japan
Japan (Great Travel Values)
Jordan & the Holy Land
Kenya
Korea
Labrador (see Canada's Maritime Provinces)
Lisbon
Loire Valley

London
London (Fun in)
London (Great Travel Values)
Luxembourg (see Belgium)
Macau (see Hong Kong)
Madrid
Mazatlan (see Mexico's Baja)
Mexico
Mexico (Great Travel Values)
Mexico City & Acapulco
Mexico's Baja & Puerto Vallarta, Mazatlan, Manzanillo, Copper Canyon
Montreal (Fun in)
Munich
Nepal (see India)
New Zealand
Newfoundland (see Canada's Maritime Provinces)
1936 . . . on the Continent
North Africa
Oslo (see Stockholm)
Paris
Paris (Fun in)
People's Republic of China
Portugal
Province of Quebec
Puerto Vallarta (see Mexico's Baja)
Reykjavik (see Stockholm)
Rio (Fun in)
The Riviera (Fun on)
Rome
St. Martin/St. Maarten (Fun in)
Scandinavia
Scotland
Shanghai (see Beijing)
Singapore
South America
South Pacific
Southeast Asia
Soviet Union
Spain
Spain (Great Travel Values)
Sri Lanka (see India)
Stockholm, Copenhagen, Oslo, Helsinki & Reykjavik
Sweden
Switzerland
Sydney
Tokyo
Toronto
Turkey
Vienna
Yucatán (see Cancún)
Yugoslavia

SPECIAL-INTEREST GUIDES

Bed & Breakfast Guide: North America
Royalty Watching
Selected Hotels of Europe
Selected Resorts and Hotels of the U.S.
Ski Resorts of North America
Views to Dine by around the World

AVAILABLE AT YOUR LOCAL BOOKSTORE OR WRITE TO
FODOR'S TRAVEL PUBLICATIONS, INC., 201 EAST 50th STREET, NEW YORK, NY 10022.